A Geography
of Saints

◇ ◇ ◇

A
Geography
of
Saints

◇ ◇ ◇ ◇ ◇ ◇ ◇ ◇ ◇ ◇ ◇ ◇ ◇ ◇

A Memoir

Penny Allen

Penny Allen

Z
ZOLAND BOOKS
Cambridge, Massachusetts

First edition published in 2001 by
Zoland Books, Inc.
384 Huron Avenue
Cambridge, Massachusetts 02138

FIRST EDITION

Book design by Boskydell Studio

Printed in the United States of America

05 04 03 02 01   8 7 6 5 4 3 2 1

This book is printed on acid-free paper, and its binding
materials have been chosen for strength and durability

Library of Congress Cataloging-in-Publication Data

Allen, Penny, 1942–

A geography of saints : a memoir / Penny Allen.

p.   cm.

ISBN 1-58195-028-4

1. Allen, Penny, 1942–   2. Ranch life — Oregon.   3. Oregon — Biography.
I. Title.

CT275.A5327 A3 2001

979.5'043'092—dc21

00-067310

AUTHOR'S NOTE

The following story is essentially a true one. Events occurred largely as herein represented, and many are even a matter of public record. Names, including the town's, have been changed, with the exception of some belonging to people who were the subjects of news stories in Oregon in the 1980s.

My thanks to Literary Arts, Inc., for a literary fellowship in 1990. Thanks also to Robin Runco Stenkemp for permission to quote from her poem, "This Country is For You"; to the late Joe Fox for his early help and encouragement, and to Theresa Stefanidis, Steve Hull, my family and friends.

A Geography
of Saints

❖ ❖ ❖

ONE

OUR FIRST SUMMER on the ranch up in the high country of Central Oregon, Peter and I were cage-trapping feral cats one by one and having them cut if we liked them, killed if we didn't. Up there in stock country, cutting animals wholesale is a common and necessary practice, although it's not usually cats. Nor is it always cold-hearted: Horses sometimes get what's called cut proud, which means a cut gelding can still get hard and mount fillies. He's got no sperm but he's got his pride.

A lean, sunburnt horsewoman named Faith Gaines told me about proud cuts. She was a local veterinarian, so I figured she knew. Faith was doing our cats in exchange for Peter's legal advice. She said to me one day, "Those good ol' cowboys wait until a stallion's had sex and then they cut him, so he keeps the male menace in him, menace to cow a steer with, the horse is absolutely carryin' menace in his brain." Faith went blank after she said that, stood absolutely still, as if the menace had got her, as if the whole cosmos had stopped and was waiting for her to move. It was eerie. I was sucked right in.

She started up again: "So, uh, uh anyway," she said tonelessly, faded out, stopped. I swallowed, waited. Palpably, then, she made an effort, used more juice to get going, got over the hump this time: "So, uh, anyway, they do it that way an' the horse knows sex, so he's always wantin' it, a real pain in the butt, an' so he presents a problem in terms of you being able to manage him the rest of his life . . . male cats too're the same, except they don't kick you in the head. Anyway . . ."

I remember not quite following Faith when she was saying this. I was thrown by the contrast between her flat delivery and the edginess of what she was saying. I got off into thinking instead about the sex I was having with Peter then and how it was not at all a pain but a lingering pleasure not quite in the butt but near there. We were like wild animals, Peter and I. My flesh chittered, traveling the distance. I stopped listening to Faith Gaines. This explains why I couldn't follow her, because you had to listen very closely to Faith. She was all subtext.

In any case, right at the beginning, Peter and I were catching the feral cats the only way we were ever able to: We waited until they came out of the crawl space under our house directly into a wire-mesh cage trap, whose door fell shut when the cat would reach for the chicken bone. Bam, it was caught, and the whole cage would leap up and down wildly. I'd take the caged cat into the town of Saints, to the clinic where Faith Gaines practiced, the crazed beast next to me on the seat of the pickup truck. The eye contact and adrenaline level caught me up, went right to where I lived, wouldn't let go. I could hardly drive straight. With each animal, neither of us could see exactly what was coming when we got to town, and with each one, I would make the choice — cut or kill — on the basis of that brief ride.

Our cabin was an authentic tumbledown ranch house, a movie set at first glance, a main house to somebody half a century earlier. By the time we got there it was quarters for whoever was caretaking a certain corner of paradise just outside Saints.

Originally, someone set the simple dwelling down on a partial foundation less than a foot high. Then they nailed massive one-by-twelve old-growth yellow pine boards vertically all around the outside clear down to the ground, except for occasional small openings around the bottom, where various fauna — not just cats but coons, porcupines, and skunks — moved in and out of the secret labyrinth under the cabin.

Our first day at the ranch, we heard a resonant growl under the house, followed by a piercing, high-pitched shriek, and the floor shook and thudded in a path from one side of the house to the other. Peter and I were in the kitchen putting his things and my things in drawers, together, for the first time. We had to decide what to do with two large woks and two prints of the Hiroshige lithograph showing people crossing the Ohashi Bridge in the rain.

At the noise, we stepped outside and shone a flashlight into the ground-level openings near where the sounds were coming from. All we could see were boards that hung down randomly from the underside of the kitchen floor.

Then Dad Cat emerged. His jowls were tinged red with blood. He was huge, big as a bobcat, with a bobcat's ears and tail. Dad didn't so much make eye contact as aggressively stare you down, and it was apparently his habit to bang against the hot-water pipes like Jackie Gleason on *The Honeymooners*.

"Shut up, Dad," Peter would shout through the wide pine-board flooring. The caterwauling would cease for a moment and then start up again.

Dad was the ideal straight man for Peter, who made me laugh, clowning hugely around the kitchen in counterpoint to his stuffy Garden City, Kansas, high school football half-time radio announcer voice — a classic performance. He was thirty-three then. There was an unresolved teenager inside him doing battle with a strong superego, and that bit got them both just right. In some ways Peter seemed younger than I, which he was, and in some ways he seemed older. Peter was unspoiled and loved to please and did please and excite me endlessly. I loved to watch the tiny dimple in the end of his chiseled nose move when he got excited. An infinitesimal indentation, the dimple would narrow and flatten whenever he flared his nostrils, carrying on in the half-darkened kitchen.

As for the ranch, it was literally an animal preserve when we got there. Just before we moved in, the house stood empty for seventeen days after the former caretakers departed on short notice. The ranch had gotten out of control in that short a time. You imagine a place will just sit there and await its new keepers, but it doesn't: Water pumps go into fibrillation and seize up, like forgotten hearts. Horses trample fences and cut their legs on barbed wire. Birds get drunk on rotting juniper berries and smash picture windows. Someone has left the side door of the house standing wide open out there in the middle of nowhere, and the rooms fill with earwigs and barn swallows and bats.

Those magical first days, the air was already hot even though it was early spring. It was dry, too, and very still, except in the afternoon, when the cicadas would start clicking their high-pitched castanets. They made a symphony together with the frogs down in the spring. The sound would build, and then sudden gusts would cross the southern landscape, picking up dust and whirling it into towering vortices that hung in the air and then dropped, suddenly exhausted, and the sound would stop. The day we came, a twister barreled toward us as we unloaded Peter's round yellow wooden reading table from a van. We stood transfixed as the wind smashed full force into the giant cottonwood tree dominating the space between the stables and the caretaker's cabin. We watched dumbstruck, like city people not accustomed to performances of weather.

The tree stopped the twister, but not without a terrible commotion as limbs fifty feet up crashed down through the massive tree to the ground. One of them snapped a hitching post in half directly in front of us as we stood there rapt. Up in the tree, thousands of leaves and twigs continued to dance in frenzy until they dropped to the ground. A porcupine fell too and lay on the grass ruptured and dying. We walked over and examined it. It had orange teeth. There was a twig of cotton-wood impaled on the claws of its right front paw. We buried the corpse, although we later learned that dead animals on the high desert desiccate long before they ever begin to smell, so we could just as well have nailed it to the barn door and kept it around to look at the way other people did.

Sometimes those first few days, dark clouds would pile high in the spectacular sky over the Three Saints Mountains to the south. By late afternoon we'd see violent displays of thunder and lightning. The sun would still be shining overhead, but a few drops of hot rain would be falling on us, blown from clouds miles away on the mountains. The fat drops would hit the dust and smell of electric trains.

"It's ozone," Peter said as we played naked in the exotic hot rain the way one does in the tropics. The horses, most of them Arabians, were excited by the thunder. They raced madly back and forth across the pasture, airborne.

Let me tell you about Peter and me.

We'd met unromantically a year earlier, at a fund-raising meeting, in Portland, Oregon.

I was a film director at the time, kind of a disappointed one, having flirted with unpleasant financial risk. No failure, really. When I met Peter, I was working on somebody else's movie, partly to make some money, partly because the director, an eccentric Englishman, asked me to. I was trying to interest ordinary people in financing scenes of his antinuclear film to be shot in fifteen countries. The Brit wanted the general public to finance his movie.

At the fund-raising meeting where Peter turned up, I didn't notice him until he was leaving, and I hardly looked at him then. He touched my elbow just as we were breaking for a glass of wine. "I have to leave. I'll be in touch. Oh, I'm with Lawyers for Social Responsibility," he said with a kind of hesitation.

"Yes, and what's your name?" I asked, glancing but not seeing, registering only his name as I turned to speak with someone else. I wasn't drawn to lawyers, felt they can't see anything for what it really is, always laying an ill-fitting grid over everything. So I didn't engage. But later I remembered the lawyer's voice. Deep. Smooth. Resonant. Mysterious somehow, I thought. I wondered why he'd left early.

A few days later the voice stopped by my apartment to look at some papers concerning the movie project. We stood near the door talking business. I was showing him something on a document when I noticed he was standing very close to me. I saw his hand make a slight gesture, a few dark hairs visible at the wrist, a cuff, a lawyer's three-piece gray pinstripe. I suddenly became very aware of him as a human being separate from myself. The hairs on the back of my neck rose up. It was animal to animal and lasted only a few seconds. He stepped away then, and the moment passed.

I dreamed about Peter that night. I hadn't been dreaming for months. I'd been hibernating, not dreaming. I was ripe for an epic, a wet dream. That night, I nearly knocked myself unconscious, thrusting back in my dream to embrace Peter against the headboard of my bed. I heard his voice and looked into his face, and there was nothing there. Because I didn't know what he looked like. I hadn't even noticed what the object of my dream fantasy looked like in real life. I was that morose.

My moroseness probably started with the eighties decade, probably the minute Ronald Reagan took office, so fast did I lose my bearings in terms of my own work. It was the end of an era. People started thinking differently about money. My community of people was breaking up. Some were moving away from the "neighb."

A decade before I'd come back to the States from all the great theater in Paris to do theater in Portland. I discovered the "neighb" right there in my own hometown, a jewel of a community, and it had grown into a big extended family where we'd all known one another intimately throughout the seventies, seeing life through the prism of our passions, becoming artists because we had something to say. But art money dried up with the Reagan recession: Social generosity became passé, and a change in tax law wiped out the limited partnership as an attractive-to-investors means of financing independent motion pictures. The culture narrowed as people hunkered down.

I'd been one of the first to say we had to grow, not live in the past, but so doing I cut myself off. I felt isolated. I'd got no good feeling from Portland for at least a year before I met Peter. It was like being stuck in my hometown. I'd begun to fantasize about going back to Paris. Work in film that had felt good in the boom of the earlier decade was reduced, in the bust, to thinking about numbers.

I was like a hungry animal, looking for an opening. I would wake up with my fists clenched, jaw aching, and would sit in the YWCA sauna longer than you're supposed to. I was down to my last five hundred dollars in a rotting Victorian house with a basement full of film cans when the Brit came along.

He needed someone to raise money for his antinuke epic in the age of accelerating nuclear missile proliferation on both sides of the Wall. The Brit was passionate, had a difficult, huge personality, and could, if he chose, move people to tears. Without either of us knowing it, he tapped into my terror. I took on the job.

I dressed up and went to see the president of the historical society — himself a huge personality with a booming voice, and the best fund-raiser in town. I bent my nose to smell the yellow lilies on his desk, sat down and made my case. We agreed on a date for an evening at his house with all the socially committed rich people he knew. My Brit would do his thing, and we'd have the money we needed.

In the elevator mirror on the way out, I saw I had a yellow blob of pollen on the end of my nose from the lilies. I decided it must have charmed the president, brought good luck.

The evening of the fund-raiser, the British film director droned patronizingly on and on, lecturing people whose only desire when they'd left home was to write a check. It felt like a disaster. My spirits sank through the floor.

The president phoned me the next day. "Your man shot himself in the foot!" he bellowed.

I still had to get the money somehow. It would take months and months. I had to hold up my end as promised: It's my fatal flaw. But the director wanted the money in small amounts only, wanted it from a large number of people, from kids having bake sales and donating $7.50. This movie was going to belong to these very people, said the director, and some part of me wanted to believe this. But this meant I could be paid only $500 a month, and I had no nest egg, no personal wealth. I felt physically smaller and smaller, folded in on myself, as if my size were somehow dependent on how much I was groveling for money. It was depressing. There was a certain grimness to my demeanor as I held meeting after meeting.

A few days after I'd dreamed about fucking Peter, he telephoned me. It was a dark, rainy afternoon about five-thirty.

"Would you like to go to a film?" Very direct, an immediacy that arrested my attention. Totally and abruptly.

"Yes," I replied as directly.

Now he hesitated. "Have you seen *The Big Chill*?"

The hesitation made me smile. "No, I haven't. . . . let's go see it."

"It starts in two hours. I'll come by in an hour and a half."

So, it was like a date, going to the movies with someone I scarcely knew yet was already wildly attracted to. Was it just the mysterious voice? At the movies I sat next to him with a heightened physical awareness. We were sitting in an old-fashioned velvet-covered double seat, a feature of Portland's Movie House, which was once some kind of society women's club.

Each time Peter shifted position, I was increasingly aware of the mere centimeters separating our knees, our thighs, our shoulders. Or not separating them. I gradually entered into that heightened state where breathing is voluntary, where the body is held in an updraft of anticipation. On the way out of the cinema, I caught sight of myself in a mirror and did a double take. I looked radiant. There was a pink glow to my usually white, Irish-looking face. My dark hair was voluminous.

I was calm as we drank a beer in a café and talked, examining each other, until Peter began to talk about a dream he'd had the night before, in which he drove his Mustang over a waterfall. My own dream came back to me just then. I felt palpably transparent, self-conscious. There was a moment of intimate confusion between us, an atomic exchange.

"Do you ever have erotic dreams?" he asked, only he wasn't asking. He was saying it. He was reading it in my eyes, or my breathing, or the way my hands lay on the table.

"I do, yes," I answered evenly, but after this advance he retreated, and in the car on the way home I was relieved. I kissed his cheekbone and ran up alone to my front door. I glimpsed his face looking up at me when I looked down toward the Mustang from the porch, and it struck me as bright, open, and satisfied. Boyish but knowing. A revelation!

I was breaking through my depression fantasizing about Peter and only too happy to have him come and sit on my couch like Prince Charming a couple of afternoons later, awakening me with his immediacy. It was then that I truly looked at him for the first time, this object of my fantasies. I was astounded to see how attractive he was. He had a Jimmy Stewart way about him — the directness, the winningness, the earnestness — what the French call first-degree behavior: engaged, guileless, with nothing held in reserve, not cynical, completely respectful, intending to be taken seriously, cerebral.

"I think I'd like to live in Kyoto," Peter said that day. And then he told me he thought of himself as actually already on his way to Kyoto, where he imagined he wanted to live. He said he'd probably been on his way to Kyoto for years.

"I probably moved out to Oregon after law school only because Oregon is on the way to Kyoto," he said in a jokey way, not joking at all. "I imagine shrines and mists and the sun rising futuristically out of the Pacific. I envision some kind of personal breakthrough happening in Kyoto, some anticipated change in the more Westernized structures of my thinking."

I was silent.

"Or something," he said. "But I haven't gone yet."

"Why not?"

Peter was sitting with a ray of the setting sun backlighting his dark, almost black hair, which he wore rather longish behind the ears in an Italian way. The light cast an aura around his angst-filled head. He was almost too beautiful.

"I'm afraid I'd be disappointed," he said, laughing real hard suddenly, cackling almost, some kind of Kansas guffaw ripping through the tortured look. He was funny.

I had the sensation of floating pleasurably toward him, relieved. It was that laugh, that wonderful sidesplitting, self-mocking laugh.

"I'm having dinner Friday . . . ," he started, stopped, shaking his head slightly, meeting my gaze with a dozen messages. It wasn't like someone flipping through his Rolodex but rather like someone settling something in his own mind before he moved on.

"I've been trying to meet people from China or Japan, so there's a dinner, some Chinese. You want to go with me?"

My head went hot. I saw the future flashing like neon and immediately felt vulnerable, foolish. I wasn't twenty-five, after all, but thirty-eight, and I had known both love and disappointment. This was no first-time thing for me.

At the dinner spirits were high, the three professors from the People's Republic of China fluent and witty in English, interested in everything. The food was superb, the lawyer-couple hosts jovial. The other guests were an American woman artist and her French husband, from Montpellier and possessed of all the unmeasured exuberance the southern French can display. It was late in the meal when Yves, in response to some now-forgotten stimulus, told us about farts.

"Zere are tzree kinds of farts," he said, his finger in the air

like a Cartesian. He pronounced *farts* with a swallowed French
r. Everyone was already laughing, partly because of the subject, partly because Yves was one of those people whose body
language is funny even before they say a word.

"Zere is zee kind where you 'ave eat somezing awful, like
bad cauliflower salad, and eet smell a certain way, and zen
zere is zee kind where you 'ave eat some beans, and eet smell
anozere way, and zen zere is zee kind where you 'ave to
sheet. . . ."

What he was saying zinged, transcendent of culture. Laughter erupted from lower depths. Like farts! The Chinese spoke
excitedly to one another in Chinese. They laughed so hard, it
was as if they had been carefully holding it in until then. As
the moment twisted and turned into near hysteria, everyone
skidding and breathing hard, Peter and I stared at each other.
The moment felt full of potential, as if we were on an adven-
ture that could go anywhere. Astonishingly, it was real now,
not a fantasy.

Back at my house later, I pulled Peter into my bedroom and
down onto my bed, wanting him in my arms and between my
legs as fast as possible. It was a couple of days later, when I
smelled his smell suddenly, before I had any kind of conscious
thought at all.

I wanted him, was what I thought.

He pulled away from me early that Monday morning, his
suit on a hanger in his hand, and went to the gym. I wanted
him not ever to go, not to leave our warm bed, not to leave. I
felt bereft.

But later in the day, as I separated psychologically from Peter, I was quite pleased to be alone. It was a stimulating state,
full of vague yearnings, both attachment and resistance to attachment. I took out a bound blank book I had bought sometime before and never written in, and started a new journal.

Why would I fall for a lawyer? I wrote. A man who plots his life out like a case, when I am so impetuous? Maybe it's the Asia thing. He wants to be caught up. To be caught up in something or someone impetuously. On a new page, I wrote: Peter got me starting writing this journal! The goad — not always a man, but this time, a man.

The next time we were together was my first time out in the country at Peter's tiny house, the house he wore like a shell. I'd felt awkward driving out there, as I realized I couldn't remember what Peter was like, who he was. I was searching my mind: How had we ever become intimate? By what series of movements? We were so new to each other. "I am going to see a complete stranger," I said out loud.

And then Peter was standing there in his doorway, and again he seemed too good-looking. His house was so private, so small, with all his belongings exposed, sitting out in the open, his stack of sweaters on top of the chest of drawers. I could scarcely look at him, but he came toward me directly, unabashedly, like an animal might, and we made love standing up. We were all over the tiny space, and somewhere in the middle of it I saw on the wall Peter's print, like mine, of Hiroshige's people crossing the Ohashi Bridge in the rain, a blue-gray river and sky crossed diagonally by a bridge, tiny people with umbrellas scurrying across, the whole pounded by a torrent of rain.

I was out of my mind with recognition. I fixed on Peter, thunderstruck. His face one inch from mine, he reached with a kiss, which turned unexpectedly into a sob welling up out of him, like keening from an abyss. Everything changed very rapidly.

We got horizontal and held each other, Peter sobbing, stuttering something out every once in a while.

"Why did you look at me like that?" he whispered, totally raw.

"Like what? What does my look say?" I whispered back.

Then, after a long stillness, he sounded calm as he said, "I can't tell what I feel."

I was sure I knew already what he felt.

Later he wanted to make it better, not hurt my feelings it seemed like, so he said, "It feels good that you want me like that." I was aware then that my wanting him affected both of us, changed both of us.

The next time Peter cried was at his little cottage again, in that economical space where his life lay bare on every surface and then spilled out into the surrounding forest, which I saw through his eyes as he took me around, showing me the creek and the rest of his territory.

Inside the house, a Navajo rug suspended from the rafters to the floor divided the sleeping area from the living/working/cooking/eating space, in the center of which there was a low couch. Over the couch Peter had draped a thick Moroccan wool rug, whose rough perfume — ambergris mixed with the redolent lanolin of the wool — had a life of its own, wafting out into the room to ensnare lovers. We made love there slowly. It was a Sunday afternoon, it was raining outside, and Jean-Pierre Rampal played Handel's *Water Music* over the sound system.

"I love you, Peter," I said too forcefully, as a result of trying not to say it.

"I love your body," he said hotly. The words reverberated pleasurably for both of us a moment, but he was then suddenly racked with sobs. This time I cried, too, a pain-letting I welcomed, I went for it so easily. Both of us were completely disarmed. We hung on to each other, and then the tape clicked off before the end of the music. It felt like an unexpected camera move, a cue, and I was suddenly both in the scene and outside it, watching. I saw our tearstained faces.

I was astounded. "Where do all your tears come from?" Peter shook his head, couldn't talk.

"Why am I crying?" I said.

"That was so crass to say I love your body," Peter said abruptly. *That was what he was thinking about.*

"But I loved it when you said that!" I said. I was laughing. "I did," I said. "I really did." I was rapturous now. Peter was moving his eyes slowly around my laughing face. He stared at me. He pressed his face against mine.

"I'm not used to this, whatever it is," he said into my hair. The rain fell softly outside. "No, it's not that," he pressed on, snuffling. "It just seems like a blank spot."

"But you're full of emotion . . . I see you wanting certain things so badly — you yearn for them. I see it." How could he think of himself as blank? I was grappling with the idea.

"I don't want you to have any expectations," he said after a long pause.

I didn't have any. "I don't have any," I said. "You owe me nothing. I don't have a picture." It was true, I had none. "You can make it go the way you want it to go."

Peter shifted in my arms and gazed at the ceiling. "It doesn't bother you, not knowing where you're going?" he asked, now more comfortably in control.

"No," I answered. "In all honesty, it excites me."

He turned, and we smiled at each other. After a while, we got up and cooked Thai curry chicken in his wok.

Midweek, contentedly alone in my creaky house, I wrote in my journal: Why is this man attractive to me? Why did I cry like that? My fantasies with this brainy man amaze me. They make me want him irrationally. I've been hit by Cupid's arrow.

I am drawn to Peter as to my other half. Or is it to get a glimpse of my own other half? I cry with him, because I feel pain instead of feeling numb. I don't feel numb now.

Does this mean I do have a picture? I wrote. Am I fooling myself, saying I don't?

On a fresh page I wrote: What is my picture? Do I want to live with Peter? Certainly not in my house, certainly not in his. We would not get along in a small space. I need my privacy; obviously, he needs his. We would not get along if we saw each other all the time. He would see all my horrible qualities. But he seems not to notice. I would feel no restraint with him. I would go wild. But then I would drain him, trample him. No wonder he is so hesitant! He's right! But perhaps, on the other hand, he has staying power, is in it for the long haul. Perhaps, yes, he would eventually put out my fire, douse me? No, he wouldn't. Why am I going on like this?

We kept on that way, country, city, city, country, two or three times a week, and everything mattered, first degree. I spent less and less time with my friends. I gradually withdrew from my old life. I was molting. Six months went by, and I came fully into a new skin.

In the city, Peter paid for movies and dinners out in the traditional man-woman fashion as I earned less and less money, a situation I was beginning to find intolerable. He encouraged me not to worry about the money, to write more and more in my journal, to seize the opportunity to do what I wanted to do. He said, "Go ahead. Do It." "But I don't want you to support me," I said. "But I am not supporting you," he said. "I am just taking up the slack." He was hard to turn down.

Every day I filled pages with stories, plots, pieces of dialogue, scenes straining not to be about people arguing over how to communicate with other people about nuclear missiles. Quite naturally, as Peter took up more and more of my thoughts, I wrote about him and about us: This does not feel like stasis, I wrote. I feel like I have moved out of stagnant, irradiated waters, and we are speeding up. We are approaching some kind of plunge, a waterfall, some rapids. What happens now?

What happened was a lovers' quarrel. He'd had plans from long before we met to go on a cross-country ski trek for a week with the gang he often did this sort of physical feat with — rafting and kayaking down rivers of no return, that sort of thing. Actually, they did more than that together. They talked, this gang: one or two man-woman couples (one of the women ever so briefly a former lover of Peter's); four lesbians: a doctor, a dentist, a lawyer, a teacher; and Peter. Spending time with them was really the only hanging out Peter did. I met them all and saw how much they all loved Peter. They welcomed me into their midst, but I felt they were something Peter should keep for himself. I wanted to go on the ski trip, but I didn't really want to go. He wanted me to go, but he didn't really want me to go.

In the end I didn't go, and fell back into blackness imagining Peter getting it on with his old girlfriend. Later, I would learn that Peter had sat and stared into space whenever the intrepid trekkers weren't on the move that cold week on skis, and he left for home a day early. He called me from some remote gas station after skiing the distance back to his car alone. "If you're still awake, I'll be back tonight about midnight."

And then, when he got there, we argued. About nothing, or everything — about me losing control of my imagination and seeing him running off with his old girlfriend and being angry and jealous.

We argued as well about Peter, wondering why he'd gone in the first place when he ended up feeling so bad, having regrets — a troublesome behavior pattern. An intimate fight.

And then I could see Peter felt low-down, as if he'd been stupid.

There was a big silence.

"Listen," he said suddenly. He took a deep breath, and took a great leap of faith.

"Would you like to caretake a ranch outside of Saints with me?" He stood, his arms hanging down, his feet planted, ready for an answer. I can see him now. He wanted to please, looked certain he was going to, and did. He didn't even care that I was sometimes a jerk.

"What?" I said dumbly. I hadn't quite got what he'd said. It was so unexpected, such a change of direction, cutting from the plane crash to the happy ending. "Caretake a what?" I stuttered.

"A ranch," he said carefully. "With Arabian horses," he added, already aware by that time, I think, of certain horse fantasies I entertained.

The fantasies were already galloping across my mental screen. I resisted them, ordered them back. "Who offered that?" I asked, something wounded surfacing again.

"One of the women on the trek . . . it's her boyfriend's family's ranch."

I weighed this, found it innocent. Peter was grinning confidently. "I thought you wanted to go to Asia," I said lamely.

"I can still do that," he said, keeping his options open, which suited me.

TWO

A MOUNTAIN RANGE runs north-to-south all the way from Canada down through Washington State and Oregon and into California, and dryland pine forests climb down the eastern side of the range and continue out eastward onto the flat lands all the way to the true alkaline deserts of Eastern Washington and Oregon, of Idaho and Nevada. The town of Saints sits just east of the mountains, surrounded by a ponderosa pine national forest, on the high desert of Central Oregon. The landscape is dry, the horizon distant, the vistas daunting.

Our second week at the ranch, Peter climbed into the battered four-wheel-drive Scout pickup that came with the place. He wanted to drive around and take stock, mark his boundaries so to speak, but the Scout wouldn't start, wouldn't even turn over. He decided to walk the fence instead and found it down in twenty-two places. He also found several fence rails tied together with flimsy yellow kitchen string. Within a few days he'd discovered nearly everything mechanical or man-made on the entire ranch was either jerry-rigged or broken. The tractor was dead, the septic system clogged, the water pump and chain saw broken. The hay barn caved in a week after our arrival. It was as if the winter had been long and troubled.

"You think maybe George and Luanne Miller're laughing at us back there in Missouri right about now?" Peter suggested to me. George and Luanne were the previous caretakers.

It was April, but the day was hot, and Peter was dripping sweat on the kitchen floor. He'd been trying to prop up the corner of the hay barn with a juniper pole for a couple of hours. He took off his sunglasses and mopped his brow with his handkerchief, a Kansas gesture.

"No, I don't think so," I said. "I think they'd given up and were sad." I was standing on a chair painting over the Millers' orange-plaid kitchen wallpaper with a glossy shade of creamy enamel.

Under the floorboards, Dad Cat growled and laid into some other beast. They shrieked and thudded against the floor. This was before we were able to get a handle on the cat situation, before we met Faith Gaines. One thing was certain: George and Luanne Miller had given up at least on cat control before they left the ranch.

It would have been hasty to suspect the Millers of negligence. We'd been told there was an area of disagreement between them and the ranch owners, something about George and Luanne wanting to buy the caretaker's cabin for years and the owners not wanting to sell. We'd met the Millers and the ranch owners at the same time — in the midst of their final parting, which was carried out in front of Peter and me, forever influencing the way we saw the place.

It happened like this: Not too long after we'd got the offer to caretake the ranch, Peter and I had decided to go look it over and meet the owners. By then I'd decided the ranch sounded great, not preposterous at all — I could write a book, start anew, find my peasant roots, try to live with someone I was in love with. Peter had been more cautious. He had wondered how much work was actually involved at no pay, for that was the going rate — free rent and use of the horses but no pay.

That first time up, we drove east through the ponderosa and rangelands of the Warm Springs Indian Reservation, south into the town of Madras, a cowboy and wheat center with towering grain elevators at one end, a stock auction at the other. It was in Madras we first saw a signpost for Rajneeshpuram, the strange city carved out of the dust early in the Reagan years by followers of an Indian mystic known as Bhagwan Shree Rajneesh:

RAJNEESHPURAM 40 MILES!

Seeing the sign was a jolt. Before that moment I hadn't thought of the Rajneeshees as being part of the landscape Peter and I were headed into, even though they'd been out there noisily on the Oregon high desert for several years by the time we drove through Madras that day.

The red-clad Rajneeshees had bought a vast ranch called the Big Muddy out on the high desert in Christian fundamentalist country and built a city on it, and the ranch was now called Rancho Rajneesh. Not only had they taken possession of the land and the landscape but, through notoriety and money and power, they'd become ruthless in their conquest of the West. They looked to be trying to make Manifest Destiny their own. Bhagwan Shree Rajneesh the man was controversial and would have called attention to himself anywhere, although he was hidden away, not available to the public. Was he a sex guru, an enlightened Hindu master, or the devil incarnate? the local and national press asked, leading the rest of us to ask the same things and ultimately making it impossible that the man should, in fact, be ordinary.

By the time Peter and I happened on the scene, there were more than a thousand people installed in the remote canyons of Rajneeshpuram. They were American, English, Australian,

German, Dutch, Indian from India, Japanese, Brazilian, what have you. The person in charge at Rancho Rajneesh, an India-born woman named Sheela, had successfully stirred up media attention worldwide. Each time she turned up on the tube, she seemed to be more outrageous.

For a year the Oregon press had spoken of nothing but how the sect had stolen the tiny desert town of Antelope from its retired old-timers. Sheela had sneered: "The town was old and dying and so were the people." American papers and television had all picked up the story and played it at length, with images of Sheela's startlingly lopsided face, one side going up, the other down, her large black eyes round and sharp. The stories never seemed to gel except as caricature, a kind of pre-millennial, end-of-the-world madness. You were always left wondering what kind of an 'enlightened person' would keep somebody like Sheela in charge.

That very morning before leaving for the high desert, I'd read something in *The Oregonian* about the Rajneeshees. The piece said that Sheela had received the Oregon Council of Teachers of English Doublespeak Award. Sheela's winning remark was "You tell your governor, your attorney general and all the bigoted pigs outside that if one person on Rancho Rajneesh is harmed . . . I will have fifteen of their heads, and I mean it. You have given me no choice. Even though I am a nonviolent person, I will do that." Next to the story was a photo of the banshee Sheela, one shoulder thrust forward threateningly, her small, dark face twisted as usual. What a joke. How did they get all those archetypically evil photos of Sheela?

As Peter and I drove through Madras that day, it was odd to think the Rajneeshees were just up the road. Maybe they aren't really there, I thought hopefully. Maybe they are only a media event. They are too easy a target. I want nothing to do with Sheela. I want nothing to do with the Rajneeshees. They have nothing whatsoever to do with what Peter and I are doing.

"You want to drive out there?" Peter said suddenly.

"Where?"

"Rajneeshpuram?"

"Now?"

There was a sudden change of scenery as Peter U-turned and headed back to the cutoff. He laughed at the incredulous look on my face. He seemed loose and contented with himself. He made me smile. He melted my resistance.

"Now?" I asked again, laughing.

Up the highway to the Willowdale Cafe was as far as we got toward Rajneeshpuram that day. The cafe was a filling station–cafe combination built in the twenties, a remote, isolated stopover perched like a checkpoint outside Rajneeshee territory. The Willowdale Cafe was a place for locals only. It was for border watching. RAJNEESHEES NOT WELCOME HERE, a sign said.

Peter and I approached the screen door cautiously. There was something ominous in the sudden silence inside. Just outside the door was a stack of *The Bulletin*, a local newspaper, with the following story above the fold on the front page:

Child Abuse At Commune Alleged

A petition alleging more than 150 children in Rajneeshpuram have been victims of child abuse was filed Monday by Eugene Attorney Charles Porter in Wasco County Circuit Court. . . .

Porter, who filed the petition on behalf of Diane McDonald of Madras, said [Judge] Jackson refused to grant his request that all the alleged victims of child abuse be taken into protective custody.

> Because of the petition, the Children's
> Services Division must immediately
> launch an investigation of the complaint,
> Porter said. . . .
> "It's not true," said Ma Prem Isabel,
> spokeswoman for the community, of the
> allegations. "The kids are beautiful kids,
> beautifully taken care of."

"So, do they fuck the kids or don't they?" I wondered out loud.

"Shhh." Peter steered me in the door.

Inside the cafe Peter and I were scrutinized, and over at the next table I saw hostile glances in our direction and heard the muffled word *Rajneesh*. This hostility I found interesting. I could have pushed it a little, but Peter seemed affronted, said, "Let's go up there some other time," and got up to go.

Back in the Mustang, I reverted to earlier thoughts of what bores the Rajneeshees were. These sect stories seem to fascinate the media and no one else. I was relieved to be back on track.

We headed south again, through dry, springtime, high-altitude air of great clarity. The air was a remarkable change from Portland's humidity and mildew.

"What's that smell?" I said, cranking down the car window, sucking in a sudden new odor. According to road signs, we were passing through a mini-badlands called Lost Creek Canyon.

"A skunk maybe?" Peter ventured, sniffing.

"No, it's not a skunk . . . something else." I sucked it in. "It's like cat musk, only sweeter and richer."

"Cat musk? I've got a woman who likes cat musk?"

"Stop the car. . . . I gotta see what it is," I said. Peter pulled off the highway onto the gravel.

Outside there was only sagebrush and juniper and hardpan.

We finally decided the smell was coming from the juniper foliage. The only person I later asked about it was a shaman type who said it was the earth calling for her man. Earth calling for her man, I wrote in a fresh new volume of my journal, this one the journal of Saints.

Saints itself seemed awful at first sight, all quaintness and artificiality, its little main section lined with old-timey, false-fronted buildings, only a few of which were actually antique. The newer buildings imitated the Old West architecture of the old. It was a theme town, a planned tourist destination, a cute lie. There were countless gift shops and boutiques, many churches down side streets. A man and woman and their two kids were coming out of a T-shirt boutique. All boasted "I love Saints" T-shirts.

Outside of town, well into the national forest, we found the lodgepole pine–log gate we were looking for. We drove in under the simple single log arch with its single fortune-filled horseshoe and onto a bridge made out of a steel railway flatcar. Below us a creek roared. On the other side, the Mustang dropped down through the riparian corridor alongside the creek, the thick forest canopy neatly divided by the narrow, dusty road.

And then we broke through to a little clearing where stood a sentinel: one of the biggest pines I'd ever seen, seven feet wide seemingly all the way up to the sky. Its bark was yellowish and dark brown, diamond scaled, like the crust of baked yellow bread cracked open and sealed by the dry heat for several centuries.

We followed the little road around to the south, where it opened out onto the postcard, the calendar shot: the lush pasture, the giant cottonwoods, the horses, the trio of white mountains poking up behind in deep focus. We gasped. I felt romantic, smarmy. Tears came to my eyes. My body jived and danced a car-seat jig.

I looked over at Peter and saw his body slowly relaxing back into the seat, as if unclenching. His arm floated gently off the armrest of its own accord. Much later, he would tell me his sphincter muscles had been spasming orgasmically, something he confessed could be counted on the first time he saw any truly great piece of property.

After we dragged ourselves away from the first Great Southern Exposure Spectacle, we drove on into the drier, desertlike part of the ranch, where the Main House was located. Just at the border between lush green and desert stood another single giant ponderosa pine, this one even larger than the first, a monster against the sky. The two trees were dinosaurs, the legacy of a not-so-distant past when the whole place was a parklike stand of giants.

We passed the remains of a smokehouse and a sagging hay barn. The ground was dust or else hardpan, shaped into gullies and dry washes, dotted with juniper, pine, sage, bitterbrush, cheatgrass, and an occasional sand lily. Once again I smelled the sweet, acrid perfume we'd smelled in Lost Creek Canyon, the smell of the desert.

Sitting on the Main House veranda with the Viorsts that first time, I could see Peter struggling to remember the doubts he'd felt earlier. The ranch was an empty vessel waiting for us to fill it. We had already decided the pay, or lack of it, was not a problem. I had the Victorian house in Portland I could rent out for a few hundred, and Peter had stashed away thirty thousand dollars from lawyering — more than enough to get us to Japan or China or wherever if we didn't want to stick around Saints too long.

And maybe I could write articles, I was thinking, make a little money that way.

"You understand we'll probably be here only six months?" Peter said, wanting to be certain the Viorsts registered his ambivalence, making eye contact first with Bob Viorst, who nodded stiffly, in control, and then with Elaine, who shook her head emphatically while miming that she'd been caught with her mouth full. Her round jolliness comfortably compensated for her husband's restraint. She and Bob were both wearing understated denim western gear, so I guess they'd been riding before we arrived. Just out from their veranda, two horses were rolling in the dirt, scratching their backs the way horses do after they're unsaddled and turned loose. The pasture where they were rolling was dry and brown, and they were raising clouds of fine red dust, which hung suspended in the hot, still air.

For lunch Elaine set out baskets of good breads, sliced cheeses, meats, and vegetables, along with garlic dip and horseradish and three kinds of gourmet mustard. A dessert tray was heaped with sliced melons and immense red strawberries. "I'm a good assembler," she said and laughed deeply in an appealing way when I exclaimed over the lunch. She had great warmth and created an aura of undeniable generosity.

As officer in charge, Viorst moved things forward. A hard-edged corporate millionaire, he had a way of sticking to an agenda. He asked Peter and me to take note of a list of useful names and phone numbers — insurance agent, veterinarian, attorney, et cetera — as well as a list of rules regarding the Main House: garbage must be placed in plastic bags, secured with twist ties, and taken to the dump; electric heat must be kept at forty degrees when house is unoccupied; house must be checked regularly for varmints; all openings to the outside, such as fans or fireplace drafts, must be kept closed when house is unoccupied.

"So how does that look?" he asked, smiling.

"That's it, huh?" Peter asked in return, still studying the lists.

"That's it," answered Viorst.

"Well," Peter said hesitantly. "It doesn't sound like too much . . ."

"No, it sounds great!" I said, rushing to erase all doubts.

Viorst leaned toward me conspiratorially. "Nothing to it, right?" Then he rose, done, ready to move on. We all stood up and followed him into the house, where he showed us a tall, carved vaquero saddle studded in Mexican silver. The leather appeared to have been nibbled off by a rodent all along the front peak and around the stirrups.

"George said he killed a pack rat in here, but I don't know how the hell one could've got in," Viorst said, and I sensed tension in his voice, but then he smiled again. Peter seemed nervous, as if his doubts had resurfaced.

I thought he might be thinking about the fact that we were actually going to be living together. I knew he wanted to do it, but he had no real idea what to expect, because he had never lived with a woman before. I'd been married once rather briefly and since then lived alone or with different men twice. In any case, I was amazed at how we were carrying the whole thing off — how legitimate we looked, setting ourselves up not just as caretakers but as a duo. All the intricacies of couple intimacy aside from sex — the textures of being with just one person instead of a group or alone — were new to Peter. He had no expectations, no baggage filled with broken dreams, no old habits. He knew only what he wanted to avoid, which apparently included just about every pattern for cohabitation he'd ever had the opportunity to observe, which is a kind of baggage as well.

"What I fear and dread most are expectations," he had said

several times early on. "On any side." I'd at first told him I'd keep him informed if I developed any, so it had become a joke. After that he hadn't insisted, so I'd forgotten all about it.

Walking the half mile from the Main House back to the care-taker's cabin on the green side of the ranch, Viorst steered Pe-ter up ahead with him, while Elaine and I dropped behind. Viorst was obviously a man's man, a maker of waves, and Elaine smoothed the waters. She took on a more confidential tone with me as she explained that the Millers had asked many times to buy the caretaker's cabin and the land it sat on, but she and Bob had always refused, not wanting to break up the property.

"So now they want us to reimburse them for the improve-ments and furnishings they've added to the house hoping it would one day be theirs," she said awkwardly. "I think Bob'll go along with the idea of some money as long as what they're asking isn't too much."

I felt caught between two worlds. Elaine seemed embar-rassed at the situation but determined to get through it as smoothly as possible. She wanted Peter and me to look at each item the Millers were trying to sell and decide if we wanted it.

We reached the caretaker's cabin and stepped up onto the sagging front porch. Viorst was whistling in a consciously de-tached sort of way, and Elaine was twirling her finger against the end of her nose. Peter was looking into the rafters to see what was holding the porch up.

Inside, the cabin was darkened and shuttered against the blazing sun, a state it would never know during our tenure.

"George isn't here, he's still at the church," Luanne Miller apologized as Elaine introduced her to Peter and me. She was still dressed for church, in a navy blue rayon dress with white polka dots. She was cute and very short, a cowboy's live-wire wife in five-inch Springolators. She teetered around, showing us down a long, narrow hallway with small rooms off it, bunkhouse style. We said no to the Formica coatrack that extended the length of the hall.

Luanne's hair was perfect, her makeup and long fingernails meticulous, but she looked like she was going to cry. We said yes to the wagon-wheel chandeliers in the large living room, no to the matching gold plush easy chair and no to the couch her son was sitting on, watching TV.

We stepped into the country kitchen. It was a large, square room, the only other large room in the house, its huge, family-sized table smack in the middle. I said yes enthusiastically to the long, wooden table and eight straight-back chairs. The kitchen had my complete attention. Around the periphery, handmade cabinets and open shelves were roughly fashioned of old wood, the boards darkened by smoke and age, redolent of a thousand pies. In contrast, the wide pine-board flooring was bright yellow. To the south, the horizontal window above the plank countertops looked straight out into the Spectacle. This kitchen, I later wrote in my journal, this kitchen is a place to die for, to be in with your friends, to laugh and talk in, to breathe in.

"Oooooh." I swooned. Viorst looked at me and laughed, stepped out of the room. Elaine looked at him, adjusted her face into a false wide-eyed innocence, and followed after. When they were gone, Luanne grabbed my hand, as if she'd seen me swoon and felt like swooning herself. "We're goin' to Joplin," she said to me, her eyes full now of real tears, spilling over and down her cheeks. "We're gonna have a piece of land of our own," she said, her gaze drifting off out the window and then back to me. "No more waitin' and hopin' and prayin' for us, we're gonna have our own place."

Luanne and I stood transfixed for a moment holding hands in the kitchen, then she turned to follow the others.

Outside on the porch, Viorst seemed surprised when he saw the red wheelbarrow the Millers were offering for sale. "What the hell?" he muttered, but just then George drove up and parked his car at the hitching post a few yards from the porch. George was the pastor of the evangelical Saints Church of the Second Coming and a former grand champion rodeo cowboy as well. He was handsome as the devil, as they say — short and lithe, in his early forties, full black hair revealed when he reached up and took off his white preacher's cowboy hat. George made a striking picture as he stood by his car in his white western-style suit and tooled cowboy boots. We all stood awkwardly on the porch looking at him, and then Elaine started us all moving toward George, who waited, rather defiantly it seemed, for us to get to him rather than meeting us halfway. Viorst introduced him to Peter and me, and we all shook hands.

Later, as we walked back to the Main House, Viorst and Peter ahead, Elaine and I behind, Viorst turned and asked Peter where we planned to spend the night. We hadn't given the matter a thought.

"We're going to be leaving shortly to drive to Portland," Viorst said. "But you're welcome to stay in one of the hunters' cabins just beyond those pines over there." He was pointing off in the distance beyond the hay barn.

Elaine snorted. "The cabins are rather primitive," she said, laughing her agreeable laugh. "I don't promise what you'll find in there." Viorst was whistling again, his protective mantle.

When we got back to the Main House, Elaine pulled me aside to say her husband had probably not realized the cabins hadn't been cleaned in over a year and were no doubt full of animal droppings. "We'll be gone in a little while," she said. "Why don't you go for a walk and then spend the night in our house?"

The Viorsts' house was contemporary, that Oregon version of Nordic clean lines and squared-off volumes that lends itself so generously to Northwest commercial-dimension timber. That night Peter and I colonized the Viorsts' bed, which afforded a perfect view of the mountains at dawn. We awoke early and talked in a dream state, the windows thrown open to morning high-desert sounds — sporadic bursts of intense birdsong and, in between, the stealthy steps and breathing of deer grazing below the windows.

At breakfast Peter was pensive. We were eating croissants we'd found in the Viorsts' freezer.

"I can't believe George and Luanne let themselves care so much about the ranch when they knew they weren't ever going to get a piece of it," he said.

"That's easy for you to say," I said. "You're a lawyer, remember?" He looked at me vaguely, as if he saw no connection between the one thing and the other.

At nine o'clock George came round to the Main House on horseback leading two other horses. He was tan and wiry, as comfortable atop a horse as a man could be. It would later be possible for me to remember him dressed as a preacher the way he'd been the day before, but I would more readily remember him as a cowboy on his horse the way he was that morning, all in black, a big black hat, and around his trim waist an enormous silver belt buckle that touted, "Grand Champion Saints Rodeo."

George showed us where all the tack was kept and some tricks to calm a horse so you could check its hooves. I was excited to be around horses for the first time in maybe twenty years. I was crazed with energy. Peter was mainly careful and attentive. George was plain comfortable with the horses. We saddled up and headed southeast a mile and a half toward the spot where George said the main irrigation ditch flowed through a grate onto the ranch.

"Now, that's the main thing you gotta know about," he said, twisting his body around in his saddle to talk to Peter. I was just at his flank, but Peter had fallen a few yards behind, so George had to talk around me. "You gotta keep that grate clean. You gotta be sure there ain't no pine needles in there, mud, what have you. And if the ditches get clogged, you gotta get somebody in there with a backhoe and clean 'em out."

We rode cross country, zigzagging back and forth to cross fences where they happened to be down. Once we crossed a tidy, deep racing flow of water about a foot and a half wide, and George said that was how a ditch should look when it was cleaned out.

"You gotta keep a watch out for barbed wire or little bundles of plain wire 'cause the horses could catch their feet on that. So you try to gather old wire like that up when you're out in the truck and got somewhere to put it," he said in his country-music accent as he pointed out various stashes of wire he'd left for future pickup. The troves were mostly at eye level, in the crotches of old, broken-down junipers.

When we arrived at the ditch grate, George showed us how to tie a horse to a tree with a slipknot for easy release. We looked at the grate — a simple, guillotinelike piece of sheet metal that moved up and down in wooden slots. We each opened and closed it manually a few times.

"I leave it at the halfway mark, keep the water under control," George instructed. Then he unsaddled his horse and taught us how to leap onto a horse bareback by clutching the mane in the left hand and heaving the rest of the body over the horse with a running jump start. He gave each of us a leg up a few times until we could do it alone.

As we left the ditch grate, I pulled ahead, making it easier for George to talk just to Peter, which was what he clearly wanted to do.

"Just follow the trail," George said to me as he and Peter fell in together behind me. I could hear him explaining how to keep the horse Peter was on — the big Appaloosa proud cut — from foundering, which it apparently had a tendency to do. He told Peter not to gallop in the pastures because of all the varmint holes, and he said if Peter wanted to ride hard out to go onto the trail system in the national forest, which completely surrounded the ranch.

"If you wanna learn about the horse trails out there, get in touch with a man name of Ed Dyer outta the Saints District the Forest Service," said George. "Dyer's the one built all the trails . . . a fine man, a Christian and man of the woods."

George and Peter fell farther behind me. I could still hear them, though, the forest was so quiet, padded with dust. They talked easily with each other, slower and slower, in tune with the terrain and the pace we were keeping. George was saying that living on the ranch was sharing in God's pleasure.

Next I heard George ask Peter if he and I were married.

"We are, in our hearts," Peter said, startling me while trying to please George.

"Well," said George, lowering his voice a little, "it's our belief folks ought to be married in Christ's name as well."

I twisted slightly back in my saddle to catch what Peter was going to say to that. I saw him look at George, sincerity flooding his face. "Well, George," he said, "I'm just waiting for the feeling."

"That's right, that's right," George replied solemnly, glancing at me with disapproval.

I galloped off and left the two of them in my dust, disgusted, thinking that marriage was probably the surest way to diminish a strong start.

It was only later, after they were gone, that we really came to know and understand the Millers as we came to know the ranch. It seemed like everyone in Saints had been out to "George Miller's place" during the Millers' nine years there. The entire congregation of the Church of the Second Coming had picnicked there more than once, the men playing horseshoes alongside the fence, the women sitting at tables in the grass near the swamp. People in town had assumed that George and Luanne were buying their place, and the Millers had hoped it would one day be true.

Perhaps the fence pieced together with flimsy yellow string was the solution of a man whose mind was elsewhere. Or maybe the yellow string had been Luanne's handiwork. We would later learn it was Luanne who had taped the kitchen chairs together when they broke, so the yellow string was probably hers, too. When Peter first told me about the yellow string, I walked the fence and looked for myself. I imagined tiny Luanne Miller in her high heels, married to George, going outside to mend fence and have a good cry.

THREE

B ECAUSE OF THE ALTITUDE at Saints, the spring
nights were cold. One minute the sun would be blast-
ing us from above a row of illuminated Cascade peaks,
and the next minute, cold air would race toward us off now-
black silhouettes, and fog would form in exact lines above the
irrigation ditches slicing down through the land. Later I saw
it was just like in Morocco, where fog hangs above the con-
crete-lined ditches snaking off the snowy Atlas Mountains
toward the northern drylands.

The cabin sat at the lowest point on the property, facing
up-country. Seen from the living room, the steam rising over
the ditches at sunset would slowly drift out of its exactness
into a serpentlike chimera hovering over the land. The effect
was theatrical, and, indeed, the view to the south was an epic
western stage set in every way: horses playing out their competitive dramas in a lush meadow bordered on one side by
towering cottonwoods, on the other by quaking aspens. A
curtain of darker green ponderosa sweeping across behind,
and in the distance, looming huge on the horizon, those
mountains, stunningly backlit. In the center of this vista was a
tight trio of snowcapped peaks huddling toward one another
like gossiping sisters. Early Christian settlers had named the
three Faith, Hope, and Charity.

It was all very overwhelming to newcomers such as Peter and myself. We were unprepared for the psychological demands of a big sky. We did not at first know how to live in keeping with such a theatrical setting, or with such pious values either, for that matter. The stage seemed somehow too wide, the Christian fundamentalist culture too chaste. The picture asked to be filled in, to have dynamic human activity in the foreground, a little sin. You could see how Sheela could be inspired to hyperbole just by looking at the landscape.

Actually Peter knew more than I did about living under a big sky. He grew up on the flat, broad plains of western Kansas, where the sky is two-thirds of the picture. I, the urban declassée, was more accustomed to the close and heavy sky over the valleys of the Pacific Northwest or of the Seine. At Saints, unlike in either Portland or Paris, the shimmering indigo of the firmament was startling. It drew the eyes upward with such force the head lolled.

"What're you doing later?" Peter asked me as we ate lunch in the sun at a weathered picnic table. We did ranch work as a team each morning, but in the beginning I spent afternoons stretched out next to the meadow gazing at the horses or into the silent vista. I was trying to see what I might take on, what there was to do on a western ranch that suited me.

Or I read. Or I sat inside the house at the round, yellow table and wrote in my journal. How to live? How to live with this man? These were the questions. I sat with my back to the breathtaking southern vista to escape its demands. I wrote about physical sensations, about ongoing fantasies. About sex.

"What about you?" I'd ask Peter in turn. Amazingly, he'd taken on characteristics of a self-sufficient Kansas Methodist the instant we came onto the ranch. He was like Henry Fonda — shockingly at home in his skin. And shockingly Protestant as well, as if the area's dominant values were contagious. Peter had a long list of things to do, was a little embarrassed for me to see he was keeping a list. He worked morning, noon, and night, had to make a dent in the endless tasks of repairing and imposing order on ranch operations. I was surprised. I'd thought he just wanted to stare into space.

"What will happen when you get to the bottom of the list?" I teased from the depths of a chaise longue where I, in a lapsed Presbyterian mode, was just then doing the job I sensed I was meant to do. I felt relieved to know Peter didn't care if I didn't feel like digging in, and I couldn't believe he might think I cared if he did. We were both struggling a bit about living with someone else.

"Well, when I get to the bottom of the list," he said thoughtfully, "I'll see what happens."

"Maybe the list will keep expanding, hmmmm? There will always be something else?"

"The place should at least function, don't you think?" he said, shifting gears. Not testily, but logically. He had inhabited the environment immediately while I was viewing it as cinema. The difference between us wasn't a problem though. It was exciting, like a curve negotiating a curve.

"Maybe I'll go riding," I might say. "Want to go?"

Sometimes Peter did ride with me. He chose a towering Appaloosa proud cut while I rode Coco, a little bay Arab mare that dominated the herd. She'd been a cutting horse. Only fourteen and a half hands high, Coco the dominatrix remained fearless and authoritarian, capable of menacing even an unpredictable sex-brained proud cut. Her mane and tail were black and huge, like combed-out dreadlocks. I liked Coco.

Most often, though, Peter said no to my invitations to ride. He preferred the Honda motorbike or the four-wheel-drive pickup or even his feet for getting around the ranch. I didn't mind riding alone, even preferred it, as it was my fantasy, not his.

I pulled Coco out of the herd and left the other horses wondering about the pecking order without her. She and I headed south into the national forest and onto the Metolius-Windigo National Recreation Trail. The Metolius-Windigo is a lonesome path cutting south through the forest for twenty stunning miles. Eventually, the trail runs into officially designated lonesomeness — the high-alpine rock and ice of the national wilderness circling the mountaintops.

When Coco and I took off from the ranch, we ended up winding through the sky toward the mountains on the Metolius-Windigo, tracing the actual horizon along a spiny ridge of igneous rock right at timberline. Skinny lodgepole pine grew thick below us on either side, but we were high above it all, exposed. It was as if the horse and I were like fleas moving along the arched spine of a giant beast. Ahead of us loomed Faith, Hope, and Charity, looking different up close, less like gentle women gossiping, more like the jagged volcanic masses they are.

Coco kicked up great clouds of dust, and we disappeared into them. She was vital, released from her tedious pasture duties, a youth plunging through the dust, perfectly surefooted over terrain that could trip up a neophyte. She retaught me everything I'd ever learned of "western pleasure" riding as a little girl galloping madly up and down coastal beaches: loose reins, voice commands, heel and thigh pressed firmly against the horse's ribs on the side opposite the turn while leaning into the turn, like on a motorcycle.

"Coco, you save my life, baby," I'd say, borrowing the cowboy's compliment paid a good horse.

After I went riding solo the first time, Peter told me it was a white Arab proud cut named Granite who moved up in the pecking order when I took Coco out of the herd.

"Ya'll oughta see 'im," he said in his best Kansas redneck voice. "Forced all them other horses into a tight little knot and then pranced around, pretty as you please, neck arched, breathing fire."

Peter arched his own neck then and pranced around, arms glued to his sides. He sidled around behind me, wanting to mount me from the rear. We were in the kitchen at the time, so I grabbed hold of the counter for support. I was still wearing my cowboy boots, but he pulled my Levi's down around my boot tops and tilted my pelvis up onto his excitement while he breathed fire into my ear for a minute or so before we slipped to the floor.

Later, a yellow meadowlark flew full bore into the picture window, not breaking it but falling stunned to the ground outside. As we watched, the bird was snatched up into Dad Cat's jaws and ripped to shreds.

Then, deep in the meadow, there was movement, and we could see a line of coyotes traveling in a phalanx across the landscape. They all stopped and poised stiffly, noses down holes, waiting. Suddenly one of them seized something, tossed it in the air, caught it, swallowed it. Without missing a beat, they all moved on to new holes and froze, until some crazed, terrorized ground squirrel belowstairs made a break for it up a hole, straight into the jaws of a different coyote, or perhaps the same coyote, who got to eat twice. These coyotes looked like a unit with no problems in communication. They'd done this before.

"Kind of sets a tone," Peter said, smiling.

"It will take years to catch the whole show," I said.

A look of panic stole into Peter's eyes.

"Oh, come on," I said. "I'm just kidding."

"No, you're not."

"Well, yes, I'm not kidding," I admitted. "It would probably take years to see everything there is to see out there . . . it doesn't mean we have to see all of it. We can see just part of it."

This was true and reasonable, and I could see Peter consciously deciding not to freak out. Instead, he mimed sinking slowly into the desert, the sands closing over his head, his vision evaporating before his eyes. He threw his arms around wildly. He was really a wonderfully physical actor.

"It'll take years, it'll take years," I taunted like a kid and ran out the front door. There was something about being with Peter that kept me engaged, ready to go. He ran after me and caught me and pushed me down on the grass and sat on me. It seemed for an instant threatening, as if we weren't playing, as if we were total strangers.

"You're very sure we won't still be here, are you?" he said, slowly tapping his index finger on my breastbone, Chinese torture style.

"I have no picture, no fantasy, nothing." I giggled, and the whole thing just became funny, not threatening anymore.

At the end of April, all the ranch she-cats came into heat, signaling the arrival of summer on the high desert. Each night as the moon waxed fuller, their tremolos filled the woodshed next to the room where Peter and I slept.

"I feel like a fool competing with them," he said one night.

"Meooooow," I said, but he meant it, rejected my play. I couldn't always guess what Peter was going to respond to and what he wasn't, which was exciting. In any case, he did not just then enjoy listening to the guttural passive hostility of successful feline mating, didn't accede as easily as I did to bestiality.

"Take a gun and shoot 'em if you can," said Larry Lazio the next day. Larry was our nearest neighbor to the east. I had mentioned to him when he stopped by that Peter and I didn't know how to get rid of our pestiferous cats.

"Pestiferous, huh?" he said, enjoying the word, moving his head around, his dark-lidded Italian eyes pixilating. Larry seemed lighthearted and of generous spirit.

"You know you're entitled to about twice as much water as you're gettin' right now?" he asked jocularly. He was sitting on his motorcycle in our front yard, grinning, another short, lithe, handsome man, this one in his fifties. Larry was the state ditch rider, whose job it was to monitor the diversion of water out of our creek.

"I'd be happy to open up your water gate full force," he went on, "but you better check first, clean out your grate. I doubt George Miller got to it before they took off." He laughed and shook his head, leaving the rest, whatever it might actually have been, unsaid.

"I already did it," Peter said. "We thought we were getting all the water we were going to get, so I cleaned out the system to make it stretch further."

Larry looked surprised. "You already did it all?" he asked. He gazed briefly at Peter, taking his measure. "You don't fool around," he said, and then he looked off into the pasture, musing. The horses were standing at the fence nearby, watching Larry's motorcycle, which idled quietly. No one spoke.

Finally, after a long country while, Larry broke the pause awkwardly, still looking out into the middle distance but addressing Peter one man to another. To Larry at least, I had become invisible — a malady of the high desert I was beginning to think.

"Who are you?" he asked Peter, still gazing out to pasture. "I mean, what do you do for a living?" There was another long silence. Larry looked over at Peter briefly, paused, then swung his gaze back out to the horizon.

It was Peter's turn to be awkward as he hesitated, rather existentially I thought. "I've been a lawyer," he said, looking at the side of Larry's face. "That is, I was a lawyer."

"Hmmmm," said Larry, nodding his head inscrutably. "I might have something to talk to you about." He started to go but then stopped and looked back. "I'll open your water gate," he said, his eyes dancing again. Then he sped off, raising a little cloud of red dust on the road.

"Was he striking a bargain?" I said to Peter, describing what I thought I'd seen. He looked at me sharply, as if my reading of what I'd seen were way off base, far from what he thought had transpired. Or perhaps Peter was hoping what I'd said had not transpired, or perhaps neither of those. He weighed his thoughts, said, "Well, you're probably right," in a kind of passive-aggressive way.

Oh, God.

"I wasn't trying to be right or anything," I said desperately, and we looked at each other a long moment, each of us spinning through a thousand revolutions, then settling. "I am not the enemy," I said conspiratorially. Slowly he nodded, grinned, and everything was all right.

That night the feline madness intensified. While we were asleep, a piercing cry rang out in the woodshed as something actually flung itself against the door between the shed and our bedroom. Peter leapt out of bed, hurled the door open. He looked wild in the moonlight that shone in on him. His face contorted, his teeth grinding. He went stiff legged and rigidly kicked his legs in front of him, first one, then the other.

I laughed. But then I saw he wasn't acting but really wide-eyed angry, staring at me with huge brown eyes. "Damn, I wish I hadn't told him I was a lawyer," he barked out and then weirdly laughed a little, which jolted loose a kind of violent gasp. He reached for me and hung on like a kid. I was thrilled and attracted by Peter's sudden shift to his unconscious self.

"Why did I tell him that?" he croaked. "I don't want people to know anything at all about me, about us. And then I tell Lazio *that* of all things. In Garden City, when I was growing up, people found out one thing about somebody, and then they thought they knew who he was and invented the rest. I'm trapped," he snarled, a raw nerve. "I've gone nowhere at all."

He was absolutely laid low. I touched his face.

"We won't tell anybody anything else," I said, feeling a primitive drive to comfort, to make it all right for him, because it did feel absolutely all right. I have no discomfort with existential ambiguity, quite the contrary. But there was something happening to Peter I didn't understand.

"I don't even want to be a lawyer anymore," he mumbled. "I'm not a lawyer anymore. I don't want to live my old life. I want to drift, to feel my way along."

"So that's what you're doing."

Peter let out a long sigh that turned into a shudder. "Soon as Lazio heard I was a lawyer, he said he might have something to talk to me about, so it's already too late."

"What's the lawyer thing about?"

He pulled back and peered at me, actually glared at me. "You hate lawyers," he said, ducking the question.

"But that's my problem, what about you?"

There was a pause before he swung back around, lawyerlike probably, picking up the thread.

"Remember you said that because I'm a lawyer, I should

know not to fall in love with this ranch because I'll never get a piece of it?"

"So have you already fallen love with it?"

"I don't know, but for me, lawyering isn't in my heart like that, it's just a performance," he said, as if reciting from memory.

"Like being an actor?"

"It feels very false. It's not where I want to be."

"It's not really you?"

"I don't think so."

"And the falseness is what you want to get away from?"

"Yes, but when I get the cue, I just go right into this lawyer persona, as if I had no choice, even against my will."

"So just don't perform. Refuse to perform. Tell Lazio you were kidding the next time he brings it up. Tell him you're really a ditchdigger. Tell him you're conflicted about your profession."

"He knows I wasn't kidding, and don't try to talk it away," he said jaggedly. "Just let me feel bad."

We got in bed, and I held him until I fell asleep. I dreamed fitfully of the dying porcupine with its claw still embedded in the twig of cottonwood and awoke with a start to find Peter now holding me tightly.

The next day dawned glorious. Sunlight caught my attention as it glinted on the pink crowns of the Saints and also, a bit closer, on what appeared to be water in the middle of our pasture. Two honking Canada geese swooped down over the house and landed in tandem on the sparkling water. They skittered along like water-skiers, spray fanning out behind.

"The pasture's flooded," I announced. "How'd that happen?"

Peter ate his bagel standing up, looking out the window at

the geese and the water. After breakfast we drove the Scout up to the irrigation district dam on the creek. The dam was a simple concrete structure, probably not more than thirty years old. It had been built specifically to back the creek water up sufficiently to fill a creek-sized irrigation ditch that serviced all the district irrigators on the other side of the creek from us. The heavy concrete gate onto that ditch could be raised or lowered by turning a humongous screw with a steering-wheel handle that was locked in place once adjustments were made by the water master. Down below water level on our side of the dam was a hole through which water poured into a long, underground pipe and thence into the smaller, open ditch leading onto our ranch. We walked down the ditch a few yards to where we found Larry Lazio measuring with a plain wooden ruler the water we were getting as it flowed over a weir.

"I opened it up last night," Larry shouted over the roar of spring snowmelt churning away from the dam in several directions. He looked back over his shoulder at Peter and grinned. "Getting any water yet?"

"Yes," Peter shouted.

"You're gettin' about one, one and a quarter cubic feet a second right now," Larry pronounced. "You usually have about half a cubic foot, but there's so much water right now, and you have flood rights . . . we'll have to watch it, make sure things don't get out of hand." He stood up, hitched up his pants, then pointed upstream toward the mountains, on which the snow was gleaming and surely melting in the hot sun.

"You ever had a flood here?" Peter asked, bending toward Larry slightly to make himself heard.

"We had a good one in 'sixty-four," Larry hollered and then chuckled at my wide-eyed reaction. "Knocked out your bridge. Just below that the whole creek took off in a new direction. It used to angle off more to the west. Now it goes straight toward town. We'll just keep a watch on it and close your gate if the water gets too brown."

Peter and I left the dam and backtracked down through the property to the grate George Miller had shown us where the irrigation network bifurcated into separate systems, one system swinging to the west in a fast-moving rush to an indentation in the earth that might once have been a pond. The other system described a slow northern crawl toward our own pasture.

"To hell with this," Peter said as he slammed open the guillotine grate George Miller had kept at half-mast. All one and a quarter cubic feet of water surged full force into the sleepy flow of the northbound network, leaving the westbound ditch to puddle up with a chorus of sucking sounds and then silence. The ditches were really only primitive furrows sliced through the land with a backhoe, so their width and depth varied according to the terrain, very much in the manner of streams. All the ditches had sprouted vegetation and filled up with pine needles or disappeared altogether under fallen branches. With the grate cranked wide open, the northbound ditch had to accommodate about four times as much water as might shoot from an inner-city fire hydrant on a hot summer's day.

The water leapt along. Peter and I kept a dynamic pace on opposite sides of the bank, leapfrogging boulders or sage and manzanita, pointing and shouting as the water swirled and eddied in the wide sandy spots. In one place the water breached the bank and half the flow rushed off to the west. We saw there had been a lateral system cutting off at that point, only now it was flattened, and the water fanned out like a delta, seeking its own way. George Miller, or someone long before him, had apparently closed all these smaller gates.

George must have always routed the water straight down through the property toward the caretaker's house and then over toward the Main House in a manner that had evidently satisfied the Viorsts on their infrequent visits to the ranch. And seeing as how George had viewed the ditches essentially as a chore, he probably never did what we were now doing.

"I'll get the shovel," Peter hollered, breaking into my thoughts. I watched him gracefully leap the ditch, his hand reaching for an alder on the other side to swing up and around, propelling him in the direction of the Scout. I turned and ran on down the main chance watercourse, where rising waters climbed up the bases of willows and alder saplings lining the banks. The water made loud gurgling noises as it sucked down into air pockets or gopher holes. On the opposite bank, the rushing water found a makeshift dam of two boards, swirled in front of it, and began to seep over the top into another lateral system, this one leading to a dead patch of willows whose switches had dried and silvered in the sun like whale rib cages on a sandy beach.

"To hell with this," I said, ecstatic, and got down on my hands and knees and pried the two boards loose from the muck with my bare hands. Water moved slowly into the long-dry channel, pushing a decade's worth of pine needles and pinecones ahead of it. I stepped into the little ditch ahead of the flow. I walked along, kicking cones and twigs off to one side. The water followed me like a dog.

I lost track of time.

Peter caught up with me where the main ditch cut across the bottom of our pasture. It was flooded over, settling into a thigh-deep lake, which was growing, spreading, actually moving down the pasture. Our eyes followed the flow. The water was moving down through a long, winding, grassy arroyo that had always been there but that had been invisible when there was only a pasture full of thick, tall, green grass. It had been totally camouflaged. Now you could see that the pasture had probably often been underwater in past springtimes.

"It's the old creek bed!" shouted Peter, the explorer with a route opening up before him. He splashed into the current in his black gum boots, the tops of which were underwater. "Or maybe a still-active alternative creek bed! Ha! That's why the pasture's so green! It's really a creek!"

Peter splashed off into the flow. I watched him and suddenly saw the whole picture, wide angle. The channel he was following serpentined down into the swamp next to our cabin, situated at the bottom of the pasture. The swamp was already filling up with water, coming alive, overflowing on down below. The cabin was idyllic down there, at such a remove, squat and yellowish brown with its green patched roof. I was thinking the roof should be red, terra-cotta red, and then my pleasure would know no bounds.

It was that evening after we'd chased water all day that Faith Gaines telephoned at a wild tilt. I answered the phone, and the woman on the other end was utterly tongue-tied. She stuttered out that she was trying to locate an attorney named Peter something, and my first reaction was that she was disappointed to reach a female voice. I later learned she'd been so full of confusion it was only with an immense desperation that she'd made the call at all. Desperation, and the vague hope that Peter, a newcomer in town, was safe.

"Every other person in town's in the Forest Service or else their husband is or else they know someone who is," Faith said to Peter by way of explaining the phone call. "Anyway, I can't go around saying that one of the Forest Service guys is a pervert to just anybody and still expect to keep on making a living in this town. I mean, I don't even know you but there's nobody else for me to ask for advice so that's why I'm calling."

I fretted for a minute that Faith had heard Peter was a lawyer from the local chiropractor, whom I'd gone to see. The chiro was such a chatty type, I'd mentioned without thinking that Peter was a lawyer. But I'd probably only helped along something Peter had started himself by telling Larry Lazio. Besides, Peter had also said he was a lawyer to the mechanic who'd worked on the Scout a few days earlier. The guy had wanted to do the work for next to nothing until Peter had insisted on a fair wage, saying that we were caretakers out where George Miller had lived and that the ranch owner would reimburse us.

"Sure, I know George's place," the man had said. "He's gone? You with the church, too?" Peter had said he'd been a lawyer in Portland but that he didn't intend to practice law in Saints. For his honesty, Peter had gotten a skeptical look. As we drove away, we'd commented on the self-righteousness right there in God's service station. We'd rushed home to the isolation and debauchery of our ranch.

Peter took the phone and went to sit on the couch. He was concentrating intently, listening to Faith. I noticed he had a hard time catching what she was straining to express. He was pulling it out of her. He squinted and gestured with his free hand, wanting to clarify, then suddenly changed position and threw his entire weight into interrupting her, which evidently wasn't easy as he got in only one word about ten times before he got to ask a whole question.

I'd been reading a book before the phone call, Yukio Mishima's *Thirst for Love*, a novel about a woman's obsession, but I couldn't keep reading because Peter's conversation was very interesting, and he was engaging me in it with his eyes. It seemed like he didn't want to be left talking with Faith by himself. I got up to leave once, to allow him his privacy, but he looked alarmed and gestured vigorously that I should stay.

During the course of the conversation, Peter looked increasingly distressed. He talked for nearly an hour. I'd never seen this before, this performance, as he might have called it, nor would I have imagined how it might cost him. It was indeed as if he'd heard his cue, and something inside him responded, as if he had no control over it, even if it wasn't what he wanted to be doing. After he hung up, he walked back and forth for another hour, wearing a path between the couch and the yellow table, repeating the conversation.

Faith had called to talk about what had happened to her son. Peter had told her he wasn't practicing law now, but she had continued talking. She had wanted to know if she could sue the U.S. Forest Service. She had wanted to know if it was possible to sue because of what they had done to her son.

"What had they done?" Peter had asked several times. I'd heard him.

"What had they done? What had they done?"

No answer for a long time. That was what had been so frustrating. Poor Peter, I was thinking. Getting sucked in. There was no fighting it. Being a lawyer's like being a magnet, and clients converge like iron filings.

Faith had said she'd had a visit from a state policeman who had told her a forester from the Forest Service may have "fiddled around with" her son. "Done something," she'd elaborated less than precisely. And, in fact, she didn't really know what was happening, because her son wouldn't talk to her. But she knew the forester, knew him well, or at least she'd thought she knew him well, had thought of him as a friend. She wouldn't tell Peter the man's name. She said it was somebody with the Saints District of the Forest Service, somebody who had taken her son Billy camping up in the Wilderness. Somebody who had taught Billy to shoot, both rifle and shotgun, she explained. And taught him how to hunt. Somebody who was like a father to Billy.

"Well, did the guy diddle Billy or not?" I shouted, frustrated.

"She's so hard to listen to!" exclaimed Peter, almost angry, metamorphosing before my eyes into a desperate person, responding to Faith Gaines's desperation, her helplessness. He seemed vulnerable to me, at risk.

"Billy met this guy two years ago, when the Forest Service sent him to talk to Billy's eighth-grade class about forestry. What an incredible jerk!" he said, pained.

"I even know his wife!" Faith had shouted so forcefully through the phone it had sounded to me as if a cat had screamed outside, and I'd gone to the door to look. The air was limpid, with a chill coming on.

Peter had gone on, talking calmly and reassuringly to Faith when he clearly hadn't felt calm at all.

"He's probably pretty upset, yes?" Peter had said into the receiver and then listened silently, painfully, for a long while. "Call again, okay?" he'd said so gently my heart had swelled. Apparently, Faith had then asked Peter if we had any pets or domestic farm animals she could perform veterinary services on, because he had then told her about our cat problem. That was when she offered to cut or kill any cat we could catch; she even had cage traps we could use.

Peter stopped pacing, sat down at the yellow table, and gazed out. "Shit!" he said.

"She's freaked out," I said.

"Right."

"And now you're freaked out, but we can talk about it, you know? You don't have to buy into her denial, yes?"

He snorted, looked frustrated, then annoyed, as if I'd expressed disapproval. I didn't speak. Things felt out of kilter.

"She needs help," he said finally, shifting his mode yet another time. "Who's anybody supposed to talk to around here? Don't suppose there's a hot line."

"You're the hot line."

He rolled his eyes.

"Aren't people supposed to talk to their clergyman?" I suggested.

"No one does, of course. George Miller was probably her clergyman. Would you talk to George Miller about something like this?"

"No, of course not. George Miller thinks people ought to be married in Christ's name fer chrissake!"

Peter sighed heavily. "I thought the law was an urban malady," he said, staring out the south window. He was absently stroking the end of his nose with a knuckle of his index finger, elbow hanging expectantly in midair. He turned and looked at me, seeking a response. I was at a loss and felt that he was grappling with a question much larger than the one at hand.

"Why did she call me?" he asked rhetorically.

I handed him a Sapporo beer. We'd taken to drinking either that or Tsingtao, looking ahead to Asia. He drank the beer, gazing out the window but not noticing the endless line of deer picking their way single file across the picture to the flooded arroyo, where they lined up to drink.

The next morning, I went by Faith Gaines's office for the cage traps. I didn't see Faith. She was in surgery with her identical twin sister, the two of them pulling porcupine quills out of a visiting poodle's snout, the receptionist told me. I had wanted to meet Faith, see for myself what she was like, and now there was not one but two of her to imagine. So Faith's stuttering came not only from denial's cruel gag but also from a twin's legendary agony at talking to anyone not her twin.

I didn't see her, nor did we hear from Faith for some time. This was typical of the sparsely populated high desert, we would learn, where the nature of stories is that they spin out slowly.

FOUR

ONE OF THE EFFECTS of stories spinning out slowly is that the people who live on the high desert seem to hold an image in their heads longer than people do in the city, where events bunch up and commingle. A simple exchange of facts takes three times as long as it might down in the city.

"Oh, it sounds like your wife flushed the toilet," the septic-tank man said to Peter as the two of them stood outside over the open end of our sewer pipe, where it emptied into the septic tank the man had been hired to pump out.

I had indeed just flushed the toilet inside. Peter would later tell me the two of them had watched as two neat turds and a wad of toilet paper floated by and dropped into the tank. Peter had laughed, but the other man had gone blank, as if a curtain had come down.

"I guess your wife flushed the toilet," the man had repeated, his face a mask. Then, a minute or two later, the man said he guessed the line wasn't clogged anymore. "It worked fine when your wife flushed the toilet," he said, still with no trace of irony. Peter had wanted to laugh again but hadn't, waiting to see what the man might say next.

"The third time he said it, the guy was so solemn, I couldn't tell anymore if it was funny or not," Peter said to me later. He said the man had returned to the subject yet another time when he suggested they might test the line once more. "Maybe you could ask your wife to flush the toilet again," he suggested, obsessively but still without affect, as if he wanted very much to do something with the subject, but could not or would not. Weeks later Peter saw him in town, and the man asked in all earnestness how our toilet was working.

Up on the high desert obsessions endure, for good or for ill. Events fix in the imagination like the dust hanging in the air long after the commotion has passed. Most observers blame the isolation, which keeps one's perspective tightly focused. Others fault the aridity and extremes of temperature (from 27 below zero to 109 above in an average year, days that would paralyze a city but that are worked straight through in the country). Up there, things don't rust or mold but persist and take on grandiose proportions. No one gauges how much in one year the batten on the weather side of a structure gets deformed, exposed as it is to the annual cycle from hard freeze to bake oven, until one day you can put your fingers in the channels left by soft wood eroding between ridges of hard resin.

Not long after we came to live on the ranch, I met an old-timer in the grocery store checkout line who told me there was a ghost who regularly haunted the ridgetop ranch six miles to the south of us. The subject had come up because of the *Enquirer* headline DAUGHTER'S GHOST HAUNTS MOTHER, which had got the old guy talking.

"Man's name was Harve Dorrance," he twanged quite believably, "and ol' Dorrance got his haid blown off by a shotgun blast sometime around the turn of the century." According to the storyteller, Dorrance was still hanging around the ridgetop and still headless.

I looked the story up in the county library in Bend. In the

local newspaper of record (then and now *The Bulletin*), it said that Dorrance had been a logger with a violent temper who'd spent time in jail for assault before he was finally killed by a Mr. Melvin, a homesteader. The paper said they'd argued over water rights.

MURDER ENDS FEUD trumpeted *The Bulletin* headline, and there were two versions of Dorrance's shooting: that of Melvin, who claimed Dorrance fired at him twice, hitting him in the chest and hat before he fired once on Dorrance; and that of Dorrance, whose head had not been blown off and who, before he died, told the doctor attending him that Melvin had shot him in the stomach so he (Dorrance) had then shot Melvin.

"*The Bulletin,*" the story went on piously, "in an attempt to get an impartial statement of the whole trouble, finds the general opinion to be that Melvin was justified in the shooting and undoubtedly did it in self-defense." Stories of Dorrance's violence followed; his former acquaintances apparently said he was a bully with brutal instincts, and, what was more, his wife was in an insane asylum, driven there by her husband. "People living in the vicinity of his mill report that the whole neighborhood has been afraid of him and that people breathe easier now that he is removed . . . the sympathy of the entire community is with Melvin." A later story said that Melvin was not indicted for murder or for anything at all. "The evidence before the [grand] jury showed plainly that Dorrance had threatened to kill Melvin and that Melvin shot in self-defense," said *The Bulletin* of May 10, 1907.

There was no further record in the library of either man. Nor was there any mention in the county archives of a ghost.

As it happened, the current owner of Melvin's ranch was a man named Hamilton Jones, who was teaching an adult evening class at the Saints Elementary School. The class was called Natural History of the High Desert, and Peter enrolled us the minute he heard about it. I did look forward to meeting another one of our neighbors. In a place as remote as the ranch, neighbors become intrinsically interesting. Who else will save your life, should it need saving?

Before the class convened even once, we had learned that Jones was a Yale man, Skull and Bones, attractive, well-off, the subject of a tremendous amount of gossip around Saints. He traveled a lot, it was said: India, New York, the Bahamas. And Jones had a lot of women visitors.

"Does anyone know the expression 'climax community?'" Jones asked us, tugging his ear as he stood in front of rows of fifth-grade wooden desks. It was the first class session, and Jones was all WASP patrician in a soft-looking lime green sweater and what appeared to be Armani trousers, definitely a cut above the way everyone else was dressed. A medieval leer played about the corners of his mouth, telegraphing his subtext as he moved behind the lectern and leaned toward us purposefully.

"Climax community," he said again. A few people in the class tittered. Most everybody there was a retiree, new to Saints like us, and we were all pleased to learn how to draw information from coyote scat or an eruption of pine sap. Some of the retirees were repeats in Jones's class, so they'd probably heard the climax-community routine before, but still, everyone was watching Jones expectantly. He was clearly enjoying himself.

"A climax community," Jones said finally, his hands rising before him dramatically, "is the species of flora or fauna that eventually dominates in a given setting if nature is allowed to take its course. Now let's think seriously about what this means."

Peter and I exchanged a look, and I leaned over and wrote "very ponderosa" in his notebook. We started giggling like little kids, and Jones enjoyed himself all the more, somehow riding on whatever energy was coming his way. He expanded, grew larger, and effectively drew us all in.

After class Peter introduced himself to Jones and to his girlfriend, Sally, who in turn invited us for dinner the following Saturday night. It was our first social engagement in the isolation of the high desert, and we both felt a sense of adolescent anticipation.

Ham Jones had bought his ranch after he came into his inheritance at twenty-one. He chose the high desert near Saints because he'd vacationed there, in the sun-drenched high country where Portland's wealthy class has summered since the turn of the century, like Hollywood going to Palm Springs. Ham had lived there twenty years now, leaving only to get a Ph.D. in zoology, specializing in crustaceans of all things. Nowadays, he went to the Bahamas twice a year for never-ending research on crustaceans, back and forth between ocean and desert, always tearing himself away from one thing to get to the other.

Ham's dryland ranch followed the curve of the ridgetop, exposed to the elements. All the buildings were lined up down behind the ridge, out of the wind. Farther below lay irrigated pastures, where Ham and his caretakers grew hay and raised llamas. He called his llamas designer animals.

"Elizabeth Taylor has one," he said, pouring the champagne. "They make great pets. I have seven Chilean llamas on their way here as we speak. The U.S. government opened the window on Chilean llamas and closed it again. Only four hundred and fifty got in, and I have seven of them."

We drank to Ham's Chilean llamas and ate a great meal Sally had prepared. There was one precarious moment when Ham bad-mouthed his past and present caretakers.

"You gotta watch out for those caretakers," Peter said ironically, abruptly affecting his University of Virginia Law School gentleman manner to match Jones's patrician air. Jones seemed not to notice the shift, and the moment passed.

"I hear you have a ghost," I said.

"So you've heard that, have you?" Ham said, smiling, wickedly pleased at my interest in his netherworld visitor. He leaned forward, elbows on the table, taking control of the moment. I took the cue.

"Tell us."

"I'll tell it to you the way I heard it from a man who was twelve at the time it happened, the horse's mouth, nothing less." He got up then and served cognac all around before starting his story.

"Melvin was a saint," Ham began. "It was only through an extraordinary effort that he was able to get water to this property — he flumed it here from a spring way up the ridge. An incredible amount of work for one man. It's not an easy property to own," he added, self-consciously associating himself with the saint.

Ham looked around from Sally to Peter to me as he talked, insisting we match his intensity. Sally had a genuine wide-eyed-bimbo look on her face as she listened. Ham had probably told his story to any number of genuinely wide-eyed women before this one, but he made it fresh. He loved an audience, and he had one.

Ham told us how Dorrance had appeared one day at Melvin's homestead wanting some of Melvin's water to operate his sawmill. They reached an agreement to allow Dorrance a certain amount of water. But instead, the evil Dorrance diverted all the water, destroyed Melvin's flume, and beat Melvin up when Melvin objected.

"Melvin just took it." Ham sighed, slumping dejectedly. "And the next year the same thing again. Dorrance destroyed the second flume Melvin had built."

That second year Melvin went to see Dorrance, Ham told us. He took with him his water-rights certificate, a piece of paper signed by Teddy Roosevelt himself. This connection to someone powerful was obviously important to Ham, and he made visible the precious piece of paper as Dorrance ripped it to shreds.

"So what happened after that?" asked Sally.

"Melvin ducked out of sight, got his shotgun, came back, and blew Dorrance's head off."

"Blew his head off?" Peter asked. I'd told him earlier what I'd read in *The Bulletin*, and he was balking at the discrepancy.

"Blew his head off," Ham said. "There was blood everywhere."

"Blew his head off?" Peter asked again rather archly.

"Yes," Ham said with absolute certainty, looking Peter directly in the eye. "Proof of it, Dorrance's ghost is headless."

"So the ghost comes back looking for his head probably?" I suggested, wanting Ham to put himself all the way into his tale, but he drew back.

"Well, who knows," he said. There was a silence. Ham leaned over and chucked Sally under the chin, leering at her.

"Have you ever seen the ghost?" Peter asked, not letting go of the thread.

"No," said Ham, "but others have, since I've owned the ranch. One woman, who'd never heard a word about Dorrance, was standing over by the ridgetop one day, said she saw him. I went with her to look but didn't see anything. She told me it was a big guy with no head."

Ham went on to tell us most of the sightings had been by macho-type men, men who might have had something in common with Dorrance. "I'm not macho enough, I guess," he said, this time grinning at me. Peter laughed, I'm not sure at what.

Ham raised his hand then, ministerlike, as if he had a pronouncement to make, waited until he had our full attention. "Dorrance came back to haunt Melvin," he said. "This is what I heard from my original source. Melvin went insane and killed himself. This is the absolute, verifiable truth. You can look it up in the records. And," he finished almost triumphantly, "everybody who ever owned this ranch since has been haunted by Dorrance and has committed suicide, just like Melvin."

"Was he toying with us or just lying," Peter said later as the Scout bounced down the rocky red dirt road from Ham's ranch to ours. I looked at the side of Peter's face in the dark. He flared his nostrils.

"It's as if he wanted us to fear him, to fear for him, to become involved in his destiny," I suggested.

Peter nodded sharply. "Exactly. He's so full of himself and wants us to be full of him, too."

"He kind of dominates the skyline."

"You want this man to dominate our skyline?"

"Maybe it's all just a good story. It's such a man's story."

"The head blown off?"

"That's the best part of the story! The part where everybody buys in, the part that makes you ready to see the ghost! There's gotta be something to account for all the maleness going on around here."

"Oh yeah," said Peter, putting his arm around me, pulling me close, so we wouldn't go on trying to talk about our different visions of Ham but would, instead, melt into a single shape on the bench seat of the pickup, like other shapes in other pickups going out to the ridge road to neck.

A few days later, Larry Lazio's wife, Marlene, told me Dorrance's ghost wasn't in the history of Saints she'd typed for a local author, but she knew about Dorrance nevertheless. Marlene was girlish and sweet, short and slender, with a big smile, head always tilted coyly to the side, gray curly hair.

"Dorrance is not the sort of thing you put in a history book," she said to me in a mock-scolding way. Peter and I were at the Lazios' to find out what was going to happen with our water, which by now lay deep in every low-lying spot on the green side of the ranch. Our cabin was an island in a veritable wetland.

Larry and Marlene had been watching *The Cosby Show* on TV, and it was still on. I noticed that their hair was mussed up as if they'd been snuggling, and Larry seemed suddenly to become conscious of their unkempt state.

"I think Bill Cosby's a great father," he said, excruciatingly embarrassed. He seemed to be talking to someone trapped behind his own eyes rather than to us.

"About the water," I said. "We're having a great time with the water."

"You are?" Larry was distracted by the idea of someone having a great time moving water. He chuckled and looked at Marlene, gesturing back at Peter. "Whadda you think of these guys?" he said to his wife.

"We'll bring all the willows and cottonwoods back from the dead," said Peter.

"Ghost willows," I said, and Larry's eyes flashed as he looked from Peter to Marlene to the TV but not at me.

"I'll give you a little more water, another quarter foot a

second, seeing as how you have flood rights," he said directly to Bill Cosby.

"Our daughter Lisa knows somebody who saw Dorrance once," Marlene said brightly, like a schoolgirl. She gave her husband a teasing glance just then, as if Dorrance were a subject bound to cause mischief.

"Larry doesn't believe in Dorrance," she said, and Larry started shaking his head slowly, trying to ward something off. "I heard he was a real tall fellow, real broad shoulders," Marlene went on, and Larry looked uncomfortable. He stepped away from his wife and shook his head at her as she said, "Not much good to anybody without a head though."

Larry's grin was gone. "I don't know what our beliefs are about ghosts," he said to Peter, even though I was the one who'd brought the subject up. I was not accustomed to being so ignored, particularly by men. It felt foreign.

Larry continued uncomfortably: "I'd have to check and find out what our beliefs are, but I don't think we go along with that."

Marlene leaned over to me and said behind her hand, "We're Church of Christ, but Larry was brought up Foursquare Gospel. Can you tell?" She giggled.

"How did that ever happen?" I whispered. "Isn't he Italian a couple of generations back? Wasn't he ever a Catholic?"

"His grandmother would turn over in her grave." Marlene rolled her eyes.

"Well, they're sort of alike, aren't they?" I ventured. "Roman Catholic and Foursquare Gospel — very passionate, yes?"

Marlene blanched. "Oh . . . oh, no," she stuttered. "Foursquare Gospel isn't Pentecostal or anything like that. It's Gospel study. Bible study."

"Oh," I said, feeling stupid. I looked at Marlene to apologize, but I'd lost her and shocked her, or maybe she'd shocked herself. She said no more. A yawning gulf opened up between us that would take us time and strength of character and good intentions to breach. The way I saw it, religion had done us no favor.

"I've got culture shock," I told Peter in the car on the way home. "This place is more than I reckoned on."

Ham stopped by one morning to ask Peter to work for him for a couple of days disc-plowing the weeds and sagebrush off a dry piece of land he wanted to seed in hay for his llamas. Peter went outside to meet him when Ham drove in on our road. I watched the two of them out the window. They planted themselves out by the hitching post and had the kind of conversation during which men my father's age jingled the change in their pockets.

Ham stared fixedly at our lush, flooded pasture — our oasis — easily big enough to feed two hundred llamas without lifting a finger, quite the contrast with his own difficult Saint Melvin spread. From a distance, he looked both awestruck and resentful.

"Is that all you're running?" he asked Peter, indicating our five horses. "It's not even a working ranch?"

Peter told me when he came in that Ham said he wanted to pay him ten or twelve dollars an hour. "What's that supposed to mean? Ten? or twelve?"

"I don't know, he's embarrassed to offer you money," I suggested. "The rich are often like that, aren't they?" I had deduced this from twenty-five yards, of course. I mean, what did I know? Peter said he wanted to try the disc plowing even though he was apprehensive about getting into an employee relationship with Hamilton Jones.

"Do I want to work for this guy?" Peter asked rhetorically. "I mean, actually have him in charge of my activities?"

"How much would you make?"

"I don't know, maybe a hundred dollars."

"I don't know, maybe it's not worth it."

"But I'd like to know how to use a disc plow."

"So then do it for that."

In spite of his misgivings, Peter did it. I don't know exactly why he did, and now, in retrospect, I don't want to guess. I could assert that there was some kind of male-rising-to-the-challenge scenario playing itself out, but in reality, Peter's behavior was often opaque to me, and I rather liked it that way. I never wanted to know everything.

I worked all day on a book review for which I would get one hundred dollars, which struck me somehow as appropriate, given Peter's day, even though one hundred dollars represented less than five dollars an hour for me when you counted the time I'd spent reading the book. I didn't care, though. I liked doing it. The activity seemed somehow more real to me than the life I was leading.

By midafternoon my mind wandered. I was thinking about how many religions have come out of desert or wilderness settings: Buddhism, Islam, Hinduism, Judaism, and Christianity. Is it just the isolation, or is there something else going on? I wrote in my journal. Is it disorientation? Is it because the sky is so big you get larger, rise up to meet it?

I went for a walk. I headed purposefully out to the desert-like part of the ranch, sat down on the ground, and read for an hour about the obsessive Catholic mystic Thomas Merton, even though Merton was not a desert person. I started thinking about the Rajneeshees, up there in their desert canyons. What was their spirituality? I'd never read anything much about them in spite of the pounds of print they'd generated. I was a blank page.

But around Saints, the Rajneeshees came up all the time, as a subject of scorn. No one talked about their spirituality, whatever that might be. For instance, the first time I'd set out to do the laundry, I headed for the closest Laundromat, which happened to be at the rodeo campgrounds. There was a general-store-cum-tavern with a Laundromat out back. Inside there was a big television set with a bunch of people around it, all of them clearly kin or next to it: brothers, kids, wives, uncles, mom and dad, who ran the place. Some of the men wore cowboy hats, and they were drinking pitchers of beer, watching their own home movies from about 1959, transferred to videocassette and shown now on the television, thanks to one brother's move into technology. The show was a huge hit, and they were all jeering and whistling and guffawing.

I'd noticed a big poster on the wall behind them. NOT WANTED, DEAD OR ALIVE, it said, and underneath was a skull and crossbones with long hair and long beard, a round woolly cap, just the way Bhagwan Shree Rajneesh looked. There was a bullet hole right through his smile.

A couple of the guys had noticed me looking at the poster. "Well, hey, looky here," one of them said to me, slicking back his hair with his hands, picking his hat up off the table, slamming it onto his head. "Wha'd'ya thinka that?" he asked me. They all looked over to catch my response. The hat said OFFICIAL WASCO COUNTY BIGOT.

"I'm impressed," I said. I could be tough, too. The gang had kept an eye on me while I read magazines off the rack and finished my laundry, thinking about Dorrance and about Bhagwan Shree Rajneesh, both of them with head wounds, one of them lurking about in Ham Jones territory, dominating our skyline to the south, the other looming in from the north. I got a headache waiting for my laundry to dry, feeling watched and unwelcome, and I felt depressed, the first time since Portland. The culture really was not hospitable, I reflected, as I sat there watching my laundry go around in the dryer. In Portland, the sadness had been the pain of a community breaking up, the well of tenderness going slowly dry. Now, up-country, it was tribal fear.

A circling hawk called long and shrill, bringing me back to the midafternoon heat as I sat now on the dry, cracked earth, not far from an anthill, with ants coming and going out of the hole at the top of the little mound. The ants were red and lanky. Some of them carried little clay pebbles away from the opening. They carried them downhill from the opening, toward me, stopping as they sensed my leg. Or rather the first ant stopped next to my leg, turned to his right, and proceeded off in that direction with his burden. The next ants stopped and turned sharply as well, making the right angle to avoid me, but the ants that followed altered their course sooner, walked down the hypotenuse.

It had grown unbearably hot. I felt how inhospitable the desert itself was in the glaring sun. I felt parched, out of whack.

Back at the cabin, I drank a glass of cold water, got a thermos of iced coffee, and wandered out to the swamp. Right away, I saw something I hadn't noticed before. It was an old, decaying footbridge floating on the water. Before, when there was no water there, the footbridge hadn't looked like anything in particular, just weathered boards half-buried in the tall grasses. Until now, the bridge had served no purpose, a dry bed beneath it. But there it was, a floating raft-bridge, more a raft than a bridge. I walked out onto it with a sense of relief and lay down, knowing that somebody else, maybe Luanne Miller, had been there before, when the water was moving just below. Had she lain down too? Did she have doubts? Did she cry?

It was still hot that afternoon, but cool gusts off the mountains began to move the cottonwoods. The huge trees leaned and then released, leaned and released, like palms in tropical trade winds. It felt hot, then cool, hot, then cool, hot, then cool.

A clutch of deer picked their way toward me as I lay there on the raft-bridge. They all studied me and then bent to drink, their faces just a foot or two away. What big eyes they have. Up above, a cloud of blackbirds darted across the pasture like a school of airborne fish, moving as one. There was a moment, just before the flock changed direction, when the birds hung in the air, suspended in a still point. They looked as apt to go one way as another, but then they all chose at once and shot off simultaneously one way, not the other.

The Scout ground noisily to a stop out front of the cabin. Peter was back early, and I heard him slam the truck door and then call my name. He rounded the corner of the house, spotted me on the raft-bridge, came over with great urgency. I must have looked at him from very far away, with misgiving, because he stopped tentatively.

"You busy?" he asked, lifting one arm, hand cupped as if to catch the response.

"What is it?"

"Ham is outrageous."

"What?" I was listening to him now, giving him my full attention.

He told me how the wind had quickened up ridgetop, the gusts starting just as he finished disc-plowing, which had loosened the red topsoil. Red dust had roiled up furiously.

"I had to wrap my handkerchief around my face just so I could get away, the dust was so thick," he said. Dust still streaked his forehead and ran down his cheeks in sweaty rivulets.

Ham had apparently jumped in front of Peter, shouting and gesticulating wildly, like a madman, no longer the urbane host, from saint to devil in an instant. "He was screaming I'd ruined his field, that the whole thing was my fucking fault!"

"That jerk. There he is, larger than life."

Peter looked down at the water and the footbridge. He yanked off his boots and socks, ripped at his jeans and shirt. Naked, he went over the fence and out into the arroyo, where he splashed slowly upstream. He moved through the water steadily, methodically, a stranger.

The blackbirds were at it again with their zigzagging, and when I looked back to where Peter had been, he'd vanished. He had apparently lain down in the deepest part of the arroyo to wash off. He had disappeared into the Great Southern Exposure Spectacle. Excited, I left the footbridge and ambushed him. We whirled together in the arroyo like dolphins in a tide pool. Grunting, Peter grabbed hold of my dorsal fin, and, like a prehistoric amphibian, he used his side appendages to fling himself up. We thrashed and humped and nearly drowned and then were still and sank peacefully into the mud.

Just then, the Viorsts drove by on their way into the ranch. We ducked down, but there we were, naked in what all of a sudden was their arroyo instead of our arroyo. I was laughing, holding on to the earlier moment, but Peter felt the intrusion viscerally. "Disenfranchised," he said bitterly. "Cut down to size."

He really felt it. First degree, absolutely. In thinking about it later, I would realize I hadn't felt what Peter had felt when the Viorsts appeared. I had felt territorially aroused, like when an animal looks around its natural habitat, sees an intruder, goes on the alert. Then I had laughed: I'd felt superior to the Viorsts as they stumbled uncoolly through our scene.

I rushed to record these insights in my journal. The differences between us are so rich, I wrote. So funny.

I eventually also wrote that whereas I had quickly forgotten my territorial arousal that day in the pasture, Peter's would stay with him, deep inside, a piece of sand that could, with time and effort, become a pearl.

FIVE

THE NEXT MORNING before we'd gotten out of bed, Viorst came whistling by the window.

Peter lurched. "Well, hell, what's he want?"

We didn't have curtains, so we could see Viorst looking pointedly away from our bedroom window, his hands linked behind his back colonial style and dangling two horse halters.

"That's why he whistles. So we'll know he's there."

We got up and watched out the window facing the pasture as Viorst tried to catch Coco and the other mare. Coco had been presenting to the three proud cuts for days, so there'd been a lot of agitation within the herd — spicy episodes of competitive aggression, males slicing at each other with their heads, while Coco, her black mane huge and wild, edged backward toward them, tail lifted, rear legs brazenly apart, her glistening vagina opening and closing slowly.

Viorst wasn't having an easy time of it. Peter went outside to help him, ended up walking all the way down to the Main House with Viorst and the two mares. I watched them till they were out of sight and studied the way Peter held himself deferentially when he addressed Viorst.

"Viorst thinks the horses have gone a little rank," Peter said when he came back.

"They're a little wild," I agreed. "I like them that way. Coco likes them that way. Gives her something to do."

"Yeah, but . . ."

"It's okay, I'll work with them, I'll bring 'em around."

Peter smiled at me. We were eating health-food pancakes with yogurt and peanut butter on top.

"What is that thing you do when you talk to Viorst?" I asked him.

"What thing?"

"The way you hold your head when you're talking."

Peter thought for a second. "I'm doing that, am I?"

"What is it?"

"When I was in law school, they analyzed our body language when we had to argue a case. It was a psychologist, I guess, and he said I did the sacrificial swan, offered my neck."

"God, it has an effect! Viorst really likes you. I don't think he much likes me. Should I offer my neck?"

"I don't know, why do you think that?"

"I don't know, he acts like he thinks I'm studying him."

"Well, you are, aren't you?"

"All I've got to say is thank God they're almost never here."

The horses needed more work, were getting too fat, pigging out on the waterlogged grass. Flood-irrigating the pasture was clearly a pleasure for us, but it could be problematical as well. The horses definitely needed more exercise. I'd noticed the big Appaloosa lying down, thought about George Miller's warning regarding foundering, and decided to put the Appy in the corral for a while, give him only dry hay. Further, I would bring all the horses in at night at least as long as the pasture remained flooded, put them out again in late morning, and each horse would get ridden twice a week. This would turn out to be partly a pleasure, partly a chore, as I would have preferred to ride only Coco.

It was while I was out riding Coco one day the following week that I found the desiccated dead body of our favorite ranch cat, a tiger stripe, the first cat Faith Gaines had cut for us. We'd named him Target Tiger, because his stripes circled into a target on his side, black on white. Target had established communication with us, sitting on the fence outside the window, staring in at us as we sat at the round, yellow table. He'd meowed insistently at us as we ate. Now he had a hole in his neck where all his blood had drained away. I guessed that Dad Cat had killed him, too much of a threat. I photographed Target Tiger's body before we buried him near where we'd buried the porcupine. I felt I was starting a series.

A spring heat wave brought days so hot, each day Peter bought a bag of ice cubes in town when he went in for the paper and the mail. We left the ice cubes in the sink and chipped away at them as we came and went. Peter was mowing the Viorsts' lawn, a task that took two full days with a hand mower. The task hadn't been on the List. I could see from Peter's body language associated with the activity that it made him angry, that he felt resentment, but he didn't say it in so many words. He appeared to be having some trouble with the caretaker role when it meant working for nothing. He did laugh when I snuck up on him once and, hands behind my back, pretended to be Viorst inspecting the work. I walked around the lawn nonchalantly whistling.

"Yes, massa, anything else, massa?" Peter said, offering me his sacrificial neck, and we laughed about it.

Peter made a decision to cut down, buck, and haul thirty large lodgepole pines standing ominously dead in a group midst the densest forest on the ranch, the area we called the jungle, because it was riparian, with heavy undergrowth. He discovered the dead stand in his wanderings and returned several times to study it. The dead lodgepoles were full of pine beetles ready to move on to fresh sap in the surrounding live pine, probably the minute they sensed their current quarters were being cut down. But the dead trees were a target for lightning to start a fire. Their location was problematical for logging, a hundred yards into the jungle from the nearest road access, so Peter had to chain-saw a few select live trees to make a path for the Scout into the dead stand. Such is the work of the forest manager.

The whole job took a couple of weeks and was enormously hard work — violent even, when one of those eighteen-inch-diameter pines crashed down through the canopy and hit the ground with a thud, shaking the earth all the way to the cabin. Peter clearly liked it. It appeared to suit him in several ways, from the violent but careful physicality to the knowledge gained about a mixed riparian forest, with its three kinds of pine, Douglas fir, spruce, and hemlock, ginkgo, and the huge, quaking aspens whose leafy branches closed the jungle canopy. The sun shone through spottily, releasing woodsy pollen perfumes, which cut the dominant sappy smell of pine sawdust.

Up in the mountains in the wilderness, the glacier let loose its winter grip and began to melt in earnest. The creek rose, and Larry Lazio gave us additional floodwater, enough to fill all the ditches we'd found so far and then some. We began to see how it might be possible, with enough imagination and hard work, to irrigate a light crop — grass or hay perhaps — on the dried-up plots scattered around Viorst's property. The water was running so heavy, the extra found its way down yet another arroyo, one that ran parallel to the "creek bed" running through our pasture. Probably this arroyo, too, was a former creek bed. The new flow ran down through the land on the dividing line between our part of the ranch — the green part where the water was everywhere — and the Viorsts' desert austerity. It took days, but finally the flow reached a drop-off near the hay barn, where it made a waterfall, glittering and flashing exotically between bleached-out cattle bones. The stream ran on down into a brackish lagoon, which overflowed into a ravine, then dropped back into the creek miles below where it had left the creek to pass onto the ranch. Closing this loop was unexpectedly thrilling.

"Look," Peter said to me, ruffling his hair, moving his hips and shoulders seductively, as he stood knee-deep in the pool that had formed below the waterfall. He was wearing blue Hawaiian swim trunks and knee-high rubber gum boots. He was already tanned dark brown.

"The water reaches a certain level, you see," he said, indicating a notch in the red clay bank where water was seeping down into a dusty pasture below. He held aloft a weathered, wooden trough, a flume that had probably been used long before to carry water to some remote corner of the ranch. Peter was jubilant, spirits sky-high as he pointed things out, his muscles moving under bare skin.

Suddenly, a chocolate Easter bunny ran by. It wasn't a desert hare, or a standard cottontail rabbit, not a magician's rabbit pulled out of a hat. It was a big black bunny with a pink ribbon around its neck.

"Cut!" I shouted. "I believed it up till the bunny."

But two more bunnies with pink ribbons ran by, babies this time.

We followed the bunnies into the hay barn, where they ran behind the hay near a pile of *Outside* magazines, a silver metal fork and spoon, a box of matches, some underwear, and a candle, still unused.

"Probably just a kid running away from home."

Peter plucked a Wild Turkey bottle from between two bales of hay.

"Uh oh . . . no, wait." He unscrewed the cap and sniffed. "Just water."

"For the bunnies, of course. The guy is kind to animals."

My ambivalence about the episode came out in the letter I wrote to the intruder. I hung it on the back of the hay barn next to a pencil on a string.

"You want to establish a correspondence?" Peter asked.

I wrote:

> Are these your bunnies? What do you have in mind for these bunnies? Will you please take all your things out of here and off the property. If you can't take the bunnies, we will take care of them. Do not come back. Please reply.

I left half the page blank for a response. By the time I was writing the letter, I was no longer thinking of a kid running away from home on the receiving end. I was thinking instead about the hoboes, all of them men, who'd been turning up on the road between Saints and the ranch since warmer nights had taken hold. We'd seen them, I from my Toyota, Peter from his Mustang, as they walked along with their dogs and their bedrolls. Or sat on a volcanic outcropping in the rabbit brush, eating a meal out of a tin can. At least one of them was probably living out there along the creek somewhere. He had probably stolen the bunnies and then stashed them in our hay barn. He was the one I was writing to.

Peter called the sheriff, not in the manner of a nervous urbanite feeling vulnerable, but very much in the manner of a slow-talking, slow-to-rile, small-town Kansan who knew about sheriffs and figured a sheriff ought to know a lot about what was going on in a community. The sheriff did know.

The key was the *Outside* magazines.

It was Buckner, he said, a Vietnam vet who'd hung around Saints for a couple of years, spent the winters in a shelter in a neighboring town, been in trouble now and then. "Buckner's on patrol out there," the sheriff said. "He's not really crazy. He just thinks he's still in Nam out there. I think he's pretty harmless, but I'll be sure and talk to him about it next time I see him. Three bunnies, huh?"

The sheriff described Buckner as, simply, a big guy. He also said Buckner drank but that he wasn't drinking now, last he heard. I wanted to know who Buckner was, what he looked like. As long as somebody was out there, I wanted to know if he was lurking or seeking solace. Was I supposed to be afraid of Buckner or was he afraid of us or none of the above? Were we the Vietcong? Were we Americans? Who were we? It was strange how all the land around us had at first seemed so empty and was now becoming populated.

No one answered my letter on the hay barn, and no one took away the bunnies or any of the other items. Perhaps the sheriff's warning had been a deterrent. Perhaps Buckner, or whoever it was, was freaked out by the demands of a pencil and a blank page.

I saw a man I decided was Buckner, on the road. He was obviously the kind of man you'd describe simply as "a big guy," and he ignored me and everybody else who drove by — all the hoboes did. They had their own subculture, their own world amongst themselves, and they noticed or appeared to notice only one another. I didn't get a strong impression about Buckner at first, but he struck me as more benign than not.

Then, just in the course of coming and going, we heard stories about Buckner — from the chiropractor, or the barber, or a waiter at the Cattle Crossing who somehow mysteriously knew us. The waiter's mouth twitched beneath his full mustache as he took a hard look at Peter.

"You're the ones who bought George Miller's place, right?" he said. Peter and I were surprised, but we shouldn't have been. The town of Saints had only eight hundred people within its limits, perhaps two thousand more hidden nearby on ranches or five-acre plots, in expensive homes or elaborate double-wides, humble trailers or rental cottages, in shacks, under bridges — about the same number of people as a large high school, with a high school's multifarious ramifications as a social unit. In high school, most of what you know about people turns out to be wrong.

The stories about Buckner pissing out a downtown second-story window on a tourist, about him dramatically French-kissing his dog to scare off a female hiker who came upon him in the woods, or about him getting his throat slit (he often showed the scar, it was said) in front of the B-Bar-B reminded me of stories about Dorrance, whose head had been lopped off by gossip, or stories about Bhagwan Shree Rajneesh, who had just become the object of hunting tags on sale at a number of local outlets. All three men seemed to be repositories for a tremendous imaginative outpouring of . . . of what exactly?

"The need for Evil personified," said Ham Jones authoritatively when I broached the subject of all the outcroppings of High Desert Paranoia around the territory.

"But it's not paranoia," Ham said, extending his index finger too far in the direction of my nose. "Things really do happen out here. I am telling you, there are forces at work you couldn't even guess at."

Peter and I were back up at Ham Jones's ridgetop ranch for barbecue. Sally had phoned to invite us to dinner as if nothing had happened between Ham and Peter, and I'd told her Peter wouldn't come up there again until Ham apologized. I also suggested Ham ought to pay Peter the seventy-five dollars he owed him for his hours on the disc plow. Ham and Sally were our only social life, so I hesitated to write them off too quickly, in spite of Ham's boorishness. Besides, he was a bit of a wit, I thought, rationalizing.

"I'll have a check for you," Sally promised. "And this *is* Ham's way of apologizing. He asked me to invite you up."

Noblesse oblige, I thought. "Don't make a big deal out of giving the check to Peter, okay?" I said to Sally.

"I'll do my best," she said and hung up.

Sally met us at the door and slipped Peter an envelope with a sweet thank-you.

"Hi, guys," said Ham's voice, drawing our eyes up to where he was getting dressed on his balcony-bedroom. "I was so busy," he said, smiling down on us, "I forgot you were coming."

I'd forgotten how much work Ham was. Peter arched his eyebrow. A few seconds later Ham was down the stairs, sweet and apologetic and charming, as if the guy upstairs had been someone else. Leg of lamb in mint sauce and three bottles of Juliénas convinced me further of my mistake. Maybe Ham wasn't such a bad guy after all.

But I didn't like the way he would start to talk about something and then stop, saying the subject might be over Sally's head. "This girl," he'd say to Peter and me, "I gotta tell you, you oughta see the way her mind tries to grab hold of an idea." It was sort of funny the first time he said it, and Sally's mouth dropped open, her eyes opening even wider than they were all the time, but the second and third times she looked hurt and embarrassed. Nevertheless, we were high-spirited, even raucous.

"You know who everybody's talking about, down at the

Saints Hotel Bar?" Ham asked, pouring shots of Glenfiddich all around. He turned to Peter and mimed a girl saying, "What is it that guy does?" Ham was grinning. "Seriously," he said, "at least three different women have asked me if I knew who Peter was."

By then Ham was looking at me. "You better watch out, I'm telling you. Better not spend too much time away from home. One day you'll come back and find him gone." He was still grinning.

Peter looked blank and said, "Huh?" Sally whined, "Haaam," in an oh come on stop-it way. I was wondering what was going on.

"The women of Saints are after your man," Ham said to me in a radio mystery voice.

"Fuck you," I said.

"Don't anybody get mad," he said. "Just joking, it was just a joke, folks. What we need is a change of venue. Anybody for a sauna?"

I was mad, but I still wanted a sauna, one of my favorite things. Peter looked alienated.

Ham's sauna was below ridgetop, leeward side, in a long, narrow, alpine-style building that housed, at one end, an unoccupied caretaker's apartment. At the other end were the laundry, the sauna, and a music room with complete rock-and-roll setup waiting, ghostlike, for Ham to come back.

The wind off the ridgetop whistled over our heads. Down at ground level, there was a sense of being tucked safely under a vast bosom. "It's a beautiful ranch, Ham," I said as we walked down the path toward the sauna. The path ran alongside a pole fence, and on the other side of the fence, llamas moved in the darkness, all of them silent except for one animal's busy, low-pitched singsong.

"Llama love," Ham explained, sounding uncharacteristically unguarded. Sweet, actually.

Once naked in the sauna, Ham was self-conscious. He struggled to hold his eyes at face level. Sally had lovely breasts, a lovely body, in fact, athletic but soft and rosy in the sauna light. I watched her pour eucalyptus oil over the rocks piled on the heater and then looked at my own naked self. I observed that I was slighter than she was, with smaller, pert breasts, but athletic as well. I wasn't dissatisfied with my body.

Peter was soaking the heat into his logger's bones. He seemed to be at some remove from the situation, and he wasn't at all self-conscious. Was, instead, taken with the good idea of it all, like a Swiss health nudist. As for me, I had missed saunas more than anything else since coming to Saints, and now I felt the tightening in the back of my neck beginning to melt away. Why oh why hadn't sauna-loving Lutherans homesteaded the Viorsts' ranch instead of cold-sponge-bath-in-a-draft Calvinists?

There were deep sighs all around. I looked once, and everyone's eyes were closed. The smell of eucalyptus was intoxicating.

Ham cleared his throat, breaking into our separateness. "I want you people to know that this building is located on the site of Harve Dorrance's murder," he said and then cleared his throat again, waiting.

"Ghost stories," murmured Peter enigmatically. "Yes!"

"Okay," Ham said after a moment. He then took a very long time to tell us the story of how his dog Jake, a black Lab, had cornered something upstairs in the music room once. Ham must have been drunk, he was pausing so long between sentences. He was telling his story in slo-mo; it made for a good ghost story, spooky-like. My mind had plenty of time to think about the four of us sitting there, naked inside a sauna somewhere in the high-desert darkness peopled by no one else for miles and miles around. Or at least you think there's no one out there for miles around until you remember that people like Buckner are out there, on patrol, whatever that means exactly. What is Buckner doing out there, day after day? I was wondering.

"This building was the site of the murder," Ham said again. "Dorrance appears only in or around this building."

Sally laughed quietly to herself, and it struck me as very sexy. I opened my eyes and looked at her, but Sally stayed to herself.

"People have heard Dorrance walking around upstairs in the music room," Ham slurred, then breathed deeply and fell silent. Then he began again. "I mean, they've heard someone or something walking around up there when there was supposedly no one else at the ranch," he said and then fell silent again.

"Wha'd they do?" Sally asked, and we all four opened our eyes and looked at one another for a split second and then I receded to my corner.

"Wha'd they do?" Ham repeated. At that moment I opened one eye slightly to look at Ham and saw that he still had his eyes open, and that he was quite desperately trying to control his rising sexual excitement.

Jesus, what next? I wondered, and just then the electrical power went off with a metallic thud and shudder throughout the building. Ham let out a long, low groan, muttered, "God damn you, Dorrance." Then he stood up, departed, and did not return, leaving the three of us sitting there naked, in the total darkness.

A long moment went by. "Somehow I don't think he went to turn on the light," Sally eventually said.

I chuckled. Peter snorted. Sally stood up. "I think I have matches in my pants pocket."

As she moved toward the door, her hand brushed against my knee. "Oh, excuse me," she said embarrassedly, then stumbled, pitched forward. Peter and I each caught some part of her, so she didn't fall. "Gawd," she said and sighed. When she opened the sauna door, moonbeams were wafting into the dressing room, so we could see to find our clothes and get dressed and say good night, which we did comparatively uneventfully.

"What in hell's going on with him?" Peter said as we jolted back down the ridge road in the Scout. I hadn't told him about Ham's satyrlike pose, now burned indelibly into my memory. I thought he wouldn't believe me, or would be offended. I didn't tell him. I started to talk about Dorrance, but Peter interrupted me.

"No, I mean, what was Ham saying about people talking about me in the Saints Hotel Bar?"

"About women talking about you?"

Peter snorted. "Yeah."

"Well, *do* they talk about you?"

"I certainly wouldn't know, I've never been there. But I don't talk about them. Why do they talk about me? Why do people talk like that about other people they don't even know? Why do they give a rat's ass what I do?"

"Because their lives are boring and empty. Because they're looking for Prince Charming, and you turn them on, what do I know?" I was staring straight ahead at the round moon, which was balanced on top of Squaw's Tit Mountain, right on the tip of the hard nipple. I was thinking about all the single women I'd seen in Saints. Or maybe they weren't single, but they were alone and dressed as if they cared how they looked, how they looked to men. One in particular I remember, in tight jeans and creamy beige cowboy boots, not the kind you'd wear in the barn, sleek blond hair, sharp eyebrows, under which her equally sharp eyes looked intently around. She had cast those sharp eyes sidelong at me in the grocery store more than once, measuring the competition, it had felt like. Was she the one asking Ham about Peter? No doubt she was already cooking up some high-desert fantasy.

"I don't give a rat's ass about Saints, Oregon," Peter said with finality as he pulled the Scout into our road.

The next day Peter was down at the far end of the property when an ancient Buick lurched into the gravel road and stopped at the hitching post in front of the cabin. I looked out the window at the car. Three men got out, stood by the car, looked around. One scruffy-looking guy walked toward the cabin. After Ham's the night before, I was on edge. My adrenaline kicked in, and I burst out onto the front porch like Ma Kettle.

"What do you think you want?" I snarled at the man. All three men stopped still and looked at me for a long, long moment. I was stricken with fear.

The man who was halfway to the porch stood with his hands on his hips, eyeing me. He glanced around at his friends and then spit tobacco juice off to one side.

"This your property?" he said, and his words fell to the ground like stones.

"Get out of here," I said, taking a step forward. My heart was pounding so loud I could hear nothing else. Miraculously, the three turned and moved slowly back to their car. One said something I couldn't hear. Another answered. The doors slammed, and all three of them stared at me with dead eyes until the Buick rounded the bend out of sight. I didn't move until I heard the familiar clunk of a loose board out on the bridge. I realized I hadn't heard the clunk earlier, when the Buick came in. Had those guys been out there a long time?

Fear is irrational and feeds on itself, of course, but it is, nevertheless, quite real. *A thing had happened out there,* just as Ham had said it would. He had prepped me for it. Had he made it happen?

I wanted to get away. The house now stood as a cage trap, human size, with me inside. I bolted outside to the corral and stood behind the knot of horses, who all craned around and studied me intently for a while, then began shifting and changing their attitudes to acknowledge my presence in their midst. Coco made a violent head gesture for me to get the hell around in front of her, away from her hot behind. I came around her and put my head on her neck. She looked at me conspiratorially.

From Coco's vantage point, I saw that our cabin was isolated and small and incredibly vulnerable. The little pine structure was no protection at all from outside aggression or uninvited visitors. It was something you could easily kick down, a place in need of protection from malevolent forces. It needed a guard. We needed a guard.

"A guard," I cried out. Coco nickered. At least three of the other horses looked over at me again. They were used to being talked to or even shouted at but saw that I wasn't talking to them and looked away. I suddenly remembered a man I had seen in New York City twenty years earlier. He had been coming out of a friend's apartment just as I was arriving. He had smiled warmly, like a friendly neighbor. It turned out the man had just broken in and robbed the place and was leaving after having skinned my friend's Siamese cat like a rabbit.

The incident had seemed terrifyingly normal at the time, although it had been a turning point, and I left New York and went back to Oregon soon after that and then to Paris for many years.

The thing is, though, in New York, after I'd got through talking to the police, cleaning up my friend's apartment, and taking the cat's body out to Queens to my friend's mother's house to bury it, I went to a party to forget it all and had a series of funny or endearing or seductive interactions, which had completely interrupted my terrified thoughts about the earlier incident. Later, what I remembered most about the cat skinner was his smile.

Now, in Saints, on the desert, those three men had driven their big old Buick into a scene of relatively deep social isolation, just Peter and me and rarely anyone else for miles around. No parties, no seductive interactions with strangers. Nothing to interfere with my fantasies triggered by those dead eyes.

So terror had begun, the mind's roller coaster plunging out of control. The intruders had made me think of something long forgotten, something grotesque. I had been truly frightened.

Now, though, standing midst these warm, breathing animals who were so comfortable with themselves, one or another of them in all normalcy passing gas from time to time, flapping an ear at a fly, stamping a foot — my fear was fading. The horses were endearing, a salvation. My feeling of terror dissipated.

I suddenly thought I understood what Buckner might be doing out there in our forest. He might just be protecting us. He might have reconnoitered the layout and decided there was something to do here. I considered the possibility that he was actually on our side, having taken it upon himself to patrol the territory around us, having sensed that we needed protecting. Foolish for me to think this way perhaps, but I felt we were much safer with Buckner out there on patrol than we were without him. I assumed, just for the sake of argument, that he stood between us and evil. Possibly he was watching our cabin now, maybe from some distance, maybe from close by, just as I was doing from the corral. He might well have watched the entire interaction with the guys in the Buick. Maybe he was observing as I regained control of my fear. This was what he had learned in Nam, how to measure the danger.

"Buckner my man," I shouted, just in case he was nearby. I waited, but there was no answer, only silence. "Protect us from evil, Buckner," I called out, just in case. I felt a tremendous outpouring of sentiment in Buckner's direction. I wanted to meet him, talk to him, come to an understanding with him, thank him, force the action.

Later, when I told Peter about the visitors in the Buick, we decided I was ready for the shotgun, Buckner or no. After Peter showed me how to use it, I went out and shot a few practice rounds at a volcanic outcropping in the middle of our driest pasture. I even took a shot at Dad Cat when I saw him trying to kill another of his male offspring. Dad had his jaw clamped around the younger cat's throat. I carefully took aim at Dad when the other cat escaped momentarily, and just as I was ready to fire, Dad turned and looked at me, gave me the evil eye. I jerked, fired wide, and no buckshot hit him.

Dad Cat looked at me, so tough he didn't even run.

SIX

ABIG GARY COOPERISH man named John Small showed up at the ranch one crystalline morning about six-thirty without phoning first. Nobody ever phoned first, not even if we specifically asked. People seemed unwilling to make arrangements other than "Tuesday" or "next week." Then they'd float across the high desert taking care of business town by town. There was an aspect of economic uncertainty to every promise. Something better might come up, best keep things loose.

That morning at six-thirty was John Small's "next week," and Peter had just drifted back to sleep in my arms when Small's rig ground to a halt out front. I slipped on a black T-shirt and shorts and went outside.

Some days before, Small explained, he'd gotten a call from Viorst asking for advice about keeping the ranch taxed as agricultural land, and Small, a land-management specialist, was dropping by for a fresh look at the property. Once there he seemed pleased to drift, to stand easily with me in the crisp morning air talking about other matters, while hundreds of yellow-and-green grosbeaks flitted in clouds back and forth between the aspens and the ground. Their wide upper beaks curved down over their lower beaks, like parrots'. They were frenetic.

"They'll be here most of the summer," said Small. "Then they're gone to Mexico." We watched the birds for a while.

"Have you gone up to see Rajneeshpuram?" he then asked, apropos of some private thought.

Small told me he'd been hired by the Rajneeshees soon after they came to the high desert to advise them about what they could do agriculturally on various parts of their sixty-four-thousand-acre ranch.

"I feel sorry for 'em," he said. "Most of their land is the worst — rocks and hardpan, cheatgrass and an occasional sagebrush."

"So was it interesting up there at Rajneeshpuram for you?" I asked him.

"I'll tell you," he said, smiling slightly just as Peter ambled out the front door to join us. "I saw some well-endowed women up there, but the men didn't appear to be of the same, ah . . . caliber." He was blushing ever so slightly at having been caught at exactly this point in his story when Peter reached us. He repeated the whole thing for Peter, only the second time through he said the women were "I don't know, I guess the word is . . . seductive. There was this one woman named Isabel . . ."

"The spokeswoman?" I asked.

But Small trailed off.

"She's really something, huh?" I pressed, pulling him back.

Small looked me in the eye. "Yes, she is. She's one of the good ones," he said with a certain amount of punch. "You should go there," he finished. "See for yourself."

The three of us spent the morning walking the ranch, drinking iced coffee out of a thermos I carried slung over my shoulder in a string bag — or at least Peter and I drank it. Small declined. "I'm a Mormon," he explained. "No coffee."

I wondered if he was going to bring up the Rajneeshees again, but he didn't. I'd noticed Small didn't have any trouble looking at me when he talked, unlike so many other high-desert men. He seemed quite pleased to be talking to a woman and equally pleased to be talking to Peter. We talked comfortably of the ranch — everything from how great it would be to grow trout in the lush pond down at the northeastern edge of the property to how you could conceal yourself at Coyoteville, a volcanic outcropping up the dry side of the ranch, way over beyond the Main House. If you could hide and hide your scent as well, you could watch the coyotes come and go.

Coyoteville had no view of the mountains. It was a miniature, jagged mountain itself, echoing the taller mountains in the distance, and from his peak a coyote gazed out into the northern light, probably at his dinner. There were ponderosa pines scattered around amongst the rock, growing almost without dirt — twisted, old-growth yellow-bellies that had sucked life out of those rocks for four hundred years or more.

"You think somebody could turn a profit here?" Peter asked Small. We had left Coyoteville and moved on to the far corner of the ranch, an arid open space that could perhaps be irrigated via the flume Peter had discovered, although it seemed complicated. The land was dusty hardpan, sand here and there, compacted by cattle hooves echoing down from the past. Cheatgrass punched through in patches. The place was literally desertified.

"No, I don't think you could turn a profit here," Small said, shifting his lanky frame to lean on some invisible support. "I'm not certain you could even get ponderosa to grow here now, even though that's what was here once." He kicked at the red dust in front of him with the toe of his cowboy boot. "You haven't got any water out here," he said, "and the land couldn't hold it if you had it."

"Water comes out here," Peter said. "Or did once."

Small looked over at Peter expectantly, his eyebrows raised. He licked his lips unconsciously. He was interested. Water was interesting. With water you could have a whole other conversation. Without water there was no point discussing anything else.

"You can get water out here?" he asked.

"Yeah," said Peter.

And they were off, gone to look at the flume, two men talking only to each other.

That night in bed Peter was slowly moving his index finger back and forth across his upper lip as he stared up at the circle of light cast on the ceiling by the bedside lamp. I watched him for a minute. "You're hooked, aren't you?"

He turned to look at me, wrinkling up his nose. "I am," he said. "It's interesting. It feels good, you know? An intriguing possibility, don't you think?" I could see he wanted my accord.

Our eyes locked. "Go on."

"Small thinks we can grow ponderosa pine out on the dry land if we can get water there, just for the first year or two."

"With that flume thing?"

"Yeah, maybe," he said, pulling himself up close against my side as if to let me know there were other things to life besides flumes.

"You serious?"

"They'd plant ten acres next spring if I can get the system working."

"Really?" He was right. It was intriguing.

"Yeah."

"But how did a forest grow there in the first place?"

"Oh, Small said there were always spring floods, sort of like what we've got here at the moment, only it used to happen naturally. The water would jump the creek banks and move down the arroyos. And Small told me we've certainly got water flowing underground, too, right under this house most likely, an invisible twin to the creek. And it's not too far underground, which is why we have the meadow. It's all subirrigated. It will stay green even after we drain it. And there was maybe even a spring down there in the dry corner that got plugged by the cattle — there's one patch that has a faint tinge of green to it, Small spotted it, as if there were water running down below." Peter paused, breathing deeply, then added: "I suppose it's a question of long-term perception . . . the Tao of forest making."

"Hmmmm," I said. "I bet our really big trees have taproots clear to China."

Peter turned and looked at me. I hadn't really meant to mention Asia. Outside, something set off the coyotes, and their hyenalike yodels filled the high-desert silence with lewd laughter. I laughed, too.

"Peter?"

"Yes?"

"Is Viorst paying Small to figure out what to do with his land?"

"Of course," he said.

"And . . . ?"

"And I was thinking of charging Viorst for my time as well."

I'd been drifting into physicality, but that tweaked me. "Lawyer rate? Is this lawyer rate?"

"Nah," he said, reaching up to tuck my hair away from my ear. "Some special rate," he whispered, his heat rising.

But I had something to say. "Peter?"

"What?" I felt his body against mine. Now or later, now or later? I was thinking, feeling like a damsel stretched between two steeds pulling in opposite directions.

"What?" he said again.

"I'll tell you tomorrow."

He snorted right into my ear, which made us laugh and wrestle around awhile. I got my hands on his biceps and kept them there as he pulled me tenderly onto him *à cheval*.

The idea I'd put on hold, I told him the next morning, was that I wasn't enjoying being penniless, that my stupid health insurance had just jumped to $147 a month, that I was now doing hours and hours of horse work every week, which was on the List so I didn't get paid for it, even though I loved doing it, of course, but I could not survive without earning some money. Now, Peter was going to get paid for figuring out an interesting problem, which wasn't on the List but was something he loved doing. He was lucky to get paid for doing something he loved, but I, in this case, was not. So I thought I'd try to make some money writing something about Rajneeshpuram, what did he think? Nothing else seemed like a possibility, but maybe this *was*. Did he want to ride up there with me, take a look at the place as tourists?

"I think you *should* write about it," he said. "I think you'd write something good. It's your kind of subject." He was fanning my creative embers, getting me away from boring financial necessity.

"Let's go up there today," he said enthusiastically.

Later, as we drove across the high desert, the radio was tuned to the Warm Springs Indian Reservation station, playing Cree and Lakota rain chants. In Madras the Dairy Queen was full of American Indians from the reservation, most of them teenagers who went to high school in Madras. North of town the land became majestic, more Old West, marked by ridges and deep canyons. In every direction, rimrock pulled the earth up into pyramids. Desert grasses were sparse, in scattered bunches. The soil, what there was of it, was hardpan, you couldn't pound anything into it, so instead of fence posts the fence wires were strung between rock jacks — square, handcrafted wooden frames filled with rocks and placed on top of the ground.

"I've been thinking," Peter said as we cut through a notch toward Antelope, the site of the first Oregon territorial post office. "Half of the money I get from Viorst for the water project should be yours, I mean, to make up for you exercising the horses and not getting paid. Seems fair, don't you think?"

"Actually, it does," I said. "Not as fair as having Viorst actually pay me to take care of his horses, but, failing that, pretty damn fair." I was a little startled at Peter's offer but wildly pleased, as we passed into what had been Antelope. The town was two short streets of old cottages and cabins, a little wooden Victorian or two, a few double-wides on foundations, one or two newer ranch-style homes. A sign told us the town was now named Rajneesh. We laughed uproariously when we saw the studiously nonstandard sign, a new-age sign instead of the usual highway-department kind. Antelope, or Rajneesh, felt like the Raj in reverse: Indians-out-from-India-to-the-colony effect. My first impression, a lasting one, was that it couldn't last.

When Peter and I arrived at Rajneesh Reception, I heard a woman's lilting, accented voice wafting out an office door. I turned to look and saw an almond-eyed beauty standing there with naked grace, as if she were standing nude in a pool under a waterfall in Hawaii. But she wasn't naked. She was wearing a red jersey dress and had white plumeria flowers in her hair.

It must have been the flowers in her hair that had made me see her naked.

The door closed just then, and our tour guide, a different woman, introduced herself to ten or twelve of us. She was an American, from Arizona. The tour was by bus and went from building to building, farm operation to farm operation. The Arizonan was not interesting to listen to: We do this and we do that and we believe this but not that. There were no Rajneeshees to be seen anywhere.

"Where are you all hiding?" I asked. People snickered. The answer was "Working. Everyone is at work."

In the restaurant I ordered a tuna-cheese melt even though I saw on the bottom of the menu that everything served was made of soybeans. It was a grave error. There are some things that soybeans cannot be made to simulate. Better off sticking to tofu as tofu.

On the way out of Rajneeshpuram's canyons, Peter and I agreed that it was a stupid tour, certainly not something you'd write about.

"Maybe there's no story there," said Peter.

"Or you mean none for me? Certainly other people are getting stories out of it."

"Well . . ."

"There's that siren behind the door," I suggested.

Peter chuckled.

"Anything interesting at Rajneeshpuram must be behind closed doors," I thought out loud.

We rode along in silence for a while.

"So thanks for the money," I said. He was a good man.

Nevertheless, I called a writer friend to see if she knew a magazine that might be interested in a piece from me about Rajneeshpuram.

"*In These Times,*" she said. "Weekly tabloid out of Chicago." When I called, an editor there liked the fact that I actually lived near Rajneeshpuram. We agreed to a four-part story, probably for only five hundred dollars. I called the main phone number listed for Rajneeshpuram.

"Who do you want to talk to?" a woman's accented voice asked me. It was a French accent. Or was it South American? The voice sounded familiar.

"You mean now? On the phone?"

"No, when you come," she said laughingly.

I'd heard her voice before. "How about the Bhagwan?" I said "the *Bhag*wan," with a *the* and a heavy tread on the *Bhag*, the only way I'd ever heard it said around Saints.

She liked my answer. "Many of us would like that, too," she said. "How lovely! But Bhagwan has been silent for years." She pronounced the name in Hindi: "Bhag*wan*," with no *the*.

"Anyone else?" she said.

"Isabel," I said. "I'd like to meet Isabel."

"I am Isabel," she said in her wafting, almond-eyed, naked voice.

Ah! The siren behind the door! "John Small told me about you," I said then, remembering how Small had become distracted speaking of Isabel, remembering as well my own vision of her naked in the waterfall.

"Ah, yes, John Small, a lovely man, isn't he? A Mormon, yes."

"Yes, he is. Tell me, Isabel, are the Rajneeshee children abused? I read about the complaint."

"No, of course not," she answered comfortably. "They are growing up differently than the local children, and perhaps this is misunderstood."

"Differently how?"

"Well, you must come see for yourself and talk with people about it."

"Okay. Who should I talk to?"

"Would you like to talk to a psychiatrist?"

I laughed. My favorite people, psychiatrists, for reasons as knee-jerk as my pre-Peter negative feelings about lawyers: For me, psychiatrists are clairvoyants.

"Who is it?"

"Siddha, his name is Siddha, he's American, a very interesting man. Do you like men?"

"Yes, especially if they look me in the eye."

Isabel laughed knowingly. "I'll arrange an appointment with Siddha for you," she said. "Call me back next week."

In the ensuing days I had an approach-avoidance conflict brewing regarding my appointment with the Rajneeshee psychiatrist named Siddha, but rodeo weekend was upon us, so I was distracted from thinking about it. We had houseguests coming, our first.

Our guests were a visiting professor from the People's Republic of China and his wife, who was arriving in Portland for her first visit in the United States the day before we would meet her. We'd met the professor at that dinner party where we all laughed uproariously at the Frenchman talking about farts.

We picked the Chinese couple up at the bus station twenty miles north of Saints. There they were on the sidewalk in their square-cut black leather jackets: Lu, the professor, formerly of Beijing but ordered south during the Cultural Revolution. There he'd met Zhang, who was of rural stock, her features more sensuous than his, her hands and body floating arrestingly, moving in a Southeast Asian fluid way, not in his stiffer, controlled northern Chinese way.

Lu spoke English. Zhang did not. We spoke no Chinese. In their presence our lives became exotic.

At the ranch we walked around the property first thing, pointing out the horses, the Main House, all the vistas, the water system that had recently become so significant to us. Zhang was excited about the water system. I liked her immediately.

Then the questions started: Why did you leave the city to live in such an isolated place? Why aren't there other people living on your ranch? Why isn't there more livestock? Why is the Main House empty? Does it belong to royalty? Why would you give up jobs in the city to live like peasants when there is no Cultural Revolution?

Lu couldn't keep up with translating back and forth for Zhang every time anybody said anything. Finally, he asked a question without translating, even though she was clamoring at his side. "How much are you paid for taking care of this ranch?"

"Nothing," Peter told him. "We get to live here for free."

Lu translated the question and answer for Zhang, who erupted in raucous laughter, Lu joining in, and the two of them argued and laughed for a while over some further point. Then Lu turned to Peter and me, folded his arms solemnly, and wiped the smile off his lips with the back of his hand, Peking opera-style.

"You should be paid six hundred dollars a month for such caretake," he pronounced. "You are . . . exploited." Just as he said this, he snapped a photo of Peter and me, in order, he explained, to capture our expressions as we learned of our exploitation. Only the picture was all wrong because we were laughing.

"What would you do with this ranch if it were yours?" I asked Lu and Zhang at lunch. We were sitting at the weathered picnic table in front of our cabin, slightly shaded from the sun by a towering cottonwood. The temperature was about ninety-five degrees, with hot winds blowing through the quaking aspens, making them dance. It was good rodeo weather. One year, apparently, it had snowed.

A pile of antlers was pushed to one end of the picnic table. We were eating apricots, tuna fish sandwiches with butter lettuce, potato chips, drinking Tsingtaos or ice-cold well water, all of it looking and tasting slightly odd because it was odd for Zhang, even the Tsingtao, which was an export beer she'd never seen in South China. Zhang liked the potato chips. She liked them so much she induced a chip frenzy in the four of us while she and Lu settled the question of what should be done with the ranch. By the end of the bag, our flooded pasture was growing rice. Zhang was high on her fantasizing.

"This is very American," said Lu, laughing with pleasure at his wife.

"I feel closer to Lu and Zhang than I do to the people around here," I said to Peter that night in bed. "I want to have everything matter again the way it does for them."

"You mean us?" he asked tentatively.

"Of course not. We're all that does matter. I mean everything else — the politics, the communal activity."

"Like it does for Lu and Zhang?"

"Yes."

After a pause Peter said he didn't think he wanted everything to matter again. He thought that era was past.

"You don't want to go to China anymore now?" I heard myself sound wistful.

There was a long pause, and then Peter's leg jerked the way it did when he was falling asleep.

I woke up with a stiff neck about six-thirty to the smell of authentic South China chow mein, bad imitations of which have been eaten for decades in Cantonese Chinese restaurants in every American town. When I went into the kitchen to look, I found Zhang cooking and talking to herself. She talked to me now, gesturing excitedly at the thick, old wood counters, and I saw that she liked them as much as I did. I think she was saying they reminded her of home.

On the way into Saints for the rodeo parade, we passed Big Buckner sitting on an outcropping of red volcanic rock a few feet off the pavement midst rabbitbrush and twisted juniper. A dog was sprawled at his feet. Buckner was eating out of a tin can with a plastic spoon. He had on camouflage pants and a leather bolero. I waved at him, but he didn't look up when we passed.

I wanted to tell Lu and Zhang then what it was like for us to live in such an isolated place with Buckner out there, usually hidden out of sight in the surrounding woods. I couldn't bridge the gap, couldn't get the story going. There seemed to be too much information missing to transmit the idea of Buckner being on patrol after Nam.

"Buckner was a soldier in Vietnam," I said finally. "But he didn't want to stop. He's still on patrol, but now he roams this territory here." I gestured to include all the surrounding pine forest. "He's still in Nam."

Lu translated this for Zhang, whose face took on alarm. She swung around to look back to where Buckner was, but we had rounded a bend, and he was out of sight.

Lu said, "Zhang is of the same people as the people in the north of Vietnam. Some of her family live in Hanoi."

"I don't think Buckner's dangerous," I said quickly. "Not at all. Not to us or you or anyone." I wanted to reassure Zhang, whose expression was impenetrable.

Peter glanced over at me questioningly, made eye contact, was satisfied, went back to driving.

*

The rodeo parade had begun, and suddenly there was a somber-faced Faith Gaines driving a horse and buggy with her twin sister. They were indeed identical. There really were two of her. Faith's son Billy was riding his own horse behind his mother's buggy. Billy sat very straight in the saddle and rested his right hand comfortably on his right thigh. He was wearing a plaid shirt, and he looked around quite naturally and unself-consciously at the huge crowd, mostly tourists packed tightly onto the boardwalks and sidewalks along Cascade Street. I called out to Faith by name, and she turned to look. She registered that she saw us, but she looked quickly away in the direction the parade was moving. Billy glanced over briefly, too, his face flooded with curiosity.

It had been two months since Faith had talked to Peter about Ed Dyer taking advantage of Billy, but their phone conversation was still writ large in my thoughts, and presumably in Faith's, for different reasons. In any case, she had not communicated her concerns to Peter or me for all that time, even though we'd seen her when we brought cage-trapped feral cats into the clinic.

After the parade I tried to tell Lu and, through him, Zhang, about what that moment with Faith Gaines might have been, about that exchange of glances between Faith and us in the middle of the Saints rodeo parade. This time I got the story going. Lu was following me, translating for Zhang, and they were asking questions when they didn't understand.

Through Lu, Zhang said, "Maybe this man Dyer did not hurt her son, but he is just on patrol out there, like that man on the road?" Zhang was so quick and bright, she was amazing.

Lu said the story would end a certain way in China. "Ed Dyer would be reeducated," he said. "And here?" he asked. "What will happen here?"

"Probably nothing," said Peter.

"Everyone will act as if nothing has happened," I said. "Even if something *has* happened. Total denial. It will stay a secret."

Lu nodded.

The next day we drove northeast across the high desert, way past Rajneeshpuram, to the Chinese museum in John Day, where once two thousand Chinese coolies had lived, building the railroad and mining for gold in the American Old West. There's a kind of shrine still there, an old stone house filled with boxes of bear claws and ginseng and tea, the walls blackened by opium smoke, the door marked by bullet holes.

The day began crystal clear and cold and built to a perfectly still, dry, hot ninety-eight degrees. Lu and Zhang were hugging and kissing in the backseat of the Mustang. Up front, Peter and I looked at each other with yearning. I felt like a teenager. We'd had no one but each other for eighty-six days straight, and then suddenly we'd had no waking moment alone together for four days. There was a lot of sexual energy in the Mustang that morning, but it would all get sublimated into more talk.

"How is it possible in your society that . . . ," Lu broke off from murmuring in his wife's ear to ask us.

"You are definitely an intellectual," Peter said to Lu with a kind of Kansas grin, catching Lu's eye in the rearview mirror. We all laughed, but Lu was intent on having us explain to him why middle-class Americans could leave their comforts and risk ending up in homeless shelters, something he'd been thinking about for months since he arrived in the USA.

"Imagine such a character," Lu suggested to me, knowing me already. "Tell us a story. Imagine a fifty-year-old man," he ordered. "A doctor."

I made up a story about a man — funny, I made him a psychiatrist — who, over the course of years, began to take himself too seriously, began to think of himself as a prophet. His wife found him odd and chose to have a life of her own, took a lover. Without whatever structure she had been providing him, the man lost his footing, became insecure, began to lose clients. One day he didn't show up for his patients at all. He started drinking. His wife threw him out. He ended up in a cheap wino hotel, full of despair.

Lu contemplated my story.

"Life wasn't what he expected it to be," Peter said to Lu, briefly turning his head from the road to lock eyes with Lu. Lu stared back. Peter broke away, turning back to the road.

"That is the part I can't get," Lu said thoughtfully after a moment. "It is so Western."

Lu turned to his wife to translate the whole story. I noticed only then that Zhang hadn't been clamoring this time. She had her head back, her eyes half closed, her lips parted slightly in a smile. She waved away Lu's translation, smiling, and he turned back to us.

"Why can't I understand?" he said.

"If it were a snake, maybe it would bite you," I said, shrugging. This time Zhang pulled on her husband's arm for a translation. He spoke, and then, quick as a flash, she said, "Oh yes . . . right in front of you," or at least that's how Lu translated what she said into English for the front seat. It felt as if we had come some distance from Lu's idea that Peter and I were exploited on the ranch to Zhang's knowing that "understanding" was right in front of you.

SEVEN

THE CREEK FINALLY FLOODED. The heat had caused thunderclouds to pile high in the sky, and then suddenly, like birth waters breaking, the rain let loose for three days straight.

Peter and I went and stood in the monsoon on the railroad-car bridge over the creek. The air sweeping down the creek just above the flood carried with it an icy rain. The muddy creek water below was thick, like pudding. Rocks and broken trees bounced along the surface of the pudding like raisins and chocolate chips. On the east side of the creek, sections of the bank collapsed, adding to the texture and color of the flow. Below the bridge the water leapt violently into a dry wash, an old arroyo empty probably since the last flood in '64. The pudding pushed dead trees in front of it the way the water in our ditches pushed pinecones.

"I want to stay here," Peter said then, inspired by the wildness into an unexpected declaration. "I love you and I want to keep doing what we're doing."

I stared at him with a stupid grin on my face while nature crashed around down below us, battering the bridge footings.

"Don't you think that's what Zhang was saying? . . . right in front of you?" he said.

I thought of all the possible things Zhang might have been

referring to when she said, "Right in front of you." I watched them fade weightlessly away one by one while Peter didn't fade but stood solidly there with a look of readiness, right in front of me.

It should flood more often, I wrote in my journal later. Asia would be interesting, but this is interesting also.

The creek stayed at flood stage for a week, reshaping the landscape. The creek bed shifted eastward six yards: nature on the move. We deduced then that the creek had been moving eastward for centuries, flood by flood.

"We're living in a floodplain," Peter joked to Bob Viorst when Bob phoned from his Portland skyscraper office to talk about the flood. Bob liked nothing better than to phone the ranch from his office and talk to Peter or me for longer than we ever expected about ranch life and weather. Any description — "huge thunderclouds and then thunder and lightning all across the southern sky, and now with all this rain, there's water actually flowing under the southeast corner of our cabin, goes under one side, comes out the other without touching the floorboards" — was enough to make Bob Viorst a happy man, almost more so if it involved some kind of precariousness in our lives.

Viorst, chortling, told Peter how the caretakers before George and Luanne Miller had been trapped on the ranch for days when the '64 flood washed out the old bridge.

"How do we top that?" Peter deadpanned to me after he hung up the phone.

Hamilton Jones phoned to talk to Peter about the weather, too. He'd got three inches of rain up on his dry ridgetop and had got religion. I was listening in on the other phone, and at first Ham sounded grateful, but soon he switched to jubilant, as if he'd won a round.

"Right now I'd say I've got just about as much water as you

have," Ham said. He knew I was listening in, so he was talking to me, too, but he was really talking only to Peter.

"You don't even appreciate what you've got there, Peter," Ham said, the challenge right up-front. "Middle of the desert, a fucking oasis . . . why don't you take a chance? Put in a crop, get some animals, *do* something, man."

It was just after that our irrigation ditches all dried up. I first noticed the water had dried up under my footbridge and walked across the pasture to find the blockage. There wasn't a drop of water in any ditch anywhere. Instead, there was fresh gravel, all the way up to the dam, which appeared to be functioning normally. Water, lots of it, continued to flow downstream. The creek was still fast and full. But below the dam where our access pipe normally dumped water into the main ditch, gravel coming down with the flood had blocked the pipe and filled miles of ditch below with scree.

As far as Larry Lazio knew, and as ditch rider he was someone who might have known, such an event had never occurred before. Peter phoned him to find out what had happened to our water, and Larry said, "There might be something stuck in there crosswise." The two agreed to meet up at the irrigation dam at six o'clock the next morning. Larry said he'd been in California for a week and had left his kids in charge. He said they hadn't known how to open our gate full bore and flush out any gravel buildup and then close it down again. He said he'd take care of it.

The next morning Peter left at dawn for the irrigation dam, and it was still cold outside when I went up there about eight. Peter and Larry were there, standing off to one side of the dam, both of them gazing down into the creek at the spot where our underground access pipe lay constipated. Larry was very wound up in what he was saying and went on talking to

Peter man to man, as if I weren't there. He was talking, appropriately enough, about the weather.

". . . never been the same twice the twenty-three years Marlene and I've been here," he was saying, shaking his head with disbelief, his eyes twinkling with pleasure at the novelty. "One year you'll get no heat wave the entire summer, no day above eighty-five, and the glacier just slowly melts and you get plenty of water right through August, and then another year there'll be hardly any snow, and I have to start rationing by July, one day, one ranch, the next day, the next, the next day, the next one." He stopped and pointed his finger at Peter and cocked his head. "You'll always get your water first, though," he said and then waited, apparently to see if Peter already knew why it was that we would always get our water before anyone else on the creek.

"Why is that?" Peter finally said, slowly pulling himself up and away from the eddy swirling below them, pulling with such effort he must have been a bit spooked. By Larry or by the gravel?

I looked at Larry. Was he promising something, saying we'd always get our water first?

"Because your pipe draws its water from above the dam," Larry said and pointed at the end of our pipe, which was, technically, above the dam, but which was also, of course, still blocked solid and evidently, at that moment, irrelevantly so. Peter nodded his head as if Larry's explanation made sense to him, and I suddenly got a glimpse of their last two hours together. I saw that Peter was enjoying talking to Larry and that the two of them were involved in what promised to be a lengthy negotiation. I was almost jealous.

"You have to be able to guess what the weather's going to do and then guess what the water's going to do as a result," Larry was saying, his eyes dancing, as I wandered off unmissed. "I personally have never seen that combination before where so much rain falls right onto the watershed after a weeklong heat wave. My kids were scared, they changed everybody's gate to flood level, everybody's got extra flood rights. Had to keep changing 'em every day and then they saw all that gravel piling up in front of your gate, they thought they were supposed to keep opening it up further and they never closed it down at all. But it's never happened before, and you'd have to have exactly that combination of hot weather and then rain . . ."

I was almost out of hearing range heading back to the house when the morning sun slipped promisingly up over the treetops, challenging the chill. I started to run and barely heard Peter saying to Larry that he, Peter, should have known what might happen, should have closed our gate himself, should have kept track of the pipe, should have taken the responsibility. I should have known even then that with Peter there would always be this taking of responsibility. To me, it seemed almost like a curse.

Peter went to the irrigation district people for help with the pipe, a subject he logically expected they might know something about. Larry Lazio had told him he didn't know if the district could do anything, even if it was their problem.

The irrigation district building was seven miles downstream. The structure itself was tiny, not much larger than a dollhouse. A sign outside said a clerk named Violet was in only on Tuesday afternoons, but it took Peter three Tuesdays to find her in and, then, to engage her interest in our blocked pipe. When he finally found her, Peter talked the leisurely discourse of the plains with Violet, and she responded well, from what he told me. She allowed him to go through all the files, which he did with lawyerly thoroughness. He discovered that the dam and all its appurtenances, including our blocked pipe, belonged to the district.

"You should of seen those files when I came here," Violet said to Peter, fluffing her honey hair. "They're fine now, though, I'm sure of it. You'll find whatever you need in there."

"Cold night last night, wasn't it?" Peter said to her as he flipped through the files. She didn't answer right away, and he looked up to find her staring at him.

"Was, wasn't it?" she said absently, staring fixedly.

Back home, Peter told me that Larry Lazio wasn't to blame.

"Not to blame for what?" I asked.

"For the blocked pipe."

"I never said he was."

"Didn't you wonder, though?"

I shrugged.

"*I* wondered," Peter asserted. "Larry works for the state, not the irrigation district. Larry does water out of the creek, not out of the dam, which the district owns. But the district covered up our access when they built the dam, so they built our access into their dam. We're part of their dam. It's complicated, but clear: It's their problem."

"Guilty, guilty, guilty."

Peter twisted the top off a Coors, looking pretty damn pleased with himself.

The irrigation district sent their own ditch rider out to look at our blocked pipe. He'd never seen the pipe before and had no ideas to offer as he stood lengthily on the dam sucking his teeth and gazing down at the pipe's blocked end.

The district board members were elusive when Peter tried to contact them. They all appeared to be preoccupied with a complex power struggle amongst themselves. One would tell

Peter one thing, then another would say the opposite, seemingly more to get back at the first one than to throw any light on the dilemma. They bitched about one another, about county and state regulations, about the heat wave that had caused the flood.

"Temperature was 120 degrees in my hay barn when the storm broke, thought sure it was going to combust," one surly cuss told Peter.

"Do tell," said Peter, like a Kansan, and they all told.

They all kept him on the phone at great length but to no avail. Finally, the board chairman told him they had no responsibility for the pipe. Peter was aghast.

"But," I suggested from behind a book, "no one local would ever second-guess them, so they get away with it. So do you want to be local or do you want to be an outsider lawyer or do you want to not think about it that way?"

Actually, Peter was intrigued by the blocked pipe, although he wasn't aware of it yet — the best stage of any seduction. For him, the problem of the blocked pipe was of course associated with a previous commitment — getting water to future plantations of ponderosa pine down in the far corner of the ranch. He had already signed on for that quite willingly, so he had the pipe's problems as a consequence.

Peter began his assault on the pipe by phoning all around Central Oregon for any kind of equipment useful for dislodging packed scree from two hundred feet of underground pipe. There was nothing, no augers, no vacuum pumps, no hydraulic presses, nothing. No scree levitators, no transmogrifiers, no vaporizers.

"Roto-Rooter guy said he'd never get his corkscrew through solid gravel," Peter said, chuckling. "Then he said his thing

was only twenty-five feet long anyway, and he did not laugh."
He guffawed then, the Kansas good ol' boy laugh, the one that
made me think what a fine-looking man he was.

But then he was out the door and up the road to the dam
on his new red Honda motorbike, bought on impulse.

When he came back, he told me about a tiny yellow flower
growing in the muck piled up behind the irrigation dam.

"It has pointed petals that curve back against the stem, you
ever seen one like that?"

"Show me."

Up at the dam I saw the flower growing out of the muck,
like a fleur du mal.

"I was going to build a barrier around the muck, protect the
flower," Peter said, pointing, "but watch the way the debris
coming down the creek gets pulled off into that eddy, see? So,
anyway, I decided to do nothing."

"Ha! Nothing!" We sat on top of the dam and looked down.

"I had to work on it, doing nothing," he said next to me. We
both looked down and watched the eddy slowly swirling.

The idyll of those days was interrupted by the Viorsts calling
to say they were coming up the following weekend.

"Gotta get that pipe cleaned out by the time they get here,"
Peter said, sitting down with the phone. He called the Saints
Fire Department for an assist from their power-jet hose, but
they turned him down.

"Couldn't take the risk of havin' our truck so far outta
town," the fire chief told him. "I dunno 'bout what you
people've got out there, but here in town we are already dry."
But we'd had a three-day monsoon, Peter told him, and the
guy said, "Hell, that was three weeks ago!"

"What does he think, we live in another climate out here or
something?" Peter said after he hung up.

The federal firefighters with the national forest agreed to come out and blast away with their hoses, but they had to come at 5:30 A.M., before high-risk fire danger time. In two minutes, Peter told me, the truck had pumped its five hundred gallons into the opening of the pipe and nothing happened. Nothing at all. And just then, an irrigation district board member had pulled up at the dam in his rig, parked, walked over to the edge, and peered down at the nonaction. It was then, Peter said, that he first grasped the scale of the problem. If the underground pipe was two hundred feet long and eighteen inches in diameter, and it was packed solidly its entire length with smooth half-inch to one-inch gravel, then it was a question of painstakingly digging out and removing several tons of heavy material.

By 6:30 Peter was back in bed with me, reeling. "The guy from the board said we ought to try dynamite," he said, kicking at the covers in frustration.

"He wants us to blow up their dam?" It was too early in the morning for intrigue, I was thinking.

"He says we could get a munitions expert who could control the direction of the blast, keep it horizontal, blow that gravel straight out horizontally." He was on his hands and knees now, acting it out as if the blast were a body-wrenching fart.

"He's crazy, he wants you to destroy the dam? They must want it replaced and they figure Viorst can afford it."

Peter snorted, rolled down on his back, feet and arms in the air, like a cartoon dead dog.

"Why don't they just blow it up themselves, blame it on Viorst?" I wondered.

Peter stared at the ceiling. "It was curious the guy was there, wasn't it? After they claimed no responsibility."

"But you found in the files that they are responsible, I thought."

"Yeah, but you don't see them doing much about it, do you?"

"Hey, you know you should make money doing this," I said, kind of jealous, this time of how opportunities to make an hourly wage presented themselves to Peter and not to me.

After breakfast Peter went back up to the dam to start digging gravel with a shovel. He ran into Larry Lazio making his morning rounds up and down the creek, and Larry laughed at him as if he'd never seen anything funnier in his whole life.

"He loved it," Peter said petulantly. "He could not stop laughing. And then he came back when I was shoveling, laughed some more."

"Well, actually, that part's nice, that he came back again, hanging in there with you."

Peter didn't answer, so I don't know if he thought it was nice or not. We were eating lunch, which he had prepared, as I was long getting back from a strenuous ride on the big white Arab Granite. We'd had to do a lot of jumping, over everyone else's overflowing water ditches.

"Well, Lazio keeps me company," Peter acknowledged. "He's very up, like a coach."

"I like Larry," I said. "Say, is there any chance he let this blockage thing happen to you on purpose, see what kind of guy you are?"

Peter looked at me, shook his head, and was silent. His body language said I had impugned some kind of rural honor even though I was kidding.

A few days went by while Peter did nothing but haul gravel out of the pipe, first with the shovel and then with the shovel attached to a twenty-foot-long plastic pipe. After that he called the state forest firefighters to come out at the end of a workday. The man who answered jumped at the chance, no restraint there. It turned out he was a hippie still in Saints after the back-to-the-land movement. He was very talkative and told Peter about hippie life in Saints before nearly everyone got driven away by the locals. The guy pumped out his tank and reloaded right from the creek and pumped it out again, all the while talking to Peter, who stood in the icy water wearing a wet suit last used by Ham Jones in the Bahamas.

After five loads no more gravel seemed to be coming out, so they stopped.

When the Viorsts drove in for the weekend, they didn't see me as I sat on the raft-bridge writing. It was only as they drove by not seeing me positioned there, watching them like a concierge, that I realized the view from the raft-bridge of people coming in was a privileged, almost secret one. An unseen checkpoint. From the road, if you happened to look over to where I was stationed, you would see a dense thicket of willows springing into life as a result of all the water that had poured through the swamp from the flooded pasture. And, just beyond in the background, the raft-bridge itself would be invisible, down low, surrounded by tall grasses, with my little table and chair and me on it almost invisible.

When the Viorsts drove in, I saw my little station from their point of view. For the first time, I felt proprietary about the ranch. I felt like it was mine, not theirs. I don't remember having had conciergelike feelings at seeing the Viorsts on the property before that moment, when the decor suggested the behavior. Or maybe I did have such feelings before that, yet I was unaware of them, and the feelings were a sign of a growing blurring of identity. Perhaps this is even the reason I was drawn to the raft-bridge, for its inherent quality as a secret point everyone had to pass to come onto the ranch. Whatever the truth might have been, that time Elaine looked over toward the raft-bridge at the last moment and through the mass of willows saw my face staring back at herself and Bob.

"Stop," she shouted at her husband. The car stopped suddenly. Elaine jumped out and came bounding over toward me. Bob followed hesitantly at a distance.

"It looks like you're on a raft!" she cried exuberantly. "Where are you sailing to?"

I felt a slight thrill. "Far away," I said.

"Is Peter around?" Viorst said, addressing me suddenly. He had his hands clasped behind his back again. He leaned forward, eliciting my response.

He was funny, made me smile. "He's up at the irrigation pipe, digging," I said, laughing like it was the funniest thing ever.

Viorst laughed broadly. "I hope he's got long arms!"

"Digging!" Elaine hooted.

The three of us laughed an orgy of laughter at Peter's expense. Finally, Elaine blew her nose, and they left down the road to begin their weekend. Five minutes later Viorst drove by alone on his way up to the irrigation dam. As he passed me on my raft-bridge, I stood up and pointedly linked my hands behind my back and pretended to examine his car. He laughed indulgently at me.

I decided to go up to the dam too and took the Scout.

I joined Peter and Viorst, who were looking down into the water as they stood on the dam above the wretched blocked pipe. The pipe lay hidden beneath us, invisible but irritated, like a diverticular intestine.

Peter was tense with Viorst on the scene. He began to outline the history of the blockage to date. He was thorough, very corporate, very serious. When he mentioned that Larry Lazio's daughter had volunteered to crawl into the pipe with a gunnysack and haul out the gravel by the sackful — Peter had cautiously declined — Viorst showed a measure of alarm. I felt awkward for my man and left.

When Peter came back to the cabin, I was reading *The Seven-Storey Mountain* of Thomas Merton, the part where Merton tries to become a hermit.

"Viorst wants me to bill him for my hours on the pipe," Peter said. He was peeling off his wet clothes. "Seven bucks an hour."

"Seven bucks an hour!" I set Merton aside.

"Right." He seemed disgusted.

"Well, I suppose it's right to get paid for it since you're doing it anyway."

"Why not *not* get paid for it?" he suggested in all seriousness.

This was an interesting notion. "Why would you do that?" I asked.

"As a means of spiritual definition," he said archly, but not entirely insincerely. I saw that he was actually considering the possibility of not getting paid for what promised to be a horrendous task, but he was also mocking himself drolly. We smiled at each other for a long moment.

"Whose idea was the seven bucks?" I asked then. "Why not eight? Or three fifty? Or fifty cents?" I felt like I was feeding him material.

"Seven is the going rate," Peter answered, dropping his hands to his sides. "It was my idea." He tossed his head and turned aside, a rather horselike gesture, I thought. He was now naked, his clothes in a pile on the floor.

"You kind of like becoming a serf, don't you?" I asked him. "A naked serf." He was still standing there, his head turned aside, waiting for more commentary, or something, from me. Was he offering me his neck?

"If you don't want to do the pipe," I said softly, "I suppose you could refuse, and we could go somewhere else. We could leave them high and dry?"

"But I *do* like it," he insisted. "I am *drifting* into it. You probably don't even know what I mean. You can't drift."

He was looking at me then with what seemed like a tinge of dislike. He had never looked at me that way before. It didn't matter what he was saying. That look was hard to take. And I didn't quite get where it was coming from or why.

"You know who else showed up at the dam after you left?" Peter said, kicking desultorily at his clothes.

"Who?"

"Buckner and his dog. He walked right past us down toward the cabin without saying a word, and Viorst just watched and then wanted to know who the hell that was, and now he wants me to keep him completely off the ranch. How am I going to do that? Punji sticks?"

So was this why Peter had looked at me accusingly? "But I like Buckner being out there," I said, exploding, jumping up, the pugilist, ready to challenge Viorst. "He's one thing I'm very certain about."

"You are? Have you been talking to him?" Peter asked me. He was surprised, maybe a tiny bit suspicious.

"No, I haven't. But I feel safe with Buckner hanging around. I trust his instincts."

"Why, might I ask?"

"I don't know, we're out here alone in the middle of nowhere, and he's one thing that seems predictable . . . what he's doing, I mean," I said. "What is this conversation really about, anyway?" I asked sharply.

Peter was uncertain what to do with this aggression. He turned and walked right out of the room, took a bath, went to bed without further discussion. I puttered around for a while to no purpose, fretted, drank a glass of wine, thought about the interaction, then went to sleep on the couch.

EIGHT

PETER WAS OUTSIDE sitting on the fence staring at the mountains when I got up the next morning and looked out the window. I'd stayed all night on the couch and slept like a babe. I'd heard him go out early, so I reckoned he'd been there on the fence for some time.

"What's going on?" I asked him when he came into the kitchen later to eat. He tilted his head and watched me eating cereal, didn't answer.

"This have something to do with the idea of drifting?" I pressed.

He sat down opposite me at the long table. The kitchen had become our ritual place for straightforward talk, a place of great comfort, its planks oiled, I imagined, by decades of confessions. There was something about that kitchen that made you feel no ill could possibly come to you there, certainly not for telling the truth. Being in that kitchen would always make it okay.

"I feel like I'm monitoring my behavior just to please you," Peter announced, having arrived at this thought and now laying it, like a dead mouse, on my plate.

"Well, my first reaction is that you shouldn't try to monitor your behavior on my account, but if I say that, then I'm telling you to monitor your behavior on my account."

"Hmmm," he said and started again: "Well, what I mean is, I think about whether something is for you, whether I'm doing the something for you, and knowing that it is affects the decision I make."

"Well, that's love, you can't fight it. Or physics . . . or something, I don't know."

"Can you understand that this is unpleasant to me?"

"Just do what you want!" I exclaimed, exasperated, I fear, with this degree of second-guessing one's emotions, of overintellectualizing one's every breath, but also alarmed, perhaps, by the idea that the thralls of love might be unpleasant for Peter. I galloped on. "You have to come down somewhere. What should I do? I tell you here and now that I don't care if you do or do not fix the pipe, or if you blow it up or write poetry about it. You don't have to try to guess what I want and do it. There's no right answer. Just do what you want to do. We don't have to do anything at all in particular, we're just here to see what happens, yes? To drift? Maybe drift together?"

Peter and I contemplated each other silently across the table in the safe kitchen.

"Right," he said finally. "See what happens."

It felt okay to me — the best we could do at the time. So many men might have retreated at that moment, but Peter stood firm. I drank my coffee and looked at him with my heart on my sleeve. I don't know of course exactly how he felt, but his tension appeared to have lessened, as if he'd been let off some hook, a hook he'd hung himself on. I imagined him letting himself off the hook.

Later that day, from my raft-bridge, I saw Peter walk across the yard and into the forest. He was carrying a little notebook, so I guessed he was going to start a journal. As for me, I was studying what was going on around the raft-bridge. A wetland going dry is interesting as long as you're not trying to make a living out of it. The watercress I had planted around the raft-bridge was dead, but my economic survival didn't depend on it. It depended on other things. I wrote about money in my journal. As it was, I was painfully close to my comfort level, financially speaking. I had to make some money, was the point. What if I didn't find anything at all to write about Rajneeshpuram? I had almost no money coming in at all, and the Portland Victorian was falling down, falling down. I need to make some money, I wrote. Once I'd written them down, I didn't dwell on thoughts of money. For me, that's the point of writing them down.

Later that day, determined to find a story to write and sell, I drove up to Rajneeshpuram for my appointment with Siddha. After what turned out to be a perilous drive down into Rajneeshpuram Canyon, slipping and sliding down the steep gravel road, I came into Rajneesh Reception. A woman I knew to be Isabel spotted me, came to greet me. She strode toward me purposefully and fixed me with a penetrating gaze.

"*Tu parles français*," she said directly, engagingly, her hand moving up her body to the plumeria flower behind her ear. "*N'est-ce pas?*" What a gesture, I thought.

"*Oui,*" I answered, startled. "*Toi, tu es française?*"

"*Oui,*" she said, continuing to hold my eyes with her own and saying, "But I have not lived always in France. And you? Why do you happen to speak French?"

"I've lived in Paris some since spending a school year there," I explained. She nodded, gaze still fixed. I went on: "And where have you lived besides France?"

"In Santiago . . . where my grandfather was with a university, and then I went to live in Polynésie Française," came the reply.

Well, I thought, that explains the flower in her hair. "Do all

Rajneeshees put flowers in their hair?" I asked as she maintained her open scrutiny of my face.

"No, not all of us. We grow them here in our greenhouse. The sun here is perfect," she explained elliptically, paused, then added: "In Polynesia, we wear a flower on the left side when we're in love."

I saw she had the white plumeria on her left side and so responded to her cue. "You're in love?"

She smiled lusciously and then finally broke her eyes away, overcome by her own private thoughts. "Siddha will be here to meet you soon," she said, pirouetting to lead me into a well-appointed waiting area that looked like the lobby of a brand-new high-desert resort lodge or perhaps a reading room in a modern library. She turned then and studied me again for a moment. I took the opportunity to ask her if she was happy at Rajneeshpuram, but she did not answer and instead selected a book from a nearby shelf, glanced at the table of contents, found the page she was looking for, and turned down the corner.

This done, she asked: "Would you like to read something by Bhagwan?" and without waiting for a response gave me *The Book of the Secrets 2*, then walked across the room to what was apparently her desk and immersed herself in a book she must have been reading before I arrived.

I found Bhagwan's book to be a compilation of discourses given in Bombay in 1972. Each discourse, I saw, was spun out in response to a single question from a follower. I glanced across the room at Isabel reading at her desk. I usually find French people, especially outside of France, interesting, and she was no exception. The French bug is a virus caught by many an unsuspecting impressionable barbarian. In my case, it happened in adolescence, when Léonore, a Frenchwoman who had married a G.I. and gone with him to live in Portland,

Oregon, taught me French. With her Edith Piaf hair and square-necked dresses, her eyebrows plucked to a thin arch, Léonore would stand in front of her wide-eyed students, fluttering exotically, mopping her décolleté with her handkerchief. We were all riveted. She so obviously had a clue about something. And it was she who had formed my image of French women.

Isabel looked over at me and said, "Try the one where I turned down the corner."

I did so and found it to be a discourse in response to "Is there any connection between opening to a Master and opening up in sex?" The question goes on to ask, "My background gives a negative and passive meaning to surrender. I know I will not go deeper unless I am able to overcome this negativity that seems to be engraved in my psyche. Is surrender possible when the opposite is planted so deeply?" Rajneesh's answer was twenty pages long and difficult to read because of frequent repetitions, sometimes of a single word, but it was the verbatim transcription of a two-hour discourse of the type spontaneously given by a spiritual master, which is, after all, an oral tradition, not necessarily a literary one.

I was thinking, as I read Isabel's recommendation, that it was an interesting choice. Of course that was her job, to make the Rajneeshees interesting to me. I knew that she was in charge of external communications at Rancho Rajneesh, of public and press relations. It was her job to figure out what journalists or visitors needed to see or do or to read to be satisfied, intrigued, and she had intuited, perhaps, that I was deeply involved, just then, with questions of surrender and control. I took note of her perspicacity, her cleverness at figuring out what might correspond to my state of mind. It made me wonder how she'd been for John Small, the Mormon land-use expert, what she'd said to him, he who liked talking to women. Small appeared to have retained a very pleasant memory of Isabel, and in general had found Rajneeshpuram interesting, not threatening in any way, unlike most other folks living on the high desert who'd never been there and would never go.

Siddha arrived after a few minutes, introduced himself, sat down, handed me a desert rock. I looked at the rock. Handing me a rock seemed like a ploy to put me off guard. Or was it a gift such as those Indians might have offered one another in that very setting in earlier days?

"You've handed me a rock," I said to him. "What's the deal?"

He laughed a little, then said it was just a way of starting a conversation, that what happens in the first four minutes of meeting someone determines how the rest will go. I would find out later that he had written a book on the subject some years earlier, called *Contact: The First Four Minutes.*

"So how's our meeting going so far?" I asked him but didn't wait for an answer and asked instead if we could go somewhere farther into Rajneeshpuram, somewhere beyond the reception area. I hadn't come down that scary road just for this.

Siddha agreed, and we walked past Isabel, who, I saw, was reading the historian Barbara Tuchman's *A Distant Mirror: The Calamitous Fourteenth Century,* which I knew to be about the similarities between the upheavals of the fourteenth century and those of the twentieth.

A driver who'd been waiting outside took Siddha and me to an outdoor café. We sat down in the hundred-degree heat, shaded by a striped Cinzano umbrella. Siddha ordered Indian chai for us. Our table was on a terrace, and the terrace was flat on the floor of the desert canyon in which the Rajneeshpuram commune sat, looking for all the world like a Dead Sea kibbutz. Siddha was about fifty, of Jewish origin, with a trimmed beard and immensely sad eyes under heavy, dark eyebrows. When I asked, he told me somewhat stiffly about his psychiatric practice in California working with victims of post-traumatic stress syndrome, many of them Vietnam vets. As he talked, a cloud of blackbirds zigzagged across the landscape, just like at our ranch. In a swoosh they were all sucked in by a cottonwood standing alone next to the stream that ran down through the canyon. Then the birds shot from the tree as one and veered off into the distance, out of sight.

When I asked Siddha how he had come to be a Rajneeshee, he said it wasn't important, that it had simply clicked for him after he'd become dissatisfied with his performance-based profession, as he put it. He said that what was important was for me to get to know the place, to read Bhagwan's writings, to spend as much time as I could at the commune.

"Is this place just a personality cult?" I asked.

"I certainly don't think so. Everyone here loves Bhagwan in his or her own way, but everyone is also on their own path."

"Do people here even see him, or is he hidden away in silence?"

"He sits with us once or twice a day, most days, in the large hall, for meditation."

"What is the connection with him?"

"It is different for each person, of course, but in general, he . . . reminds us."

It was hard to take in and evaluate Siddha's offered description of a calm, measured guru-and-followers pattern of living compared with the idea that the sect had cruelly wrested Antelope from its old-timer residents.

"Do you like Sheela?" I asked then. "You think she's doing the right thing? Making enemies?"

"Sheela? I think she's very misunderstood, but I think she is doing what she thinks needs to be done. She is following her own path."

"Is she doing what Bhagwan tells her to do?"

"No, he doesn't think about this sort of thing. I think he asked her to find this place, and now she is on her own."

"And you think that's good enough?"

"I think you must watch and see for yourself and . . . talk to Sheela if that's what you want to do. Now, tell me why *you* are here," Siddha said, and he folded his hands in his lap to listen. I wondered why he didn't accept my questions as evidence of why I was there, but I didn't say so. He struck me as both rabbinical and psychiatric, wanting to shift the attention onto me, but he also seemed truly uninterested in Sheela and her ways. Given my preconceived notions about psychiatrists, I didn't resist his tack. I was much happier to be talking to him than to Sheela, this was certain. I had my own vague yearnings. I told him about living on the ranch, about how much we loved the water on the land, and about Peter. As soon as Siddha heard about the water, he became enthusiastic and said that I must meet the Rajneeshpuram Water Man, who would show me the fabulous water system at Rancho Rajneesh.

"Tell me about Peter," he said then, and I told him about Peter's desire to change the more Westernized structures of his thinking, about his wanting not to be a lawyer anymore.

"Maybe," Siddha pondered slowly, "maybe Peter would like to come up here for a workshop, learn to meditate, slow his heartbeat."

"You might steal him away from me," I said.

He took a long look at me. "You really think that?"

"I don't know. But it would be manipulative on my part to suggest to Peter that he come up here if he didn't want to. It would be making him part of the story I'm supposed to write." My words hung thinly in the air like dust. I continued: "Don't you think it's a bit of a challenge living here in Central Oregon?"

"What do you mean exactly?"

"Well, in your case, your collective case, people in these parts don't seem to like you too much. In my case, it's hard because it's a man's world here . . . the men talk only to each other. What am I supposed to do?"

"Get a lobotomy?" We both laughed, a bit out of control, comic relief. But I became painfully aware then how false it felt trying to remain fully armed against being hornswoggled by a snake-oil salesman, as if this man were going to trip me up simply because he was one of those notorious Rajneeshees. In fact, I rather liked him for his humor as much as his intellect, and it was difficult to understand so far why the Rajneeshee community was so hated out there on the high desert. As Siddha and I parted back at reception, he found me a copy of a biography of Bhagwan Shree Rajneesh written by an Indian scholar who lived there at Rajneeshpuram. Interesting, I thought, these people who gave me books to read.

When I read the biography later, I learned that Rajneesh was a person who waited, sometimes lazily so, until something happened to him, until somebody asked him to perform. At home in India he'd floated downstream like that, and someone had always fished him out, asked him to speak. He'd done so, and people had followed him, made a home for him, supported him, and then he'd gotten talked out (or lazy again) and fallen silent, gotten back in the river and floated downstream. Of course, I had, and still have, no personal capacity to swear to the details of the man's life, although I heard the startling news up at Rancho Rajneesh that he had just begun speaking again. Ending four years' silence, something up there had now drawn Rajneesh out, pulled him out of the river, gotten him giving daily discourses again.

I made four or five more trips to Rajneeshpuram before I got to hear Rajneesh speak. Why did I keep going back? First of all, I didn't have anything to write about yet — just a couple of new acquaintances, plus a third one, Videh, the Water Man, who each time I visited showed me another section of the intricate water system the Rajneeshees had built to green their bone-dry desert land. I couldn't wait to see each part of it, from the spring up top to the large earth-fill dam with its lake behind it, to the multitude of tiny check dams below, which caught and released water as needed into a series of mini-wetlands.

Each time up at Rajneeshpuram, I talked also to two or three other people for an hour or so. Most people there, Isabel told me, were not willing to talk to outsiders. Doing so interrupted their meditative lives, she said, made them think about their own egos, which they didn't want to do. She did find me some interlocutors, however, and I found some myself. I listened to their stories, asked questions. They were all people between thirty and sixty, often with intellectual and/or professional backgrounds, some willing to talk about themselves, some not, some likable, some not, some fun, some boring. They told very different stories, but all were ultimately similar, with the person having come to a point of frustration or anguish, where life made no sense anymore. The resulting quest for something that made sense had led each of them to Rajneesh and, thence, to Rajneeshpuram. Their stories, in their most blatant and tedious sense, were like those told by born-again Christians.

Interestingly, the actual commune, the communal living itself at Rajneeshpuram, was important to everyone I talked to (especially the bad commune food, consisting primarily of tofu and cooked dried beans fashioned into one thing or another), and they all talked with pleasure and at length about commune life, so much so that I was constantly and nostalgically reminded of my earlier quest for community in the "neighb" and of my present life as half of a rather isolated couple. It was clear to me that my interest in collective living was shared more by people at Rajneeshpuram than by the local folk around Saints. Talking to certain Rajneeshees satisfied a side of me that was getting relatively shortchanged on the high desert.

I felt bad for the true communards at Rancho Rajneesh who were unaware of hostilities felt by many Oregonians. Most Rajneeshees were isolated, meditating twice a day, never leaving the ranch, never reading the papers or watching television. Some of them seemed vaguely aware or willing to say they were aware that there was a faction of people around Sheela who were into power, who made all the decisions, raised and spent all the money, decided where everyone would work and what to build. But no one really wanted to discuss (or was interested in) the fact that the guru's nonparticipation in decisions had inevitably created a power vacuum that was being filled by ambitious types.

I saw Siddha each time I was there, usually at the end of the day. When Bhagwan Shree Rajneesh suddenly began speaking, giving evening discourses to a few followers each day, Siddha was eager for me to sit in on one. He said he would try to get me invited.

"Don't hesitate!" Peter exclaimed vigorously, when I told him about the possibility of hearing Rajneesh speak. I remember thinking — something about the forcefulness of Peter's response — that it was he, not I, who really wanted to hear the guru. "This is so bizarre!" Peter had said. "In the middle of Central Oregon fundamentalist Christian territory! What an amazing opportunity!"

A woman from Isabel's press office called me then, saying,

"What's the name of that rag you're writing for?" She was hostile, and I almost dropped the whole thing. When I told her the name of the magazine, she said I couldn't come hear Rajneesh just for that little mag. "It'll have to be something bigger."

Annoyed, I did drop the whole thing, for a while. Then, remembering my hope to make some money with an article, I got a friend at *Esquire* to vouch for me, should anyone ask. Isabel's people did ask, and, as a result of this ruse, I got invited to hear Bhagwan.

When I arrived at Rajneeshpuram, I was taken to a blond-wood Scandinavian-looking bathhouse to shower and wash my hair with the scentless soap provided. Bhagwan, it was explained, was allergic to perfumes, most soaps, and deodorants, and they took no chances. The bathhouse was chilly, and there was no hair dryer. Outside, the sun was setting, and it was cooling off. I was already cold, but as I followed the guide at dusk to Bhagwan's quarters, she told me I would have to shed my cardigan in the anteroom. Rajneesh was also allergic to wool. And, "oh," she said, "he can't tolerate temperatures above fifty-five degrees, so his room may seem a little cold to you."

It all seemed like a Brechtian estrangement designed to throw the novice off balance. I was struggling, by that time, not to be utterly dismissive of whatever might follow.

But it turned out to be, on the surface anyway, a rather benign experience. There were about twenty of us, mostly Indians from India, obviously the guru's close circle, and we were sitting cross-legged on the floor facing Bhagwan, who also sat cross-legged on the floor in a long robe. I had smelled his odor briefly when he came into the room. It was a purely human smell, not at all unpleasant and quite intimate, the kind of smell you might smell on your lover's body. The smell evaporated rapidly. The cold air made the room sterile.

The guru sat calm and relaxed. His skin was mocha-colored, and his gray-white hair was long and nicely brushed away from a bald pate topping a roundish face that held dark, moist, expressive eyes. He talked slowly, circuitously, for two hours. I grew colder and colder. I stopped listening for a moment and spent some time thinking about what happens as one's body temperature drops, wondering if it was a way to stimulate religious conversion. I started to tremble, and my teeth were chattering. My hair was still wet. It took great concentration, focusing first on Hawaii, then on New York City or Fez in August, to stay warm, to keep from freezing to death. People all around me were in all normalcy passing gas from time to time, shifting their weight just like horses. That diet again, I thought, remembering what the Frenchman Yves had said, about farts: "Zen zere is zee kind where you 'ave eat some beans."

Bhagwan's discourse itself was like a sermon. Not like a Presbyterian sermon, in which, when I had them inflicted upon me as a child, the disembodied sobriety was boring. Bhagwan's sermon was engaging, like a History-of-Religion sermon, or a My-Personal-History-with-Religion discourse, in which he sounded like the professor of philosophy he had been long before, at a university in India. He talked about Faust, Marx, and Frank Sinatra (the old do-be-do-be-do joke as a way of saying meditation is an experience of the existential moment, which is why a crowd can never have the experience of truth, only an individual), about the beginnings of Christianity, replete with tales of oligarchic power struggles and palace intrigue. Here I wondered if he was subtly referring to what was happening at Rancho Rajneesh. Stylistically, he circled around his subject, often repeating expressions or words. He surrendered to it, surrounded it, frequently smothered it to death, but he sometimes summoned up an emotionally charged movement within my otherwise rational brain.

Bhagwan looked straight at me. I was shivering, writing in my notepad, looking back at him. He then said that anyone writing about him was a fool, wasting time, a fool who should instead write something about herself.

I didn't stop writing. I sat there and wrote: This is what he does? He tells people not to be compulsive, and they're horrified he has seen through them, and they throw themselves on his mercy? Am I going to let him tell me what to do? Would that be to surrender? Kind of a forced surrender?

I kept on writing like a yeoman, unembarrassed, almost until the end of the discourse — at least another full page after the part about the fool. Now that I look at my notebook, I see that my notes aren't very legible, I'd been shivering so hard. In fact, my hand had eventually seized up, couldn't grasp the pencil. And then, later, when I'd got into my Toyota to drive home, the car had done a three-sixty on the gravel road. It had seized up as well. Scared the shit out of me.

At home, when I told Peter about the evening, he focused primarily on the car, insisted on having it checked out, which I couldn't afford.

"I've kept it serviced regularly," I argued. "I'm sure it was a fluke."

"I'll pay for it, I don't care. There might be something wrong with it. It's only a couple of hundred bucks," he insisted. I loved that it had mattered so much to him.

As I sat in the sun on my raft-bridge the next day to write about that freezing evening in Bhagwan's chambers, it was impossible to re-create the sensation of being so cold that my hand had seized up. Instead, I forgot about the guru and baked my hand contentedly in the heat in a rickety chair in front of a crooked table shaded from the direct sun by a straw mat suspended from two upright stakes. It was truly the desert. I relished the heat. It was ninety-five degrees, and it was the kind of dry heat that keeps animals asleep all afternoon, not debilitated, but sublimely at rest.

The drought had persisted, a concern for all who were intent on growing something. As weather, though, it couldn't have been more enchanting. People in Saints — in the post office, in the grocery store checkout line, at the gas station, everywhere — were unusually talkative about both the worrisome drought and the wonderful weather. I thought it funny that everyone in Saints was obsessed with heat, drought, and the possibility of fire, while everyone at Rajneeshpuram felt the heat of Bhagwan speaking again. The mood of Rajneesh's latest discourse could dominate the Rajneeshee community atmosphere, make it hot or cold, gusting or raging or bringing relief like a breeze. Everyone at Rajneeshpuram was inspired by so much talk from Bhagwan. Compared with the people in Saints, who characteristically seemed to prefer not really to converse at all, just to emit a sound or two, stick to the basics, the Rajneeshees were overstimulated. They were intense, expressive, the air they breathed on you was hot. They were on fire.

It was suddenly very still on my raft-bridge. I stopped writing, looked up.

All the frogs in the swamp had fallen silent long before — not dead, presumably, but hanging in suspended animation somewhere within the drying muck. I'd been told that interesting fact by Ham Jones, that such phantom frogs could wait in the benthic layer for as long as it might take for water to pass their way again. Without dying. Like Dorrance the ghost, I'd said, waiting for Melvin to pass by.

The cicadas started up suddenly. Unlike the frogs, they were unaffected by the loss of water, of any moisture at all.

They hummed in the reeds as usual, stimulated intermittently into song by any sudden noise, a slight change in the wind, for instance. Or had it been the sound of a branch cracking underfoot?

"Hi, Buckner!" I sang out. Just in case. Had a little flash I was in Nam, a touch of high-desert madness. I thought I saw someone move, deep in the trees in front of me.

No one answered.

Later, Peter emerged from the forest far across the meadow, carrying his little notebook in his hand. Out of the corner of my eye, I saw him appear off behind the corral, a red shirt coming out of green and brown. I watched him go inside. I went in and heard him on the phone with the irrigation district, playing hardball.

Over dinner he said, "I'm going to force the irrigation district to fix the dam, build some kind of grate or coffer dam." We were eating pasta with clam sauce and a kind of high-desert focaccia I'd bought at the new upscale bakery in Saints. Outside in the dusk, the horses were lined up at the fence, staring in at us sitting in the lighted window. They looked like they were watching television.

I studied Peter looking at the horses looking at us. "Is this lawyer work?" I asked him, with complete affection.

"No, it's not, but somebody has to make some money, don't you think? You know how much it costs us to live here?" he said.

"How much?"

"Eight hundred a month."

I was surprised. "What costs eight hundred dollars?"

"Oh, gas, telephone, electricity, health insurance, not yours, I realize you pay for your own, but you don't pay the Chevron bill, let's see, dinner out in Bend, membership in the State Bar . . ."

"Membership in the State Bar?"

It must have slipped out.

"Yeah," he said sheepishly.

"You're still a member? You never gave it up?"

"Uh huh," he said, his body doing an elaborate squirm and shuffle.

I leapt across the table at him, laughing. "You lawyer, you," I said, nose to nose.

"You woman, you," he sputtered. I'm not quite sure what he meant by that, but both of us seemed to want to wrestle just then and wrestle hard, down onto the floor, banging against chairs, no holds barred. I was comfortable using all my strength wrestling with Peter. He could contain me. We were lurching around the room connected, when suddenly the phone rang.

Peter got up off the floor to answer, and I gathered right away it was Faith Gaines talking about her son and the Mountain Man after three months' silence. I got up to give Peter his privacy, but he gestured for me to stay, just as he had done before. I turned on the lamp and saw that he looked miserable. Why did he want me to stay and listen? I wondered. I lay down on the rug and looked at the ceiling. Somebody from before our time had scratched the name Joel in the darkened timber.

"Now, tell me what this deal is again," Peter said to Faith. Twice he asked. A third time.

"Hmmmm," he said. "Dyer now admits to mutual masturbation. And so Billy admits that it happened. Are you sure they're not talking to each other, agreeing on this?"

Apparently Faith didn't answer at all, because Peter gestured to pull an answer out of her. Getting nothing, he then said, "And so, they're dropping the investigation? Is that what you're saying?" He waited endlessly without saying anything at all. Then: "What if that's not all that happened between them?"

And then: "What do I mean?" Peter looked down at me then intently, as if to say with his eyes and shoulders that Faith was resisting his questions completely. "I mean, something more than just mutual masturbation."

Silence. Then he said, "You don't think so? You're sure he would tell you?" A long pause. Nothing more, apparently. He started again on another tack: "What exactly is the deal they're offering?" Peter sat down on the couch, snapped off the lamp I had turned on. He preferred sitting in the dark, which somehow suited the long periods of intense silence. Then, finally: "Why won't it just keep happening?"

I understood from the few words here and there that Ed Dyer was applying a lot of pressure on Faith and Billy — I couldn't get how, exactly — to accept some kind of deal from the district attorney that would let Dyer off so that the whole matter could be shelved. Watching Peter this time, I was less able to see exactly what was happening to him; he was sort of hiding in the dark. This struck me as interesting: He wanted me there, but he wanted to hide from close scrutiny. As a result of not being able to see Peter very well, I got more involved in imagining what was happening to Faith Gaines, as if I were listening to the radio. I now had met Faith and could picture her, had already listened to her talk in her office about proud cuts, had already seen her disturbed affect, her emotional logjam.

Peter gave Faith advice: "Call up the district attorney, tell him Billy wants to talk to him in his office. The district attorney is prosecuting this on behalf of Billy," he said. "The district attorney is your lawyer. I am not practicing law now." It was simple, but Peter had to say it several times, explain how it should be done. Then he hung up.

A big silence ensued. It seemed as if Peter was not going to tell me what Faith had said this time, was just going to sit there in the dark, leave it at that.

"What's Dyer doing to her?" I asked finally. I sat up.

"Dyer is . . . amazing," Peter said, and I had the impression I was dragging it out of him. He really would have preferred not to examine the matter further, not to look at it this way and that, the way I would, not to expend any more psychic energy on it at all. Or perhaps he already thought of his conversation as privileged, confidential, a kind of lawyer-client relationship?

"Is this already confidential?" I asked him.

"No," he said firmly. "I am not her lawyer. The district attorney is her lawyer for the time being, or, if she's unsatisfied, she should get a lawyer specializing in this sort of thing."

"Wouldn't you really rather I not listen when you're on the phone? I hate it when someone listens to me talk on the phone."

"No, I really don't mind. I like it when you're there."

"Why is that?"

He paused a long time, did not answer the question, but eventually decided to tell me about the call. "Dyer came by Faith's clinic," Peter began, "and cried and said, 'I just love Billy. I couldn't do anything to harm him.' Dyer told Faith that what he and Billy did together was what men do, men who go out hunting and camping together, mountain men, real men, Indians, Everyman."

"What does she think Dyer and Billy did together exactly?"

"He told her they touched each other's penises, and Dyer said to her, 'I know it's against the law, but I don't know why.' He said, 'It's better than getting fourteen-year-old girls pregnant, boys are so oversexed.'"

"Is all this angst just for mutual masturbation?" I wondered. "There's got to be more to it than that."

Peter looked down toward me sitting on the rug, and the moment took on gravity. "God, it's hard to listen to . . . Faith," he said bitterly, one of those near-Freudian slips, it seemed. I'd felt sure he was going to say it's hard to listen to *you,* meaning *me,* but he'd said Faith and now he continued on about her.

"Faith was completely taken in by Dyer!" he finally spat out. "He spent time talking to her, bought her a cord of wood, things like that! Now she's hysterical, and Billy is terrified of Ed!"

This is what it's like to live with a lawyer, I was thinking — at least to live with a totally empathetic lawyer.

"The thing is that Dyer probably does love him in his twisted way," I said sadly.

"What?" Peter snapped.

"I don't know, doesn't every guy have a circle jerk somewhere in his past?" I ventured softly.

Peter looked hard at me.

Finally he said, "Wouldn't you be hysterical if it was *your* kid?" He stayed true to Billy.

"I would, I would, I would," I answered. "I would indeed, but I probably wouldn't have been caught so unawares — she's very naive."

"She is naive," agreed Peter, lightening a little. "She's naive, and I'm naive."

"Yes, and I'm naive as well."

Peter snorted.

"If you want, I'll talk to her next time she calls," I offered, "and you won't have to . . . you know, advise her, get sucked in. You don't have to talk to her again if you don't want to."

There was a pause. Our eyes met. Peter nodded slightly.

A few days after that, I took another cat into Saints to the vet clinic. Faith's long, thin, bare arms hung motionless at her sides as she spoke to me. I was unnerved by her.

"Anyway," she said, as flat as the stainless steel examining table in front of her. She took the cage with the growling cat in it and set it on the table. "Uh, uh, anyway, the Mormon Church knew what Dyer was doing for twenty years can you imagine and kept it to themselves and never told the police or the sheriff or spoke of it at all, and uh, anyway, a couple of those boys that Dyer was with are all grown up now and doing the same thing to younger boys in the very same church serves them right don't you think?"

Her logic was sure, in any case, although it was difficult to adequately comprehend how all of this had been going on for years in a population that would so adamantly disapprove of such behavior, such a small population that everyone was sure to know about it at some level, yet no one had ever spoken of it, brought it to the surface. Faith turned then, looked at the caged, snarling animal on the shiny metal surface, and said, "Thinks of himself as a mountain man, you know, I mean, a mountain man. Shoots, hunts, wears pelts. Straight out of the Old West." She trailed off, allowing me visions of a man's man, this guy in rawhide and furs, slashing his way through the forest with an ax. But she was talking again, or at least stuttering, trying to talk. She was a puzzle, not really saying all she was thinking, but at the same time forbidding me to ask. "Anyway," she said and stopped.

Later, over dinner that night, Peter and I talked aimlessly around the subject of children and sex. Outside in the Southern Spectacle, the sky offered a purple-and-silver crucifixion effect behind Faith, Hope, and Charity. I wondered what the Indians had called the three mountains.

I ventured to tell Peter about an incident out of my past. It was the story of my childhood best friend's brother, Jerome. I was vaguely aware of Jerome, who worked as a box boy at Safeway. Jerome wasn't a stranger to me, wasn't frightening, was someone I saw at my friend's house, two doors down. One day we were upstairs in my friend's house, and Jerome was there, in his bedroom. He must have been about seventeen. I was about nine.

My friend and I walked by Jerome's room. He was lounging in bed. "C'mere, gimme a hug," he called to me, and I responded, a little shyly, as I had no experience hugging men other than my father. When I got there, Jerome lifted the bedcovers, pointed to a part of himself I'd never seen before on anyone. It was interesting, and he said, "Here, touch it," and I did and it moved, which startled me, and I giggled. He giggled, too, and reached down and took my hand. With my open hand in his hand, he stroked his penis, which bobbed larger and larger and pointed at me in such a way that I felt confused, turned away, and left to find my friend in her own room next door.

Nothing told me that there was anything wrong or unusual about what Jerome had done, and, in fact, the incident fit into no context in my life. I forgot it until years later, when the memory was elicited by something I was reading about sexual abuse. I was learning about the subject of sexual abuse in the context of a puritanical culture, the United States, and was a little shocked or startled when I remembered Jerome. I was a little shocked as well that I had forgotten it, and that the memory, once called up, was not unpleasant. It was later, during a college year I spent in Paris, not a puritanical culture, when I read *Nana* by Zola, or something by Colette perhaps, that I saw that what had happened between Jerome and me was a gentle awakening indeed. I've never been able to fault Jerome, on the contrary.

"Jerome was warm and loving," I told Peter. "What's wrong with that?"

"He didn't grab hold of you?" said Peter, cross-examining.

"No, he let me walk away. He was smiling sweetly at me."

"Letting you walk away's the important part," he said, making the call. It occurred to me Peter would make an excellent judge.

NINE

PETER WAS OUT on the creek, five miles upstream from the ranch. Larry Lazio had asked him to take a look at a spot where the Forest Service planned to log the national forest.

"It's a neat place" was what Larry had said about it during one of their slow, laconic conversations up at the dam while Peter was continuing to haul gravel out of the blocked pipe. Larry had not faltered all summer in his role as cheerleader for Peter's slow struggle with the pipe, and he especially showed up whenever Peter was trying out some new low-tech invention. Later he would phone to find out how the work had gone.

Sometimes Larry had news about the irrigation board's continuing discussions on their nonresponsibility for the pipe. The phone conversations between him and Peter were raucous, a pleasure to overhear, with lots of Kansas guffawing on Peter's end. I'd answer the phone, and Larry would laugh and say, "Peter sure doesn't know how to quit, does he? Ha, ha, ha."

Up at the dam, from what I observed, their conversations were so slow they were the kind where you'd better not wager at any given moment that the talk had not already spun itself out before you got there. I showed up once and saw Larry do a double take and lose his balance when he glanced up at me standing on the edge of the bank. I was wearing a red-and-magenta-plaid cowboy shirt with red gabardine shorts and red espadrilles. I thought I looked rather French if I thought about it at all. The red on red was apparently too much for Larry, though. He looked away furtively, maybe horrified I might be a Rajneeshee, since they always wore red clothes. Then he self-consciously picked up the conversation with Peter as if nothing had happened. A man's world.

Peter told me Larry was always physically comfortable, even perched precariously above the spillway on the dam. He'd sit there, his knees pointed at the sky like a frog's, watching the water below, while Peter would poke at the pipe with his pincers. During these long, drawn-out conversations, Larry often told Peter about interesting places to see and explore up the creek and on into the Wilderness. He told him, for instance, about the Cache Mountain Toll Road, which had once been a pay-as-you-go pass for driving cattle across the Cascades. (Maybe it was really Cash Mountain?) Each spring in the 1870s, cattlemen down in the valley hired cowboys to drive herds up through the pass to the meadows on the high plateau, where the steers fattened up at no expense before fall slaughter back down in the valley. This was before all the best grazing land around Saints got doled out as homesteads, which was only after all the good land down in the Western Oregon valleys was already taken.

Much of the high-country western-movie terrain around Saints is still there, undeveloped, still intact, still relatively wild, primarily because of its inaccessibility in the ruggedness of the Cascade Range. Much of the land anywhere around Saints is federally owned and contained within Wilderness or National Forest or Bureau of Land Management acreage, and all of this sits on what is essentially a thinly covered flow of lava running east from the Cascades. From this dead-rock plain, you can stand out in the rugged terrain, look to the west, and imagine the wet valleys over the mountains and on west through the evening haze toward the sun setting in the vast Pacific beyond the serrated Doug fir horizon of the low coastal range. As night falls you can look to the west and imagine the line that divides today from tomorrow sliding lazily overhead like the contrail of a jet.

Peter and I generally went to the places Larry mentioned, no matter how inaccessible. Sometimes Peter went first to re-connoiter, then he'd take me. The sites were always interest-ing. A forest is, first of all, a landscape, and people can know and love a forest the way people know and love a coastline, or a mountain. Sometimes Larry's favorite spots were dangerous to get to, demanding major effort and respect for drop-offs or rock slides or chasms to be leapt across. Larry was testing us at the same time he was revealing his secrets. Peter had gone out now to look at a new secret site, this one just up the creek from the ranch. This was the "neat place" Larry thought the Forest Service was planning to clear-cut.

Peter came back and told me he thought the planned clear-cut was all a mistake, a bureaucratic error. "It's too preposter-ous otherwise. It's hard to imagine they'd just blatantly violate the law and log alongside a creek that way," he told me. "Wanta go look at it?"

"Sure," I said, closing my books for the afternoon.

By truck, Larry's secret place was only five miles from the ranch. We'd driven by it unawares, but now we walked to the edge and looked down. It was a sudden drop-off, a little Grand Canyon. A hundred yards below, a magnificent white-water cascade surged through a pinched, boulder-strewn gorge. It almost didn't look violent from such a height. We bush-whacked down the cliff in the heat and climbed up on a car-sized boulder sitting midstream just below the falls. There the air was refrigerated by the creek, and it pulsated in alternating drafts of hot and cold, hot and cold, hot and cold. The beat punctuated the energy exchange that naturally occurs around masses of water in free fall.

Millions of tiny water droplets filled the air. It was a cold shower, a total pleasure. Peter and I laughed and made animal noises and clambered around on the rocks like mountain goats.

"Come up this way," he said, moving slowly up the wall of the gorge just downstream from where we'd climbed down. I saw where we were heading before we got there, for it was one of those miracle giant trees, those flukes that never cease to amaze as wild nature becomes harder to find. Halfway up the gorge wall, clinging to the steep slope, was this giant, gnarly, fire-blackened, ancient Doug fir, its foot stretching fully ten feet toe to toe, top to bottom, as it grasped the slanted, rocky, wet earth like a giant octopus stuck to the side of a whaling vessel. The tree was so big, it was creating the weather in that gorge. The tree was making it rain. The tree had been making its own mini–rain forest down in the gorge for several centuries by the time we came upon it.

Up the slot in the other direction, just above the falls, the land flattened out at creek level and made a wide bank, a kind of landing. It was the sort of place you'd have migrated to for the summer if you'd been a Paiute a few centuries ago. There would have been salmon in the creek in those days, and you would have caught them in nets and baked them on vertical racks around a fire to eat each day and to smoke for winter. Here, the trees were scattered. Giant, ancient ponderosas, a whole covey of them, stood in a parklike stand as if waiting for a ceremony, the earth open and clear at their feet.

"God," I said to Peter, "I think you're having more fun than I am."

"Guess again," he said, and he led me through the trees to show me the tags the Forest Service had stapled all around the area, marking an impending timber sale. CLEAR CUT, the tags said, and the sale encompassed the landing with its huge ponderosas and all the gorge upstream and down, all the way down to the rainmaker Doug fir, for it, too, was expendable. So long, mini–rain forest.

Peter and I both got angry about the timber sale, but in different ways. I ranted and raved over dinner, felt quashed by an invasive and corrupt bureaucracy, drank too much. Peter became analytical, judicial. I threw up in the bathtub. Peter drafted a letter to the Saints district ranger asking about logging along the creek. Then he phoned Ham Jones.

Ham was all ears. I could tell by Peter's shift on the phone into high-male gear. Ham wanted us to drive up to his ranch that very night, but Peter agreed to dinner the next night. Peter was excited. He could hardly wait to talk to Ham.

"The Forest Circus'll kill you, they'll wear you down with blah, blah," Ham was saying the next evening. He was looking at Peter with a newfound admiration as he cooked steaks for us outdoors on the patio behind his chalet. Sally made the rest of the meal in the kitchen. We drank chilled Oregon Sémillon, nibbled on dipped vegetables, watched Ham perform.

"That's just great, that's just great," he said to Peter, kind of fawning over him, projecting powers onto him. Peter looked pleased.

Ham went on, talking euphorically about the landing we'd visited along the creek, a place he said was actually marked on an old pioneer map he'd found tacked to the wall of his barn. "You know what I mean? You know what I mean? My God, man! It's an official place, man. It's called McDougal's Landing. It's been named! It fucking exists!" Ham was warming up.

He told many stories that evening about the ignorance and arrogance encountered in the Forest Service. He was bright, witty, very funny, and this got Peter telling stories about practicing law. They were funny, the two of them, and I think I'd been laughter-deprived without knowing it.

We laughed and laughed and laughed, and I got the impression as the evening wore on that Ham was challenging Peter to succeed with the Forest Service where he himself had failed. Or maybe he was just recruiting him.

"Are you recruiting Peter?" I asked, when the stories had spun out. Ham chose to ignore me and just talked to Peter, carrying on for another half hour, all male. Sally got up to make coffee and then disappeared. Ham turned to me and fixed me with a look. "Why don't you help Peter fight the Forest Service?" he said, arching a brow.

He caught me by surprise. "I'm already doing something else," I stuttered.

"What?"

I didn't know what to call it, didn't want to get indignant. "My quest up in Wasco County."

"Are you still going up there?" Ham said with disdain. I could feel the rest coming.

"You're being boojooed, girl."

"I haven't taken sides."

"Doesn't the Bhagwan know there's no room for another religion?"

"Maybe he does know that."

"Anybody who elevates himself to some sort of supposed enlightenment and then surrounds himself with people who wait on him hand and foot and believe he's God is pathetic," Ham said disgustedly, very Yale, very Skull and Bones, very forceful.

I didn't have an answer. I'd already said I hadn't taken sides, and it was a shadow argument anyway, really about something else.

Peter got hold of a copy of the national forest plan, as well as an environmental assessment for the timber sale along the creek. The sale was clearly in violation of the forest plan, which was apparently a legal document.

Peter put on his lawyer suit and wing tips, went to see the district ranger. I watched him as he got in his Mustang and drove off. He did not appear to be doing a lawyer performance at all. He did not look tortured. He seemed whole, into it, very first degree. There was a new light shining in his eyes. I had witnessed no lateral motion, as if he were slipping surreptitiously into a parallel persona. Or at least I didn't catch it if it had happened. I longed to be a fly on the wall down at the ranger station, to witness the exchange, see how it played.

When he came home, Peter told me the ranger had thrown him off. "This guy just kept saying over and over that I was the only person, the only one, who had ever complained about logging along the creek," Peter said. "It was like it was programmed into him. It was his only response, no matter what I said: No one cares but you."

"Did you offer him your neck?"

"Probably I did, but he didn't know what to do with it."

Peter looked perplexed more than anything. But also caught up, interested, focused. A couple of days later he was still mulling over several possible moves, several courses of action, when the following letter to the editor appeared in *The Bulletin*:

> Strident voices that unrelentingly assail
> without understanding the goals and prob-
> lems confronting our forest managers
> should not be surprised if their slightly

> muddled thinking is not greeted with a
> chorus from Handel. What the gentleman
> in Saints fails to understand is that the For-
> est Service is not committed to managing
> the forest for maximum esthetic value dur-
> ing his, compared to timber crop cycles,
> short life but rather for the continued yield
> of the area for generations to come. . . .
> Timber is still the lifeblood of Oregon and
> if he is not prepared to deal with this real-
> ity perhaps he should notice the highway
> that brought him north runs south on the
> other side of the centerline. (back to Cali-
> fornia) His glitzy "If I can't have my way
> I'll take 'em to court" attitude should be
> carefully considered by prospective sup-
> porters.

It was weird, and somehow embarrassing. Here we were —
here Peter was — hidden away on a ranch in the middle of
nowhere, rarely setting foot off the property, almost completely anonymous. He drives into town to have a chat with a
forest ranger, and, all of a sudden, the story turns up in the local newspaper of record. Some total stranger is addressing him
in Mark Twain hyperbole, insulting him, lying about him.

The incident went to the core of Peter's being. I'm not sure
what was worse for him — having the complexity of his point
of view misrepresented or being called a Californian, a terrible
insult to Peter's Kansas self-righteousness. The small town of
Saints had poked its finger all the way into Peter's private
parts and tweaked his balls. It had got his full-fledged attention. He was not somebody to just let this sort of thing slide
by, just write it off.

"What the gentleman in Saints fails to understand!" Peter
hammed, pained, in his most exquisitely tortured Virginia
senatorial mode as he postured stiffly around the kitchen like
someone impaled on self-parody.

Ham telephoned to laugh, and to tell us there was a woman in town saying that Peter was spreading lies that there was a timber sale along the creek. She, too, was saying that we were from California. Peter got angry, but only for one explosive outburst, then he moved quickly to cap his anger. Within a day he was depressed, the way you get when you cut yourself off in the middle of a righteous rage. He stopped working on the blocked irrigation pipe.

During that period I had a series of disturbing small-town encounters myself. The first had to do with a Jazzercise class. I liked the class, but I also didn't like it. I liked it, because I wanted to be in a group of people doing some physical routine together. I liked it also because it felt good after an afternoon hunched over writing on the raft-bridge. But I didn't like it, because it was a stretch to feel as one with that particular group.

One day in late summer there'd been eight or ten of us waiting outside the little dance hall where the class was held. It was black-ant season on the high desert, when giant black ants were everywhere. Larry Lazio had told me groups of insects cycled through the high-desert region every year in regular and predictable patterns: There was a week when pear-sized moth corpses would accumulate on the town's sidewalks in veritable heaps, there were so many of them. Another time we had a week of walnut-sized, luminescent-blue scarabs: The raft-bridge was miraculously illuminated with shining blue polka dots. I never managed to get a scientific explanation for these visitations.

Now came a ten-day period when an army of giant black ants crawled right through the walls of our cabin, swarming over the floor and across the beds. Great black ants were all over the roads, all over the hot sidewalks of Saints. The sidewalk outside dance class was thick with black ants, and two girls were stamping right and left, killing as many as they could.

Suddenly a pale, long-haired young woman off to the side of the group said in a low-pitched, possessed voice, as if issuing a curse: "Remember those ants when you die and go to hell, for they will remember you! In hell, you will take on all their suffering and all the suffering you have inflicted on every other helpless creature!" The woman froze, caught in her vision, her neck taut, her mouth a rictus.

The girls stopped stamping, frozen as well, as if bewitched. This paralysis was soon alarming to me. I realized that everyone there, myself included, was somehow paralyzed. Why was no one laughing? What was going on? It was as if we were struggling to wake up from a collective lucid nightmare, and couldn't. The moment went on and on, and I couldn't move, I couldn't speak, I couldn't end the sensation of social awkwardness or possession or whatever it was. It wasn't until the Jazzercise instructor opened the door from inside the building that the spell was broken, and we all were able to move and speak, although no one spoke of what had just happened.

What the hell was that? I wondered, and I wonder still, remembering the sinking sensation of being in the thrall of strange powers. Nothing like that had ever happened to me before. I played it over and over in my mind during that fateful dance class and for long afterward, trying to see what had happened exactly. It remained unexplainable. There was some information or conviction missing.

My second strange small-town encounter had to do with photocopying. In Saints, clerks unabashedly read what I asked them to copy wherever I tried — at the bank, the video store, at city hall (there particularly), at the newspaper office, or at the tiny print shop I favored until it mysteriously disappeared. The little print shop was on a back street with, out front, its own quaint, freshly built western boardwalk. Inside, the clerk, Elly Starr, would stand behind the counter and carefully read what I handed her to copy, just like all the other clerks in town. But Elly was different. She played fair. She would always tell me something revealing about herself after reading what I'd handed her, a kind of equalization of the risk. The first day Elly read the word Rajneeshee in my material, she smiled at me with assumed complicity. Her large, green eyes glittered purposefully. Her blond hair appeared to gleam like a golden aureole. Every part of her seemed to lift as if she were floating slightly.

"You must see this," she said to me, rummaging through some papers. She found what she was looking for, copied it, gave me the copy. It was another letter to *The Bulletin,* this time from herself:

> Being aware of all the problems concerning Antelope Rajneesh, I read with interest your article on "Tips from the Bhagwan." I was wondering how many other religious orders around the world would have allowed outsiders to experience their "Most powerful" of rituals. It also occurs to me that the Rajneesh, as with the majority of all religions, pray, adore, salute, or glorify, the one God. Are not religions meant to feed our souls? If you can't make it as a Baptist, we have the Jewish faith. Can't be fed by them? Why not the Catholics? That doesn't work? How about the African Methodist Episcopal Church? There are over 150 religions listed in the Encyclopedia for the United States alone. Only one of these will feed your soul. So do we fear all the others?

I was fascinated and asked what kinds of consequences the letter had provoked.

"None, really," she said, "or, actually," she went on, lifting her index finger into the air, "a very loud silence. You know there are forty-eight kinds of silence here?" Elly made eye contact then, zeroing in intimately, an uncommon occurrence in the local social environment. She lifted her eyebrows all the way to her hairline. She was funny. I laughed.

"What are you doing here?" I asked her. She laughed again, and we ended up going for coffee at the Saints Cafe over on the main street of town. We sat in a corner booth. Elly told me she was from Ohio, that she had worked there as a psychic for a police department, done a little ghost busting on the side. All of this she said as if these occupations were ordinary. When her husband had disappeared one day a decade ago ("went out for a pack of cigarettes," Elly told me), she had moved to Saints with her five blond children. "It worked out perfectly, in terms of the kids," she said with great pride. "All five are working artists." She put both her hands on the table in front of her and folded them, signaling a shift in subject.

"I am a Christian," she told me then. "I go to a different church in Saints every Sunday, sometimes Catholic, sometimes Episcopal, sometimes Jehovah's Witnesses, what have you, and," Elly said, "this is what I have to tell you: I hear the Rajneesh condemned from pulpits, from ministers speaking in Jesus' name, and it shocks me."

Elly came on very strong now, and she drilled her eyes into mine. Sitting in the booth with her, I felt like I was sitting next to a magnet, or a powerful vacuum cleaner, and I involuntarily took hold of the edge of the table to keep from being sucked toward her. She was intriguing but alarming somehow, in the sense of having your mind bent out of plumb, and I began to develop the feelings of resistance I often get when

people bring up Jesus Christ insistently. I have a knee-jerk reaction: I want to run. Right then and there, in that conversation with Elly, I decided my desire to run was a problem. It
was something I was going to have to explore if I insisted
upon continuing with my project, my subject, my quest up in
Wasco County.

With some effort, I reached the end of the exchange gracefully. I was congratulating myself for not having bolted as Elly
and I walked back to the print shop, where I'd left my car.
On the boardwalk out front Elly turned to me dramatically,
smiled, and said, "Next time you have something to photo-
copy, come before noon and we'll talk over lunch. I am part of
your story."

"What story is that?" I wondered out loud all the way home,
sputtering, angry. I was annoyed with the whole episode, but
especially I was annoyed with Elly saying that new-agey thing
about being part of my story. I hate it when people I don't particularly like imagine they know what is going on in my mind
and drop one of those Confucius-like lines on me. It's so pre-
tentious, so intrusive. It's like being shit on by a bird.

There'd been a frost already, and it was only August — an
early warning of the coming change of season. Peter and I
added getting in the winter's wood to our morning chores.
Hauling wood was a great absorber or neutralizer of mental
frustration and low-grade ennui. I was in a bad mood, and it
was a job Peter did perfectly well even though depressed.

We were able to get all our firewood right on the ranch.
We'd find a dead tree, the more accessible the better. Peter
would chain-saw it down, buck it into logs and then rounds.
Together, we would load the rounds and haul them home in
the Scout.

We eventually rented a hydraulic splitter to split the rounds into approximately four cords, which was what Larry Lazio estimated we might need for the winter. We picked up the split hunks of pine as they fell from the hydraulic press and threw them into an immense pile, one chunk after another in a regular rhythm. I wore leather gloves but still got the gluey sap on my skin and clothes.

My mind wandered as I performed the rhythmic chore. I thought about Elly Starr as a bird, shitting on me as she flew in a circle. It seemed apt. I moved from that to thinking about flocks of blackbirds that wheeled and turned as one in the sky over our ranch and over Rancho Rajneesh. I wondered if the birds when they turned as one were having an experience of truth as a flock — as a crowd — and if the truth in the sky over our ranch were different from the zeitgeist hovering over Rajneeshpuram. Probably it wasn't. An intuitively orchestrated turn executed simultaneously by a hundred birds along a rising air draft is just that and is true only insofar as it's true that it happens.

As I went on thinking about those sorts of things while we made firewood, I decided Bhagwan might be wrong about people never having the experience of truth as a crowd, only as individuals. "I'm looking for an example of crowd truth," I told Peter.

We left our wood in a pile, didn't stack it in rows the way people in Saints were doing. Were we the only ones doing it that way? I don't know. Probably not. But everywhere, it seemed, at every cottage and cabin and double-wide across the high desert, people were stacking their rows of wood higher and higher around their dwellings. In Saints, the houses looked like forts.

TEN

I WENT TO THE COUNTY LIBRARY looking for old pictures of the towns of Saints and Antelope. I found some that showed me how much alike they were in the 1870s — similar wide spots in similar dusty roads.

Saints never boomed then, but it was boomy now, a phony-baloney fake Old West town with intense tourism. Antelope did boom briefly, back at the time of the earliest white settlers. Its hotheaded first citizens had anticipated hitting pay dirt as a regional center for selling and shipping sheep and wool — a reasonable vision in a landscape ideal for flocks of sheep. So the townsfolk put their money into getting the railroad to build a spur to Antelope. According to the anecdotal history books I found, wooden storefronts with tall fake second-story facades shot up along the main street. At the time there'd been two banks and seven saloons.

Best of all in Antelope, though, the early settlers had planted trees everywhere — cottonwoods, poplars, weeping willows, mountain ash, and lilacs. The trees had grown and become tall and graceful in the desert breeze. Now, they were full grown and gave a marvelous physical definition to the town, a place shaped and measured out by groves or lines of trees, or by the perfect single weeping willow in someone's backyard. The tiny town was geographically imposing, a clus-

PENNY ALLEN ◇ 162

ter of dwellings in a draw where three lonely country roads came together from the north, the southwest, and the southeast.

Sadly for those pioneers, Antelope did not thrive as anticipated. The railroad spur went to another town, and the people with big ideas moved on. As time passed the town did not rot or rust but instead persisted, almost unchanged, a ghost town, with a kind of hopefulness that clung to it at least long enough to inspire the novelist H. L. Davis to write *Honey in the Horn* about it.

I checked *Honey in the Horn* out of the library at the suggestion of Margaret Hill, who had been mayor of Antelope when the Rajneeshees turned up. I found the novel to be a wry account of the unmet expectations harbored by those early settlers around Antelope, with all their driven intensity. The book was full of real stuff: shenanigans over water rights, land grabs, rebellious women. It was as if nothing had changed at all.

"You'll never understand what we've gone through with the Rajneesh," Margaret Hill told me, her angular, sixty-year-old self tilted in the doorway of her ranch-style house in Antelope. With one hand firmly on hip, she was shaking her other hand at me angrily, a motion that began at her waggling shoulder and ended in her finger almost in my face. She was provocative, a bit ferocious even.

"I am *from here*, Margaret," I fetched up just as ferociously, shaking my own finger back at her as if I really were only and always from there, not just back on a fluke. I was already tired of this argument, the one about having to be from a place before you could say anything about it. But I went on with my claim: "Right west of here, my grandparents were orchardists. I'm one of you, in a way, third generation. I am not a tourist. I have the same dirt on my shoes."

She stopped and stared at me for the longest time, I had gone so far. Did I pass? I wondered. Perhaps she was wondering, too, about exactly how much I was one of her people. Perhaps she didn't believe me. Nevertheless, I was saying with complementary body language that my grandparents and some of their children and some of their children's children had been and still were orchardists and solid Christians in a nearby valley. There was probably some subtle ambiguity in the language, though, because I had no fondness for my dead grandmother and no doubt revealed it now. As I had known her, she was a cold, remote, American Gothic type of Christian, her tight lips pulled downward toward a set jaw, a woman who had never shown much feeling toward me or toward my brother or toward her daughter-in-law, my mother. My grandmother had not recognized me as one of her people. Nor had my mother, she who had come from the city to capture my father, been one. My mean-spirited grandmother had blamed my mother for my father leaving the valley and going to work in the big-city shipyards during the war. So angry and disappointed had my grandmother been, she had turned her rancor on the local Japanese American orchardists and argued in favor of putting them all in camps. Years later, when my father had died of lung cancer caused by asbestos from those shipyards, my grandmother had faulted my mother for his untimely death. "You didn't give him enemas," she wrote.

Shortly thereafter this same grandmother had disowned me for getting a divorce. Outraged, my mother had challenged her mother-in-law's will. I eventually got my seven thousand dollars in stock, which became the down payment on the tumbledown Portland Victorian.

Margaret Hill seemed to be working her way through this unspoken story, as if it were written on my face. I smiled at her at that moment, knowing that she wasn't like my grandmother at all, and for some reason she smiled back. She offered me a piece of chocolate cake.

Margaret was not at all stupid or petty. She was actually quite a lady and rather sexy, in a gray-haired Sophia Loren kind of way. She had fairly recently married — a second marriage — a proud man who flirted and exchanged meaningful glances with her. Margaret had been the Antelope school English teacher, but she now occupied a position of leadership in a besieged community. The media always went to her, and so did I, to start with.

A couple of hours into our first visit, Margaret, whose experiences with the Rajneeshees seemed to have involved mostly rude and abrasive ones, told me about the only time she had ever seen the guru, whom she called a dirty old man. This was her story: She and her husband were out in a narrow, dry, rocky wash of a canyon in their truck when they came across a Rolls-Royce that had gone off the road into the creek a few feet below. The Rolls was now high-centered on the rocks in the creek.

"We looked at that Rolls-Royce Silver Cloud down there and knew it had to be the Bhagwan himself," Margaret said, her color rising, "because he has any number of Rolls-Royces, and no one else around here has even one."

She breathed deeply, started again: "We climbed down there and tapped on the windshield to see if he needed any help, and the man would absolutely not look at us, would not turn his head and look at us. His companion, an Indian woman, I believe, got out of the car and told us they'd radioed for help from the Ranch and preferred to just sit there and wait, thank you very much. That man just sat there, hidden behind his double-glass smoked windows, never glancing at us, not even breathing the same air we were breathing, not even knowing or caring where in the world he was."

Margaret stopped talking. She was trembling, her chest rising and falling, her hand shaking. Her teacup chattered into its saucer.

"I can't . . . ," she stammered, unable to go on. She started weeping. She was ashamed not to be able to continue, not to be able to cope with it.

But she had really already said it all, as far as she was concerned: The guru didn't know where in the world he was, and Margaret had taken this lapse of his, rightly or wrongly, as aggression. For Margaret and her husband knew exactly where they were. They were in the territory of their clan, which they would know blindfolded but which the Indian guru did not choose to know at all. The difference was existential.

How to go beyond this strange territorial warfare? I would ask my journal as soon as I left Margaret's house to enter my own little portable territory: my car. It seems like a time warp, I wrote.

I sat in the car, looking at the trees of Antelope moving gently in the breeze. I was actually in Peter's car; I was now driving the Mustang on my outings because of that strange incident when my Toyota had seized up and whirled around on the washboard gravel road the night I heard Bhagwan. In contrast to my boxy little Corona, Stang, as Peter called his car, was big and heavy and enormously solid. Stang was also extremely powerful — you could be going eighty miles an hour up the highway and floor it to pass easily. Nothing like the Corona. The Mustang's engine was one of those engineering feats that prove to be too high a standard to maintain, as later versions revealed. In any case, I felt safe in Stang, even though driving it was like driving a boat. It had a lot of play to the wheel, and I had become extra cautious on all the twisting canyon roads, especially the one descending into Rajneeshpuram. Once or twice, late at night, I'd felt I lost control, sliding a little too much on a turn, losing contact with the road altogether when the Mustang bounced in a rut.

"Jesus," I said to Peter an evening or two later. "I got lost going north out of Antelope instead of northwest toward The Dalles night before last, up some winding desert canyon for thirty miles! There was no way to turn around! And when I got to Moro," I roared, full of the desert wind, "one of the old false fronts was on fire! It was surrealistic! Desk clerk at the motel said it was arson by the property owner, wanting out. Look what kind of life these people are living!" I screeched in epic lament, and he responded in kind.

Peter and I were out doing what we did most evenings on the ranch during that period: We were doing our territory, walking it, looking at it. Observing where we were. As we walked I would tell Peter stories about the people up north. He liked hearing them, was very responsive, although he may have feigned interest at first in order to please, to not be preoccupied with his own concerns, to not be a drag. It seemed right to try to entertain him. I could make him laugh at my stories of high-desert small-town behavior. He was a terrific audience, and he seemed to want all my stories. We would laugh and laugh, always holding hands, walking along. Laughing was something we did very well together, and Peter would forget himself, would start to glow slightly in the dark.

Because there was nothing funny or redeeming about them, I didn't tell Peter about my scary moments in Stang, losing the road. I avoided telling Peter things that might alarm him, because these emotions persisted with him, and his alarm would still be clinging to him like slime when mine was long gone.

Instead, I would tell him about my day down on the John Day River talking to Kelley McGreer, to whom I was sent by

Margaret Hill. Kelley was a forty-year-old college-graduate spud rancher, a wonderful example of a modern, educated American farmer, running the family farm like three generations of his family before him. As fate would have it, Kelley's farm lay just across the John Day River from Rancho Rajneesh. The first time I met him, Kelley told me about his wife, Rosemary, who had gone on *The Merv Griffin Show* opposite the notorious Sheela.

I'd found Kelley out in front of his barn, wiping his hands on an oily rag. He'd been at work on a big tractor when I interrupted him. He was a short, good-looking, sandy-haired guy with a gold tooth up front that showed when he smiled or squinted. Was the gold tooth a lack of vanity or instead a touch of raciness in an otherwise conservative man? He told me right off Rosemary hated it when the Rajneeshees claimed to be farmers. "It drives her wild," he said. "It gets her right here." Kelley pressed his hand against his solar plexus, then paused. "So she got pulled into a fight, right there on national television. Sheela said the Rajneeshees were just simple farmers. Rosemary ended up saying one or two things she probably ought not to have said."

The Rajneeshees had sued Rosemary for something she'd said. The McGreers had countersued, and the two sides had gone full bore into the long-term stress of a legal fight and then a trial, and now Kelley was standing here crying, twisting the oily rag, squinting his eyes so as not to cry, but it was too late.

"I felt bad during that trial," he forced out, utterly uncomfortable, his forehead holding a terrible tension. "Emasculated," he said. "Rosemary's dad had just died, and Rosemary'd had surgery and was vulnerable, and I just couldn't protect her. I could not protect her! And the goddamn Rajneesh psychiatrist who examined Rosemary for the trial testified she was getting some good out of having the Rajneesh driving her mad!"

Kelley held my eyes for a good, long while after he said that. In the silence, as we stared at each other, I heard him breathing and felt myself breathing. A flock of geese lifted off the wide, flat John Day below us, honking. They flew off over Rancho Rajneesh. It was so beautiful, so peaceful, yet for Kelley so bleak.

Later, when I was saying good-bye, I thanked Kelley for talking to me and told him I wanted to meet Rosemary. Then I asked him what the name of the Rajneeshee psychiatrist was, the one who had examined Rosemary and said she was getting something out of the Rajneeshees driving her mad.

"Siddha," Kelley said.

"Christ!" Peter shouted at this point in my story. We stopped walking and looked at each other in the dark. "So now what do you think about Siddha?" he asked, gesturing emphatically with his hand, which was still holding on to my hand. I was pulled off balance, and Peter caught me. It was funny and kept me from having to answer the question.

We were stumbling along, wending our way up the dry arroyo halfway between the Main House and our cabin. A lot of deer were out doing their territory that time of late evening as well. They crashed away from us noisily, bouncing like kangaroos whenever we came close. A great horned owl swooshed down toward us, changed course suddenly, and vanished, having sensed we weren't prey after all.

"Goddamn!" said Peter, still reacting to Kelley's story. It was great to have him to talk to, to tell my stories to. Maybe I wasn't getting an article out of my quest, but I was getting stories to tell Peter. I'd go on long enough to get his sweet empathy eventually. And it was true I was often confused about what to think. I would change my mind about everyone on all sides from one day to the next. I couldn't take it up in Wasco County longer than three days running without a reality check.

The night after the hallucinatory fire — the alleged arson — in Moro I'd gone to an Evangelical rally at the armory up at The Dalles, the Wasco County seat, situated on the Columbia River. The armory was sold out. Four thousand ticket holders had listened with rising color and intensity as a Hispanic evangelist named Mario Evillo exhorted us to "hold strong against the Bhagwan, who is, most assuredly . . . the *Devil!*" Strangely, I had to pee like mad when Evillo said the word *Devil,* as if the Devil had one of his cloven hooves squarely on my bladder. A palpable sensation was sweeping through the armory at that moment, although it no doubt affected other people differently than it did me. I do not believe in the Devil, but I do believe in social psychology, and Evillo had me and everyone else by the short hairs at that moment. The potential for mass behavior, for experiencing as a crowd some kind of truth, or lie, seemed extraordinary. We were all caught up in the grasp of Evillo's upraised hand, waiting.

But Evillo let the moment pass. He lowered his hand, breathed deep, and shifted back on his heels. Was he getting a grip on himself, chickening out?

"We must hold out against an *extremely evil force,*" he said quietly then, almost whispering. He did not tell us to act, which he could very easily have done. Something had held Evillo back at the last moment that evening. And, interestingly, his evangelical interruptus left me and perhaps many others uneasy and unfulfilled. As I walked outside the armory, I thought about what I was going to do next, who I was going to beat up. I'd been invited to stay overnight at the house of a woman who ran an anti-Rajneeshee group, but I didn't feel like it. I telephoned her and backed out.

I stayed instead with the mother of an old boyfriend I hadn't seen in years who gave me the telephone number of a man she knew in The Dalles, a watchman or guard who would tell me he had seen a woman at dawn one day pouring sugar into the gas tanks of state-owned vehicles. The miscreant had then driven off in a car registered to Rajneeshpuram. The mother of my friend explained to me that this had occurred during the same period as an extraordinary epidemic of salmonella food poisoning traced to three different salad bars in restaurants in The Dalles. A year earlier, 750 people had been sickened in one day after eating in three restaurants in The Dalles. I remembered having heard about this in Portland, where I had regarded the story as opportunistic media speculation following a banal case of bad hygiene, or perhaps mass hysteria. Plus it had turned out the police had never been able to make a case against the Rajneeshees for the poisoning.

Now that I had begun to experience the forces at work in that corner of rural America, I started to feel that the Rajneeshees, or at least the faction around Sheela, had probably done this evil act, had tried to poison the townspeople: There was something subcontinental about the nature of the crime — mass poisoning of the opposition — if one is to believe the stories told in Salman Rushdie's *Midnight's Children*. Wasco County locals had been convinced that Sheela and the Rajneeshees were guilty, or guilty by association, and now I, too, believed it.

What was interesting about what my friend's mother was telling me, though, was not the facts or the proffered telephone numbers that would allow me to verify everything for myself, but rather the fear. Her trembling voice bounced along unchecked, like tumbleweed blowing across the high desert.

She became even more alarmed when I did not respond to her story with sufficient intensity.

"People tell me so many stories" was all I could say for myself. Then, just when it had seemed that the interaction was going off the deep edge, that I was going to have to leave, the lady suddenly remembered I wasn't the enemy. She saw how tired I was. She made me some Sleepytime tea and tucked me safely into bed on a sleeping porch next to a creek where I dreamed of animals running.

The next day, heading home, I stopped off in Antelope to see Darlene Osborn. Margaret Hill had wanted me to see Darlene. Margaret had told me she thought my sympathies were starting to go with the Rajneeshees.

"I think it's natural," Margaret had said. "You have more in common with them."

"Like what?" I'd asked her disingenuously, and she told me she knew I'd lived through some of the same cultural history as many of the Rajneeshees. "I don't have my head in the sand," she said. We didn't explore that any further. Margaret had given me a grandmotherlike look meant to silence me, and it did. Then she'd given me Darlene Osborn's phone number, and when I had called, the voice was injured, torn from privacy.

"No, no, no," she'd said in a tiny voice and started to cry.

"Margaret told me to call you."

She was silent a long time, so long that I was able to visualize Margaret's strength and sense of civic duty working their effect on Darlene, who was sighing.

"All right," she said finally in a forced pitch, and I felt awful about it.

Now, seeing this tiny old woman as she opened the door of her farmhouse just outside Antelope — a trailer on a foundation, nicely surrounded by gardens of annuals and roses and vegetables — I felt very intrusive indeed. Darlene was small and innocent looking and somehow lyrical like a schoolgirl as she led me to two straight-backed wooden chairs. She sat in one, folded her hands in her lap, and placed her feet in loafers and blue argyle socks side by side in front of her.

"I have never had any trouble filling up emptiness with imagination," Darlene began, breathing deeply, exhaling slowly. "The way it used to be in Antelope, there were the forty of us retired folks, but we didn't have to talk when we saw each other. We were used to each other, didn't have to put on airs for each other, the way you don't have to pay attention to your little sister if you don't want to."

"It sounds idyllic. What happened?"

"Water. It was all about water," Darlene answered right away. "There wasn't enough water to have put a town here in the first place, so water was always our quest."

I quite fell for Darlene Osborn at that point. To have her use water supply as an organizing principle, something I am likely to do myself, was terribly satisfying. Darlene sat there, speaking about water. She spoke with her eyes closed.

"One year," she said like a storyteller who begins, unprodded, "the state condemned the Antelope spring as unsafe to drink. All the men in town got together and built a reservoir, and we started collecting the surface water running down the canyons. And then that year, when the state people came to test our water, we passed. And because we passed, the school got to stay open, and we stayed alive as a town. All the children from two hundred square miles around came here to school every day. I loved the children. I loved seeing them every day. We wanted the school to stay open, so we had to pass that water test every year. That way, we would have children another year in Antelope."

I asked Darlene to walk with me through Antelope. She said yes, and we got in the Mustang, drove there, and parked. We walked up the main street past the boarded-up storefronts, past the little wooden cottages under towering poplars and cottonwoods. The wonderful Antelope trees were moving, and the wind lifted the heat off your face.

"Listen," Darlene said in a little voice. I could hear water gurgling nearby. "It's our ditch," she said. We were standing in front of Darlene's former house in the center of Antelope. Darlene was not looking at her old house. She was holding her head twisted stiffly away as we walked by. She cleared her throat, her head twisted.

"When it was dry, the water from the reservoir was not adequate, so one year, we all voted to pay to dig a well for Antelope," she began again, walking on. Her neck relaxed visibly as we moved down the street. "The first well was dry," she said, "and all our money was gone. There was talk then of people giving up and leaving Antelope, but instead some of us just started raising money, slowly but surely, with auctions and whatnot. We did that sort of thing for years. And then our second well came in. And then we had to pay for a pump. And then we had to pay for a fire truck and then for a fire hall to put it in. Life's demands keep on expanding."

We had reached the bottom of Antelope. There was no one else, of any stripe, on the street. Darlene looked at me and said, quite simply, "Now it's all theirs." And then she wept. I got cotton mouth and couldn't swallow or speak and heard the rush of time passing alongside memories of Greek tragedies performed outdoors on dry, windswept hillsides, of women wronged, beating their breasts and wailing for justice.

It was toward the end of our walk back up through Antelope to my car that Darlene felt like talking again. "Not long after the Rajneesh came," she began, "Sheela wanted to build a printing plant, and she was outraged to find out that the law prohibited her from building a printing plant on a ranch, because it was agriculturally zoned. So she got the idea of buying a house in Antelope to turn into a printing plant. So Sheela appeared before city council to request special permission."

"Yes, and what happened?" I asked, seeing the whole thing now, the impending animosity. "The council turned her down because of water-supply problems?"

"Yes," said Darlene. Her voice had thickened, and she faltered, went on in a whisper. "It was shocking."

"What was shocking?"

"Sheela said shameful things," she whispered. There was a long pause.

"What did she say?"

"She said we were all just waiting to die . . . but other, worse . . . I can't."

"But we *are* all just waiting to die, aren't we?" I asked. I couldn't believe this was really it. Darlene gave me a penetrating look, a look of dread and anticipation that both forbade and compelled me to ask, "What else did Sheela say to you?"

Darlene seemed not to be breathing. "That our husbands . . . ," she whispered airlessly. Then she inhaled. "In the beginning," she said, "we heard rumors . . . then a newspaper in Los Angeles had an article . . . an article . . . that a sex cult had bought a ranch outside of Antelope, Oregon." She halted there, and it appeared there was nothing further. It was a full stop. She wasn't going to tell me what else Sheela had said, even though by then that was all I really wanted to know.

Darlene began again, but in a new vein: "And after the city council meeting," she said, in control now, finishing with the story she wanted to tell, not that other one, "there were Rajneesh in town videotaping us, everywhere we went. And then Sheela's husband came around to every house and made offers to buy. Nobody accepted, but we only found out later he was talking to everyone, because we were too ashamed to even necessarily bring it up with each other. So the Rajneesh took advantage of this. Finally, somebody couldn't take it any longer and sold. It was awful. It was the beginning of the end. They were the weak link in the chain. We were all frightened. One night, I was getting ready for bed and looked out my kitchen window, up the draw toward Antelope School, and I saw a caravan of headlights moving slowly, ghostlike, down into town."

Darlene turned to look up the draw, remembering the moment. "I knew it was the Rajneesh," she said, not breathing any more at all. "I called out for my husband, and I knew suddenly that they were going to keep on doing what they were doing no matter what, that these were not people who would save our lives if they needed saving, the way it was before. These were people who didn't care if we died."

Darlene's body arched. Submissively, like a beaten child, she held out her arms toward me, wrists in the air, imploring, begging to be called to account. "I wanted out! I couldn't hold out any longer," she said. "We sold our little house to the Rajneesh the very next day. I am so ashamed."

By that point we had reached my parked car. Such was Darlene's moral force, I now felt personally responsible for what had happened to her. I wanted only to get her home safely to her husband so he could save her if she needed saving from the Rajneeshees, but I could not get the car door on the passenger side open to let Darlene in. She opened the back door herself and got in. I clumsily got in behind the steering wheel and hunched up tensely. I drove back to Darlene's house. At her gravel drive Darlene said, "Stop, please," and she got out of the car, looked at me pityingly, turned, and walked up to her house.

"The two-hour drive home was just tears," I told Peter, exhausted.

We were at the bottom of our bone-dry pasture in the moonlight now. My stories weren't funny that night, and Peter seemed exhausted by them as well. He was holding his lower back as if it ached. I'd forgotten his potentially fragile mood in my rush to tell all. But actually, come to think of it, I had thought he was no longer depressed. I had imagined I'd seen Peter moving lately toward some distant light in a new direction. I thought I'd seen him acting as if it were time for something else, as if it were simply time.

"Something's wrong," Peter said then, tensing, and we both saw the fire. The dry grass along the edge of the pasture was on fire, a curve of low, flickering flames. There'd been a gathering of the Viorst clan that day, and it was there, in the shade of the cottonwoods bordering the pasture, that they had set up their barbecue and dumped the coals out on the ground when they left.

"Christ," Peter said disgustedly. "They think it's going to rain or something, take care of this?" We scuttled around, trying to put out the fire, stamping on it, kicking dirt on it. We stumbled onto a pile of ice cubes the Viorsts had apparently dumped out after the picnic, and we used them to smother the fire. It was over quickly and simply, not a big deal at all, although we did tramp around the area for a half hour just to make sure. Caretakers. A day in the life.

We headed home across the pasture, passing through the shifting pod of sleeping horses. I stopped and put my hand on

Coco, and she made a sound deep in her chest, nicker, nicker. She smelled musky, warm, inviting, and I pressed my face into her neck and breathed there for a moment. Peter waited, calm now since putting out the fire.

As we moved off again toward the house, Peter said, "I think Buckner stole our hatchet."

What a startling thought. "Nooooo, not Buckner."

"Yes, Buckner."

"Our hatchet's missing?" I couldn't even get it.

"Yeah," Peter said. "I'm sure he took it."

"He's starting to take things?"

"He took the hatchet."

"He came up onto our porch and took the hatchet?"

"Evidently," he said, gazing at the stars as they popped on. Peter was untroubled, apparently unconcerned by Buckner's secret visit, or visits.

"He was standing on our porch?" This was the part I had trouble with — the thought of Buckner standing on our porch while we weren't home. Of course he would know when we weren't home. It was the easiest thing to know. He could easily camp out in the forest a hundred feet from the cabin, and we might never know.

"Maybe he went in the house?" I suggested then.

"Oh, I don't think so."

"Why?"

"Oh, I don't know, but he left something in place of the hatchet."

"What? Oh, why didn't you tell me this?"

"It just happened, and I am telling you."

"What'd he leave?"

"I think it's a bullet casing."

"A bullet casing! From Vietnam?"

"I guessed so."

"In exchange for a hatchet?" Well, of course not, not literally, I answered myself. There was obviously something else going on. "Are you worried about it?" I asked Peter.

"I'm not worrying about it," he said.

"Well, what, did he just throw it there?"

"No, he set it on the ax handle."

"Christ! And you're not worried about it?" I was breathless, but Peter remained calm.

"No," he said. It seemed extraordinary and pleased me and excited me as well that Peter wasn't worried about this Vietnam vet on patrol on our porch. This was more interesting to me than whatever Buckner might have done. I realized that Peter must have decided not to do anything about Viorst wanting Buckner actively kept off the property. This I found very interesting.

"I'm not worrying," Peter said firmly.

"You're not?" It was a game now.

"I'm not."

"Third time: You're not?" I was starting to laugh.

"I'm absolutely not." He made the sound of an arrow being released and hitting wood. *Phtttt thoink.*

ELEVEN

IT WAS INDIAN SUMMER on the high desert. The days
were hot but the nights frosty. The sun was low in the sky
now and fiery as it cast its magic-hour rays through a fair
amount of particulate matter hanging in the air as a result of
occasional small forest fires in the Cascades. The southwest-
ern vista was streaked all across with smoke and turned purple
and orange at sunset.

I'd been writing all afternoon on my raft-bridge. When I
stood up, stretched, and turned around to the south, I saw at
the bottom of the pasture what looked like a dream. There
stood a huge, proud-chested buck with an enormous rack of
antlers; he was gathering his does and yearlings into a herd.
Each individual animal was dark against the bleached-out,
silvery grass. The deer weren't grazing. They were jumpy,
bunched up in tense little knots that exploded apart here and
there.

Another buck, almost as large as the first, stepped from the
trees on the opposite side of the pasture. The two snorted like
bulls and then went for each other without further preamble.
They crashed together, not quite head-on but at an angle. The
sound when they struck — even from a distance — was sickening: a high-pitched shriek, the torque of antlers caught. The

first buck, sprawling, snorted and heaved himself up, neck arched. He turned to drive his herd back a distance.

This had all happened fast. What followed had the sense of slow denouement. While the big buck moved back and forth in front of his dominion, the smaller buck stood up slowly. I could see he was injured. He backed up, then turned and trotted unsteadily back across the pasture. As he moved, his head fell slowly forward. The heavy rack kept pulling his head down and down. The buck slunk, stumbling, his neck hanging oddly. He lurched into the fold of the woods, where he most certainly collapsed, his neck broken.

I turned from the scene then and saw Buckner. He wasn't far from me at all, just behind the willows in the swamp. He was actually nearer the cabin than I was, but on the other side. He was looking off across the pasture to where the injured buck had exited. He'd probably observed the whole spectacle along with me.

This was the first long look I'd had up close of Buckner, who was quite good-looking in a wild-man sort of way, with dark, tangled hair. He had a Rambo look about him, with ash streaked on his face, but I didn't get the idea that Buckner was imitating Rambo or anyone else. It seemed more likely Buckner had invented the behavior. His brown, muscled arms were bulging from a sleeveless vest, and he had a big deer-skinning knife strapped to his arm.

He turned and caught me staring at him then, and he stared back, as if we were trying to bridge some gap. Even though we were from the same culture, the same race and nationality, about the same age, an unnameable gulf yawned between us. I wondered if he'd ever read my note about the bunnies on the back of the hay barn. Or answered it. I hadn't looked in months.

"Hi," I called out.

He saluted.

"You may collect the deer meat," I said, like some goddamn colonial matron. Where did that come from? That wasn't what I'd wanted to say at all. I really wanted to thank him for scaring away those three dead-eyed guys in the Buick. They had never come back. And who knows how many others he might have warded off. But I didn't say anything, and now I imagined the gap between us widening.

His face broke into a smile. He was missing a couple of teeth on one side. "Much obliged, ma'am." Nodding his head and smiling at me still, flirting actually, he took a few steps sideways across the pasture, then stopped to see why I was still looking at him. I wanted to ask him something, anything, but I remained tongue-tied.

"I'll bring you some backstrap," he called, making friends.

"Great," I said. He stopped looking at me, turned his head, called his dog. "Chin," he shouted, or something like that. The dog came running, and Buckner walked off across the pasture with the dog. A hundred yards off, he turned again to look at me.

"Never mind," I shouted, but he probably couldn't hear me. I don't know if "never mind" meant that he should keep the best part of the deer for himself, "never mind" about giving me any backstrap. Or did I mean that "never mind" he shouldn't bring it by, that I didn't feel comfortable having him come to the house with the meat (why? what might happen? what were my fantasies? that he might rape me? that he might expect me to duplicate the way some girl in Asia had pleased him?).

Buckner stopped looking at me then and disappeared into the Great Southern Exposure Spectacle, as a naked Peter had done some months before when he'd lain down in the flooded arroyo. I stood watching the empty scene for a few moments, kind of flushed, fantasizing on about Buckner, then remembered pleasantly what had happened when I'd gone after Peter in the flooded arroyo. When I recalled how it had ended, yes, with the Viorsts driving by, reclaiming their territory from the caretakers, it occurred to me this must be something of what Buckner was experiencing now, with Peter and me living on the ranch, right in the middle of his hunting run. That made us neither friend nor foe so far, simply the competition, another set of his species to be accommodated or dominated. I liked the possibilities of that relationship, but I didn't know how the bullet casing fit in. The scene with Buckner had seemed so like a western, the two of us meeting awkwardly in the pasture, isolated in the middle of nowhere. Now I'd been standing there in the same spot for two hours — feature length — and the action had never abated.

I went in the house to phone Peter and tell him what had happened. He was down at the Main House in the sunroom, where he'd set up a makeshift legal office for poring over Forest Service documents. I told him about the deer and about seeing Buckner, who was probably now about halfway between where I was, in the cabin, and where Peter was, in the Main House.

"He's probably dressing out the dead buck right now," I said. I heard Peter shift in the leather desk chair down in the sunroom. He was compartmentalized into the Forest Service just then, and I could tell by his nonresponse he really didn't want to get into it until later. I guess I felt a little put off. It seemed such a workaday response to extraordinary activity.

"Is this why you hate the law?" I asked belligerently into the phone. "Is this what it does to you? It takes you completely away? I could be here by myself."

"Hey," he said.

"Why does it have to be so austere?" His work on the Forest Service suddenly felt to me like a withdrawal, a distancing. I recalled that Peter had once told me how he used to escape from his mother: He'd go to the basement and play violent war games. Was I paranoid to make this association?

"Are you playing war games down there?" I asked him.

He laughed, and made the sound of an arrow being released and entering human flesh. *Phttt thuwuup*. He was very good at it.

"I'm not your mother. I'm your lover."

"Thank God."

"Well?"

"Well, I want to do this." He shifted again in the big leather chair.

"Great!" I said, actually meaning it, albeit ambivalently. It's true I had been seeking his company in the short run, but I genuinely applauded his engagement. Something in me felt relieved now that he finally wanted something.

"But," he said, "I watch my mind engage as if creating a perfect argument really mattered. Who am I trying to please? Does it please you?"

"Does it please you?" I asked back.

"I don't know. Maybe I'm doing it because I think you want me to do something like this. Maybe I'm doing it for Larry Lazio. Maybe for Ham. How do I know if there was anything there before Larry first said something to me about the forest along the creek?"

"But have you found something there now?"

We talked on the phone from two sides of the property for a long time, and then I got tired and wanted to go to sleep. "Good night, Jean-Paul Sartre," I said and hung up.

I called him back to ask if he would like to go up to Rancho Rajneesh for a meditation workshop so he might be able to see if there was anything to it.

"With you?" he asked.

"No. By yourself. For seven days."

"Don't you think you ought to do it as part of your . . . thing?"

"I can't seem to," I said. "I'm too into watching them, too much the sociologist. Or else I'm secretly afraid I'll just click and join up. But maybe it could be interesting for you."

"Hmm," he snorted, and we hung up again.

Why did I suggest that? I wondered, my hand still on the receiver where I had cradled it into the base. I shivered. The house was dark.

I built a fire in the woodstove and thought it through: How manipulative of me, I thought. I decided not to mention it again.

The next morning, when I went out the front door on my way to feed the horses, I found an object hanging on the front doorknob. It was a medal. After studying it, I figured out it was a Purple Heart. It belonged to Buckner, I supposed. First a bullet casing, now a Purple Heart! Was it a gift, to thank me for the deer meat? An invitation to further exchange? A condemnation, as in angrily throwing your medal received for extreme valor on behalf of your countrymen on the steps of the Pentagon? I couldn't guess what it meant, but it didn't strike me as an idle gesture. I had no idea what Buckner might do next. Thinking or fantasizing about it had the potential for becoming a major but secret preoccupation.

Right about that time, something odd happened to Peter, something which made moot the whole question of his needing anyone's help to find out what he truly wanted. He had a flying dream, the kind all seekers are waiting for even if they might not know it. He reared up in the middle of the night, scaring me to death. I woke and saw him poised there in the center of the bed in the pale moonlight. I thought he'd heard something outside, some hideous shriek in the night.

"What is it?" I hissed, heart pounding.

"I flew," he said. "I was in a kind of cave high above the creek, and I came out and jumped off the ledge, and I flew. I didn't fall to the ground, I wheeled and turned. I saw the creek down below."

I felt a chill up and down my spine. I didn't want to wake up. Maybe I was asleep and dreaming this myself. I stretched and was asleep.

The next morning when I got up, Peter was studying a Forest Service map of the elevations along the creek, looking for clues. He thought he'd found where the cave of his dreams might be, said so, got in the Scout, and drove off. There seemed to have been no question in his mind that the cave was real and not a figment. Of course, he was right. Peter found his cave. Most often in life, we do not find the cave of our dreams, so we make decisions rationally, or desperately.

Now, much later, I wonder how this series of events was different from any kind of religious conversion or spiritual surrender.

In any case, Peter's cave wasn't far from the waterfall, the landing, and the giant Doug fir. It was, as a matter of fact, within the boundaries of that notorious, perhaps felonious timber sale. Peter told me the cave had no relics, no potsherds, no arrowheads, although it had obviously been home to somebody — perhaps Buckner? — somebody who had pried open a few tin cans and warmed them over a fire, blackening the ceiling near the wide opening. Peter camped out in the cave that first night after dreaming it into existence, and he would occasionally return there for years afterward. He showed me the cave, but I never stayed there with him. I left it for him alone.

From what people said to Peter when he started poking around in town, he got the impression that logging of the big ponderosa pine on the national forest had intensified in recent years as harvestable timber on private land grew scarce, but pickings on this subject were so slim his appetite was whetted without him ever getting his fill. This was the part of the law Peter loved: following the paper trail to a case. Once he was convinced there really was a case, he had the patience required for developing it, for tracking its every aspect, for nailing it down. In the case of the timber sale, he was convinced the Forest Service was breaking the law: violating its own legally adopted plan, logging next to a creek, logging an archaeological site, and who knew what else? Next, Peter had to develop a constituency. This part was perhaps my idea. As a matter of fact, in retrospect, I realize that Peter may well have involved a wide range of townsfolk in how their forest was managed just to please me when all he really wanted to do was the law part. I don't know. In any case, Peter and I entered a more collaborative phase of our relationship. This was okay with me, desirable even, but I had no wish to replace anything else or bring anything else we had to an end.

Peter was not depressed anymore. In fact, he had such renewed energy he decided to go back to pulling gravel out of the irrigation pipe, just to finish it, to get it off his plate. It was an awful task. Clearing the last section of the blocked pipe was the worst chore, the kind where the equipment is breaking down but it's too much trouble or too late in the game to start over with new. It was grit-your-teeth work, "a task a Methodist might excel at," Peter said. By trial and error he elaborated on his basic working tool. His earlier invention, the white-plastic-pipe-with-tin-can-attached, became a series of white plastic pipes, one replacing another as each got over-stressed from being twisted down and then horizontal into the bigger pipe belowground. Each plastic pipe would break off, leaving part of itself or its detached tin can for Peter to retrieve with the next tool he built.

It was autumn now, and the sun's rays were oblique, so their warmth didn't reach down into where Peter was toiling in the pit. It was chilly, painful work. He bashed his knuckles raw pushing and pulling tubing in and out. I would go up to the dam to see him with a thermos of hot tea, and he would be grateful out of all proportion for the warmth, for the company. He would point out his other visitors — three turkey vultures roosting in a dead cottonwood just upstream. The huge black birds with their red wattles were hunched in a row on a dead branch, poking at themselves, grotesque. They glared at Peter with beady eyes. "They're waiting for me to expire," he said.

It was stoicism that kept Peter at the job, but Larry Lazio's steadfastness helped. Larry picked right up on the fact that Peter was back at the dam working, because Larry was out working on the creek himself.

The creek was low that late in the season. The drought had never abated, and the mountain glacier that fed the creek was sucked dry as a dehydrated ice cube. Larry was kept busy all day rationing scarce water to irrigators. He still came by to see Peter periodically, and the two of them talked. The talk was important to Peter — this transfer of one man's territorial memory to another.

"Ed Dyer," Larry told Peter, "knows the national forest like it's his yard, just like his own private rock garden. He's the one made the Windigo Trail along the creek all the way up to the Wilderness — hacked it out with his own hands practically."

Larry stopped, Peter reported, then proceeded with an uncharacteristic rush of words. "I heard he just got transferred out of Saints District. I don't know why. Heard he was still around though, he might be hard to get ahold of. You should ask Faith Gaines . . . at the vet clinic?"

"Why Faith?" Peter asked, wondering if Larry was privy to Dyer's story with Billy.

Larry went a little flat at that point in the conversation, Peter told me. "Took her son camping" was his laconic reply. Peter figured by Larry's awkwardness he knew at some level.

Peter told Larry he was aware of who Faith was, told him we'd had some of our feral cats in to her office for neutering. Larry laughed about that, and, according to Peter, the earlier awkwardness evaporated into his usual contagious laughter. Larry was an interesting mix.

Peter said to me later, "Everything seems connected . . . always the same names keep coming up. I walked into the Saints hardware store, asked the guy at the counter if he knew where I could find Ed Dyer, and everybody there turned around and stared at me. I just want to talk to Dyer about logging on the district. I don't know about talking to Faith about how to get ahold of Dyer. She'll talk about Billy and the mountain man again, or maybe she doesn't want to talk about it anymore, I don't know. But if she does, there I'll be, and she'll just think I'm stupid or a jerk if I don't go into lawyer mode."

What a dilemma. "Down in Portland," I said with comfortable remove, "they say there's only a hundred people. Maybe five hundred in New York. Here there's only three." Peter laughed at this, but not without a certain touchiness. "Steer Faith to me if she starts in," I offered again. "I'm willing to talk and listen. I'm not forcing myself."

*

Peter arranged to meet Faith for coffee at the Ski Inn in town. Afterwards, he told me she'd talked about the horse clubs around Saints, about the trails through the national forest, about the logging alongside almost every trail in recent years. When he'd mentioned that Ed Dyer must know something about why the Forest Service was logging recreation and archaeological sites, because he was the one who had built all the Windigo Trail, Faith had stared into her lap, hadn't said anything at all.

As for Ed Dyer, Peter decided not to get in touch with him. He claimed not to be curious about him. I was a little bit curious about Dyer, about the mountain man thing. I wondered if he wore furs. I also wondered if Dyer, the Forest Service employee, was involved in something shady related to illegal logging. Was he going to end up the object of Peter's legal pursuits? I could think of no reason to call him for an interview, though; his case didn't even exist yet, or had not yet surfaced publicly, so I didn't call him.

Peter took townspeople out to the marked timber sale on the creek to see how they reacted, to hear what they had to say. There were loggers, hunters, millworkers, real-estate brokers, anybody around town who called him up. Quite a few did call. The phone rang a lot then, and it was almost never for me.

Peter sent people out to look at the timber sale on their own if they knew the forest well enough to find the site for themselves. Many did. People around Saints knew their forest.

I had the idea that Peter was benefiting from the karma of past caretakers at the ranch. They had all been ministers seeking congregations. The history of pastorship was in the walls of the cabin, and Peter was now trying, like any minister, to get people to take him at his word, to believe what he was saying as contrasted with what the other guy was saying. The other guy in Peter's case wasn't that cloven-hooved guy, the Devil, but the Forest Service.

While Peter was drumming up followers, I went north to Wasco County almost every week. For sheer drama and spectacle, I was more interested in the Wasco County Wars than the Forest Service Wars. I was also getting to know people on all sides quite well by that time. I was drawn to my ongoing relationships with them. I also reveled in the high-desert landscape, with its new autumn perfume of ripe juniper berries, the desert condiment.

Up at Rajneeshpuram, migrating Canada geese were dropping out of the sky by the thousands onto the lake sparkling behind the dam the Rajneeshees had built on their creek. I had become friends with Videh, the Water Man, an American who loved systems, water or otherwise, a techno-nerd who'd worked in film sound in his pre-Rajneeshee life. I was impressed with the elegance of their system, which held water on the land, as opposed to what had happened in the past, when the runoff from sudden torrential thundershowers would wash all the topsoil down into the John Day River. Now, tall grasses and waterfowl were everywhere. Even more than our ranch, Rancho Rajneesh was a wildlife preserve. That September their ranch became for the first time in history a flyway for thousands of migrating sandhill cranes.

I was out climbing up and down gullies with Videh one day when we saw the first of the cranes. We hunkered down in the tall grasses fifty yards from the noisy birds and watched as one big male stretched his tall frame and began to move like a principal dancer. With his wings extended upward, the bird stood easily six feet tall. He looked human as he wheeled his wings like an Indian dancing. For long minutes the bird pranced through this mating dance, bobbing his head in a roosterlike strut, falling back now and then to let several other

birds flame up briefly like the corps de ballet. Then the dancing stopped, and the action moved closer to the ground, where
it was hidden from sight behind the reeds.

Videh was ecstatic. He could not contain his pleasure at the
cranes. He saw the crane presence as a sign the Rajneeshees
were doing at least one thing right, although he was funny
about it, not dogmatic. Actually, he had no reason to edit his
pleasure in front of me, as I was full of exaltation myself. On
these extraordinary but not infrequent occasions on the high
desert when I saw wild nature in action, I would automatically
become awestruck. Afterwards, I would always think of these
incidents as signs of great good luck, luck being the skeptic's
religion.

Out in the parlors and kitchens of Wasco County, my interlocutors were unimpressed when I mentioned the crane
visitation.

"I've seen a dozen sandhill cranes this year on the John Day
River," Kelley McGreer told me. "They're everywhere. That
was a sign of *nothin'*." Kelley was incredulous I'd been impressed. It was Kelley who had bared his soul to me, talking
about his wife, Rosemary, and now he was baring his gold
front tooth to me again, grinning. It gave me pause to think
again about what a good-looking guy he was and about how
provocative it was to have a front tooth done in gold instead
of porcelain, especially when you have a grin like Kelley's. He
was attractive, and he knew it.

I had gotten to know both Kelley and Rosemary by then —
enough so that I felt comfortable phoning them up from
Saints to ask if I could spend the night at their house. Not
only was it free lodging — instead of seventy-five dollars to
stay at the Rajneeshpuram hotel — but staying with the Mc-
Greers was also reassuringly secure, like staying with distant
kin. If I had to hold my breath all day long in Rajneeshpuram,

keep my dialogue edited so as not to prevent people from telling me whatever they might want to, I could take a deep breath at the McGreers' and relax: They wouldn't throw me out. I was almost family, I felt, although I never put it to the test.

At Rajneeshpuram I was never quite certain there wasn't an ecstasy-spiked apple in a proffered fruit basket, or a microphone under my hotel-room chair to catch some unedited outburst when I thought I was alone or, better yet, a bugged telephone to overhear a conversation with Peter when I recounted some contradictory information I'd just discovered. When I suggested these doubts to Isabel, she said "Penny!" with mock horror, fixed me with a long stare, then shrugged, not answering, just looking sidelong at me once or twice. "I know you're never going to write anything," she said then.

With Isabel the talk was stimulating, but it was also a power game: She had power over me. I continued prying into Rajneeshpuram at her pleasure, however sophisticated her pleasure was, and she could terminate my visits, my sessions with Siddha, at will. I played this ironic power game with Isabel, but once or twice, when my irony disappeared, hers did, too. When I criticized her invitation to the press to photograph the Rajneesh SWAT team at target practice with their Uzis, she said, sadly, I thought, "Well, we have received a few death threats lately, and we must respond, mustn't we?" It wasn't that she was in over her depth but rather that she couldn't see where things might be headed, and there was no irony in that, only a palpable level of concern.

With the McGreers I could have been talking to my cousins who actually lived in the area, people I never saw in real life but perhaps secretly wanted to see. I could and did say to Kelley and Rosemary much of what I was thinking, even when it didn't correspond to what they thought. Yet they continued receiving me.

One night I had just driven over to the McGreers' from the dusty canyons at Rancho Rajneesh, and Kelley gave me a frozen daiquiri when I arrived. I was parched. It was hot outside at ten o'clock, and the McGreers had their air-conditioning on. They had their feet up, relaxing. Kelley had been cutting hay all day, and Rosemary had spent the day in Portland, shopping.

Rosemary had dramatic taste. She had designed and decorated the McGreers' new southwestern-style ranch house, whose windows looked down from a bluff onto a spectacular horseshoe bend in the river and across to the wild, remote part of Rancho Rajneesh. The house dominated the site, owned it.

Rosemary was short, like her husband, but whereas he was all pointed chin and ears, she was round-faced. She did not look like a farmwife. She wasn't wearing a print cotton dress. She was wearing a suit and looked like a businesswoman and was one, in charge of the books for the family ranch operations while Kelley was outdoors, the physical one, pulling a crop out of the same earth year after year under always-changing conditions. His father and grandfather and great-grandfather had done the same before him.

As a more recent arrival, Rosemary was more involved than her husband in defining what she was doing out there on that land. She had made a statement in building a grand house that dominated the setting. And then when the land across the river had come into Rajneeshee hands, Rosemary had gone right on saying what she was about, gone right on trying to dominate the setting.

"To call yourself a farmer," she said to me once, explaining the crucial part of her beef with her neighbors, her face tight-lipped, her eyes angry — she was not a woman you'd want to cross — "let's see you make a living at it."

I had looked over at Kelley when Rosemary said that, and he had winked at me and told me to watch out for his wife.

Now, as we three sat with our daiquiris in the gathering night, Kelley fixed me with a look. "Who are you in all this?" he asked.

I leaned forward suddenly, looking at the backlighting behind Rosemary and Kelley. "Can I take a picture of you guys right now?" I said.

"I've got it!" said Kelley, index finger in the air. "You're Jane Fonda!" He then laughed long and hard at his own joke. When he stopped laughing, I told him that, no, I was just a simple farmer.

Kelley raised his eyebrows when I said that and glanced over at Rosemary, who was a study in cool, tolerating the banter. Kelley swung his eyes back to me. "So you're a farmer?" he asked and took a measured sip of his drink. "What do you grow then?"

"Horses," I told him. "I take care of horses. I exercise them, doctor them, groom them, sometimes I even get shit on my shoes."

"You don't say."

"And we'd be irrigating the land, but our irrigation pipe got blocked by a flood."

"When's that? Last spring?"

"Yeah."

"And it's still blocked?" Kelley leered.

"Yeah," I allowed.

"Now you don't wanna let that happen to a farmer." Kelley cawed. He grinned, showing his gold tooth, and I took his picture. I was happy to see Kelley grinning like that after having seen him cry when we first met. He was moving on.

The next day, after leaving the McGreers, I drove over to Rajneeshpuram and had it out with Siddha. "What's this about your expert trial testimony that Rosemary was getting something out of the Rajneeshees' intrusion into her private paradise? That was shitty what you did to Rosemary Mc-Greer," I blurted out, tired of his calm, considered answers for everything. I went on accusingly, wanting to get a rise out of him: "It made me cry when Kelley told me about what you said, and who knows what you did to her? Do you even care?"

Siddha reacted. He was prickly when he told me I should read the transcript of the trial, "so we both know what we are talking about." I agreed he had a point there and said I would. "I've got a transcript," he offered, "and I'll have our printing office make you a copy." "Fine," I said, and we dropped the subject for the time being. As I left I picked up the copy of the thick transcript from the Rajneeshee printing office, along with a bill for seventy-eight dollars, ten cents a page. I was furious, because seventy-eight dollars represented a large sum of money to me just then, and I felt swindled, as if Siddha had been trying to make some point about me writing the article I was supposed to do but found myself unable to write.

I went and found Siddha again immediately. "Seventy-eight dollars happens to represent a substantial portion of my monthly income!" I shouted at him.

"Why are you trying so hard to earn as little money as possible? What is this silly game? You're an educated woman," he riposted.

I was outraged and stomped out of the room, but not before writing a miserable check for seventy-eight dollars. As if life weren't getting hard enough financially, I had to listen to a crackpot as well.

Back home I discovered that many of those precious 780 pages contained a lot of blank space, a lot of silence, a lot of blah, blah. I cried on Peter's shoulder about the money, about my big mouth, about the silly legal profession that wasted so much paper. He looked at me empathetically and gave me half of the $429 he'd just received from Viorst for work on the pipe, buying my peace of mind.

I read the trial transcript, mulled it over with a lot of other things that were happening, brought it up again with Siddha the next time I saw him. "It seems to be your theory," I told Siddha, "that it's all right to interfere in other people's lives because we're social beings, and it's our nature to do so. Or, in Rosemary's case, that the Rajneeshees gave her something to vent her emotions on when she had so much going on inside her that needed venting but wasn't getting vented. So that just about excuses any kind of disturbance or interference, doesn't it? Where do you draw the line? Before or after violence?"

We were sitting that day in the Rajneeshpuram mall restaurant, which only a week before had been in a different building entirely. Everything was modular at Rancho Rajneesh and got moved around constantly, a fact that lends itself invitingly to deconstruction. Were the Rajneeshees like gypsies, or nomads, living and breathing in a spot only as long as it worked, very "into the moment"? Or were they a moving target, always one step ahead of expectations, one step ahead of the law? Or were they immoral opportunists, sleight-of-hand liars and thieves, potentially murderers?

Siddha eventually responded: "You cannot have a relationship with another person," he said, "without interfering in that other person's life. That is the nature of relationships."

"Isn't this whole experiment up here an abject failure?" I came back. "Not to mention irresponsible?"

He sat in front of me and tapped the ends of his fingers together, fell into the psychiatrist's silence, left me with my own thoughts.

Okay, I'll go on, I thought. "You, Siddha, you messed with my life by suggesting Peter should come up here to learn to meditate, and then I interfered with his life by suggesting it to him, and I feel sure he took it as interference. Am I now responsible for whatever happens to him as a result of my suggestion he come up here? Do you feel responsible for whatever happens when you suggest things? Did you feel responsible for the effect your words had on Rosemary McGreer?"

Siddha listened, remained undefensive. He was pretty good, actually. "What if the point is to interfere with other people's lives," he asked me, "rather than to avoid connection?"

"Don't you ever experience performance anxiety anymore?" I asked him. Performance anxiety is an interesting subject, and I knew Siddha had experienced it in his pre-Rajneeshee life, Jewish guilt and all. "Don't you worry professionally about making the wrong choice, about having made a wrong choice? You don't worry about such things? You manage to be completely guilt free?"

Siddha waited a long time before answering, seemingly to hear anything else I had to say. Finally, in all intimacy, not pompous in the least, he said, "Of course I try not to make the wrong choice, and of course the anxiety is always there. Sometimes the anxiety seems to go away or it becomes lesser, but what do you know? It is always still there. But I no longer have the paralyzing fear I used to have about doing a bad job. The point is to watch what is happening in front of you, to the Other, and also to yourself, and to watch your choices form, and to continue to watch the consequences of your choices, not to look away but to have full awareness of it all."

The next time I sat in the McGreers' den, slightly tipsy on a daiquiri, I watched Rosemary shifting authoritatively in her leather chair. She tossed one leg up over the arm, settled back again. Were the Rajneeshees a good Other for her, something useful to measure herself against? I watched her, watched myself forming an opinion about her, didn't stop watching her or watching myself watching her until Kelley started to talk about a conversation he'd heard that morning in Madras at the fertilizer outlet. Supposedly, according to Kelley, some guy in the area was getting together a kind of death squad, a militia, a posse comitatus that would use high-powered rifles to fire down on Bhagwan Shree Rajneesh from the top of the rimrock circling Rajneeshpuram canyon. Someone was thinking of assassinating him, in short.

"Looky here, the guy at the fertilizer place says, Why not? Ain't that the way they used to kill renegade Indians in the past?" Kelley explained, laughing, and I wasn't able to tell if he was making the story up or not no matter how long and hard I watched him. Some things appear to be true simply because they fall within the zeitgeist, within the realm of possibility, so it doesn't really matter whether they're made up or not. If they haven't precisely happened yet, they could just as well have happened, or they could easily happen the very next day.

"Who was this guy at the fertilizer place?" I asked Kelley.

"Hey, now . . ." He was still chuckling.

"Was it somebody you knew?" I ventured, thinking of Ed Dyer, high-powered hunting rifle in hand. Ed Dyer, the mountain man, killing Indians. I wasn't really sure of what I was thinking. My own mood skidded and veered off then, adrenaline pumping slightly. Kelley was gazing at me, strong and sure. "It wasn't anything," he said, like a dad, strong and sure and reassuring, like a dad. But it was too late. I was already starting to get a picture.

God, I wondered, is seeing these sorts of things the beginning of high-desert madness? More to the point, was somebody going to get killed unless I interfered? Was somebody going to get killed if I did interfere? Was the spectacle I was involved in up north really there or was it simply a narrative that I was eliciting and provoking? Was anyone actually relying on me to reproduce this narrative, or was its importance always in the original telling? "Who are you in all this?" Kelley McGreer had asked me. Once I connected all the dots, would there be a picture or, as Kelley asserted, was I making the picture up?

TWELVE

I WAS SURPRISED to learn that Peter had actually finished hauling gravel out of the pipe and never even mentioned it, except to toss it off casually. "Oh, it's done, I
forgot to tell you," he said, when I asked him one day if he was
going up to his work hole. He was uninterested in celebrating
the end of his heroic task, since he was already quite taken up
with another. He'd been working the phone and around town
for some time, putting together a public tour of the gorge area
up the creek where the Forest Service planned to clear-cut.
The idea was to have the Forest Service personnel out there
with the public and to get them to explain what they were doing while everybody who cared was standing there, right in
front of them, all parties together in that great place with its
irresistible powers.

The day of the tour, when Peter and I pulled up in front of
the Saints Ranger Station, there were more than forty people
waiting outside. The first person I caught sight of was Larry
Lazio, hanging back in the ranks, leaning against the wall. But
he was there, glittering, a nugget of gold midst the gravel. On
the steps of the building stood the Saints district ranger and a
few of his underlings, not interacting with the public, all
bunched together in their olive green uniforms. I caught sight

of Faith Gaines looking intent, as if she had unfinished business.

"Great work, Peter!" I exclaimed about the size of the crowd, but he looked apprehensive.

"Oh, no." He sighed, sinking back, gesturing out the window at the woman who had earlier called him a liar around Saints and caused that embarrassing letter to the editor to appear in the newspaper. But then Peter swung open the car door and stepped out purposefully.

To my amazement, standing right up front, her eyes full and round and green, her hair curly and golden, was Elly Starr. How had she heard about the tour? I wondered.

"How . . . ?" I said to her, and she said, meaningfully, "I knew."

Just as we were loading into a caravan of green Forest Service vehicles, there came Ham Jones's four-wheel-drive Jeep, out of which Ham unfolded slowly, not even aware he was late. He looked tan and relaxed, fresh from the Bahamas, crisp white shirt with sleeves rolled up above the elbows. "Hi, Babe," he called out to me just as the cub reporter from *The Bulletin* zeroed in on him with her camera.

We shuttled in Forest Service vans from one proposed logging site to another. There was one funny moment when the district ranger pointed out a particularly attractive stand of massive yellow-bark pines as an example of how the forest would look after the planned logging. Then it turned out the example stand was part of the new timber sale and scheduled to disappear. Everybody laughed except the ranger, who was red-faced and overweight and out of shape and gave the sad impression that he had never before been out there on the ground.

At the next stop Peter guided the group down the gorge to the gnarly, blackened Doug fir. Everybody was suitably amazed at its existence. Below, the river shot through the slot. Larry Lazio inched on his belly out onto an overhang and clung there, looking down. Everyone was moving slowly, not rushing it. Time passed. Then we all made our way upstream to the landing at water's edge.

I walked with an old logger named Jack, a third-generation local who'd worked on the forest for fifty years, one way or another. He looked the part, with his huge torso stuffed into a red buffalo-plaid shirt, his suspenders like parentheses around a bulging belly. His face was crumpled leather. A finger was missing on his left hand. Chopped off? Ripped off by a choker chain? As we hiked along, Jack appeared to be distressed by the timber sale. "Whyzzit right next to that clear-cut over yonder?" he muttered. He kept mumbling to himself or to me or to no one as he took in the conditions. His immense forehead was pulled forward into a deep scowl so he looked like a rhinoceros.

At McDougal's Landing, everyone fanned out and talked in small groups. I was thinking that Peter should be pleased, it was turning out so interestingly. Faith Gaines was interrogating two Forest Service employees. She looked as if she had a lot to say, and the rangers were listening hard, their faces straining to catch her drift. I would have liked to overhear what she was saying but stayed apart until I saw her standing alone later. I went over to her and said, "Anytime you need to talk, just give me a call, okay?" She registered on me blankly and nodded.

After a few minutes the geography of the landing took over. Everyone gravitated to the center of the site and waited. "Now, I know what you're all thinking," the district ranger said and then fell silent. He looked as if he thought he might have stuck his foot in his mouth again. Before he could go on, my pal Jack spoke up, his arms aggressively akimbo above his big belly. "I think you're runnin' outta options, is what I think," he announced succinctly. Everybody turned to look at him and waited, but he didn't say anything else, just stared heavily back.

Elly Starr spoke up next. "Trees have spirits," she said slowly, like a storyteller, "just as we humans do. And the young trees grow and develop their spirits better when they have larger trees around them as examples."

Someone tittered slightly, and Jack craned his weathered neck around to look at Elly. A couple of Forest Service men looked at each other and rolled their eyes, but most everyone else seemed awkwardly frozen in that high-desert mode I was becoming familiar with.

Time stood absolutely still for a good, long beat, and then Ham Jones spoke, drawing the weight of the moment onto himself as if he'd heard his cue. He spoke in the voice of God, as we call it in the movies. "Surely everyone here today can see the magic in a place as lovely, as richly endowed as this, this cathedral-like, old-growth ponderosa climax community?" Our eyes all moved from one huge yellow-bark pine to another.

"This place is called McDougal's Landing," Ham continued. "I call it that. We *all* call it that, I imagine. It's on the map, even on Forest Service maps." I puffed up proudly, feeling as if I, too, had called this place that name for generations. Ham glanced at the district ranger for his reaction. The ranger's face stayed totally blank. Ham cleared his throat, began again: "When I say to someone, 'Let's take a lunch and go to McDougal's Landing,' a picture of this place comes into my mind, a picture with a long history."

Ham was now turning from one person to the next as he spoke, his eyes making contact, eliciting a coming together.

"What do *you* call this place?" he asked a Saints old-timer, who self-consciously mumbled "McDougal's Landing" under his breath.

"And you?" Ham said to another, waited for the nod, moved to the next. "And you?" he said to the lady who had called Peter a liar, and even this lady nodded yes. The next person smiled and lifted a hopeful shoulder even before Ham asked. Then several people quickly changed position in a kind of mounting excitement.

Ham rode on the energy projected upon him. "This is a place with a long story to tell," he intoned, gesturing expansively around him, his slow delivery giving weight to his remarks. "First, the Indians knew it, they left artifacts behind, and later, after white people came here, the site was named after an ordinary hero, a settler named McDougal, a few decades ago, who kept a dairy going out this direction. This man McDougal would have brought his family here on Sundays for picnics, I imagine. And now, it's because this place exists that our generation can connect to his, and all of us here today, it's a way for us to connect with that past, and maybe even with . . . the future."

Ham was captivating. He was elegant. And graceful. I watched Larry Lazio watching Ham admiringly, his head nodding almost imperceptibly, a slight smile on his lips, his eyes shining. Larry was inspired. Everyone was inspired. Even the fat district ranger was inspired.

"I can speak to that," he said when Ham ended. "We'll pull the sale away from the creek."

There was spontaneous applause. I felt a primal thrill.

Later, back home, Peter and I talked about what had happened.

"Ham was stupendous," I said.

"That's what people go to Yale for," Peter said matter-of-factly.

"I'm glad he went to Yale then," I said, wanting to celebrate.

"I'm glad he spoke up," Peter said, smiling. But his smile was ironic. It wasn't the smile of someone taking his pleasure. Was it the affectionate smile of my father enjoying my exuberance? Or was it the knowing smile of a professional fighter, already three moves ahead of the moment? Or was it the smile of an exhibitionist about to show off? Or was it the disappointed smile of the man who had done all the work, created the consensus, and had his thunder stolen by the guy who showed up to close the deal?

I felt myself backing away from the edge of glee. I fell back instead to a different, more restrained angle of repose.

One cold morning after having gone outside in my pajamas, fat socks, gum boots, and parka to feed the horses and open the corral, I was back in bed getting warm again. The nights were starting to be much colder than we were used to or prepared for. We had already begun feeding the horses in the morning — a flake each of good hay with alfalfa in it — because they were thinner and hungrier than before, their coats shaggier. The grass in the meadow was of diminishing quality now in late autumn. But we hadn't really gone to great lengths to keep our own house warm and draft-free, until the night an icy wind blew on us in bed all night long. We spent the next morning plugging all the holes in the bedroom wall and putting clear plastic over the windows. Still, the house was cold in the mornings until the woodstove started really pumping. Nighttime temperatures were dropping to right around fifteen degrees, and it wasn't even winter yet.

Buried under the comforter until Peter got the fire going strong, I heard the phone ring. Peter answered, and then he came in and said it was Faith Gaines, and she wanted to speak to me.

On the phone Faith told me that her son Billy had finally spilled his guts. "There was more to it, there was more to it, there was more to it," she repeated over and over, unable to formulate anything else. She was manic, desperate.

"There was more to . . . what happened to Billy? Is that what you're saying?" I asked her, remembering that Faith had clung to the belief that there had been only mutual masturbation between her son and Ed Dyer.

"Well, uh, uh, anyway, Ed found out he was going to get arrested, I think the court called him and told him, anyway, he found out he was going to be arrested, so he forced Billy to say the thing about mutual masturbation when he was questioned, and —"

"Forced Billy? How?" I interrupted Faith to ask.

"Well, Billy said Dyer told him he'd tell *me* what they'd been doing together if he, if Billy wouldn't say it was both their idea, you know, what they did," she answered shrilly. This was the Faith that Billy was surely seeing now, too, and it must have been terrifying for him to see his confusion mirrored in his mother's eyes. The truth, whatever it might be, had been ripped out of Billy in a painful fashion, I was certain.

"So what happened? What did they do together? *Who* told you this? Billy?"

"Billy said to me that he told the officers who came to talk to him, they wouldn't let me listen, they talked outside, he told them just what Dyer told him to say, that they just masturbated each other. But then, after the officers left our house and went to Dyer's, Dyer turned around and denied everything! He said it was all Billy coming after *him*, not the other way around! Ed just broke their agreement and ditched Billy! The whole thing blew up in his face!" Faith said, so intense now I thought she might snap in two. I had grown used to listening primarily to Faith's tone rather than to her words for hints about what she was really thinking, since she seldom said things directly, but now her affect was strong.

"How do you know all this?" I asked. "Did Billy finally talk to you about it?" I was still flat on my back in bed and now even more chilled than before. I had been concentrating on extracting Faith's story for a half hour, and I still didn't know what had happened between Billy and Dyer or how she had finally found out what she now knew. I wanted to talk to her in person. I wanted to gather my resources, to ring off, to start again later. I asked her to meet me for lunch in town at the Ranch House Deli.

At noon I drove into Saints in my Toyota, which had been thoroughly checked out after the whirling incident. The mechanic had found nothing wrong with the car. On the drive into town, I searched the forest on both sides of the road for Buckner. I hadn't seen him for days, and I was used to seeing him fairly regularly now. We hadn't received any offerings from him in what must have been a week. Halfway to town I thought I saw Buckner's dog, Chin, but I wasn't sure. Could have been a coyote.

The deli was done completely in local pine — floors, walls, ceiling, tables, booths. I picked a booth, sat down, and waited. There were five or six other people there having lunch. Faith arrived, wearing jeans and a long-sleeved cotton blouse in a blue that matched her eyes. Her face and long hair were plain and unadorned. We got lunch, and I ate while she talked.

"Anyway, Ed did call me, anyway, even though Billy had already told me everything Ed made him do when he found out Ed denied everything," she said, not keeping her voice low, starting in right where she'd left off on the phone. "There was a lot more to it than that."

"Than what?"

"Than . . . touching each other."

It was important she'd finally got the story, even different stories, from both of them, although I was going to have to piece it together for myself, I saw. For Faith had come to a full stop after the "touching each other" and was now stirring lump after lump of sugar into her coffee as she stared into the cup. My mind began to focus on whether she would find it too sweet when she finally took a sip. She took a sip, and the coffee or its sweetness got her started again.

"Uh, uh, anyway, Ed said that whatever he and Billy did, Billy wanted it, too, and that no matter what happens now, that he and Billy could do whatever they want in a few months when Billy turns eighteen. And I couldn't do anything about it. And anyway, you know," she rushed on, the emotion gone again, the affect now flat as armor, just a rat-a-tat-tat delivery, "it wasn't till Ed said that that I realized how stupid I am." She paused, stirred more sugar into her coffee, drank some.

"When Ed said what?" I asked tentatively.

"When he said that he could do what he wanted with Billy when Billy turns eighteen."

"But he'll say anything now. Why did you think *you* were stupid?"

"I thought Ed had been making a play for me, that's what I'd thought, and it was . . ." She blushed then, one of those ever-so-brief flashes I was beginning to wait for and seize upon midst all the undifferentiated muddle. How could she make the emotion matter and prevail? But she had started again.

"I should have known," she said plaintively.

"Why should you have known?" I asked her and reached to touch her arm.

"I just should have," she said awkwardly and looked down fixedly at my hand on her arm until I slowly moved it away. "When Hope and I were teenagers," she began then, "we had this way of talking no one could understand," she said, "and we used to completely fool people and switch clothes even, and no one could tell which one of us it was. Ha, ha. And, uh, uh, anyway, if the Mormon Church knew Ed Dyer was butt-fucking their children and didn't say anything, what do you think, do you think they told the Forest Service, and if they did, why did the Forest Service have Dyer working with kids? Don't you think I should sue them?"

"The Forest Service or the Mormon Church?" I asked, noticing that a few people eating their sandwiches had fallen silent and were obviously listening. Faith didn't seem to notice.

"What about Billy?" I asked her.

"He doesn't care about suing them."

"No, I mean, how is he? How is he taking all this?"

"Well, he cried, but then he's never had a father."

Later, back at home, I wanted to tell Peter about Faith, about her extraordinary juxtapositions and omissions.

"I can imagine Billy crying," I said to Peter, "not understanding what is happening, not liking what Ed did to him, but not having known for sure until now if he was supposed to like it or what . . . not liking it, but not wanting to reject Ed, who was like a father to him, who loved him . . . not having liked it physically, what Ed did to him, but actually terrified of Ed, who is apparently a big guy . . . a big guy who taught him how to shoot a rifle —" Unexpectedly, I burst into tears. Peter tried to comfort me. He put his arms around me. It felt like a willed gesture. It felt unfelt.

I had the impression that something about Ed and Billy's

story was twisting and skewing things between Peter and me — that even my telling Peter about it compromised us somehow, because it compromised him. Just listening to me compromised Peter's refusal to be responsible for Faith, was that it, in his mind? Or something. Maybe he'd grown up worrying about his ass in relation to some man? I noticed now how Peter and I both became physically hobbled when this subject came up. We were like jerky marionettes. We could no longer behave naturally. It made me want to kiss him and lovingly push my finger up his behind to show him it didn't matter.

Then, I felt like such a predator. Billy Gaines's angst was clearly contagious. The whole horrid story was catching. To know about it was to suffer it. I felt depressed and turned away from Peter to go lie down. He watched me confusedly as I walked down the hall to the bedroom. I could feel his confusion on my back as I escaped.

What a cruel place we were living in, I thought, looking at the ceiling. The ceiling was white, with glitter mixed into the paint. I thought about how Saints went right on about its business with never a trace of pain visible on the surface, although pain obviously lay thick and viscous just under the taut veneer. The boosters of Saints went right on civilizing the place even though it was secretly out of control. You ran up against a lot of boosterism in a place like Saints, where there was a future to be gained, a reputation at stake. I thought about how it was the women doing the civilizing, the boostering in Saints, controlling social behavior within the community, just the way the women had tried to do up in Antelope. It was the women in Saints who wanted libraries and public health programs and never a discouraging word. The women who wanted emergency-medical-treatment squads and marathons, and bicycle races and improved aerobic capacity and poetry readings. Women who wanted civilization. Civilization and conformity and fidelity and secrecy. And with secrecy comes inauthenticity and denial: If you have a problem, keep it to yourself. Elly Starr had told me, "Obsess or repress, those are your choices here."

I was so tired. I slept all afternoon.

Faith called me regularly. "Why didn't Billy tell me?" Her now-insistent, emotional voice would leap through the wire from her kitchen to mine. "I mean, uh, uh, anyway, it's not like Billy and I never talked . . . he's seen me reach into a horse and massage its prostate gland until it ejaculates, and we collect semen for artificial insemination, he's asked questions . . ."

The important thing, I thought, was to listen, to hear it all, to be patient when she was emotionally blocked and encouraging when illumination shone briefly. I didn't have to let it overtake me. I could remain myself. I could try to be there for Faith.

I wondered about Billy. Who was listening to him? Who was he talking to? I didn't think he had anyone. He was keeping it all to himself, I was certain.

Faith asked me one day if I was going to Ed Dyer's hearing at the county courthouse, because he had finally been arrested and charged with abusing Billy.

"Of course I am," I answered. "I'll be there."

"Something's going to happen," Peter said darkly as I left to go.

"There, at court?"

"Maybe there, I don't know, but something horrible's going to happen."

I went to the hearing. I was there so Faith could look around and see that I was there. I wasn't the only one. Half the town of Saints was there.

The courtroom in the Justice Center was low-ceilinged, modern, bland. As soon as I walked in, I spotted Ed Dyer, even though I'd never seen him before: Ed, the mountain man, who was tall, and hardy, and robust, and intimidating, a big man indeed, this maker of trails through the forest. He was wearing ordinary clothes, no furs, just a kind of hayseed suit that was too tight on his large frame and looked from a distance as if it smelled of mothballs. But he was large. And confident-looking.

By contrast, Billy looked small and innocent and young, withdrawn into himself. He was sitting up front in a plaid cotton shirt. His features were spritely and successfully masked whatever might lie behind them. He was sitting next to his mother, who also looked shy and young in a plaid cotton blouse, barrettes in her hair. They both looked very brave.

When Ed Dyer took the stand, I looked at Faith, and she appeared emotionless, blank.

Dyer explained in an even, protected-by-religion voice that he had often wanted to seek professional help for his problem, but that he had always hesitated because of the ruin it would bring upon himself and his family, his wife and children. "Most of the boys that I molested by their terms, by the terms of the law, I really loved," he said, and he looked directly at Billy Gaines, who was only fifteen feet from him.

The hair rose on the back of my neck. Dyer was looking at Billy with love.

Dyer went on, still looking at Billy: "I know that Billy back here, sitting there, I know that he probably hates me now, because of the problems I brought on him and his family. But I truly did love him and enjoyed his company and all the good things we did. And I'm painfully regretful of that problem and that situation. And if there was any way I could erase it, and make his life better, I would sure do it." There was such intimacy in his look that several people in the courtroom looked down into their laps. I didn't. I kept staring at Ed Dyer, but my throat had gone dry.

"Who initiated the sex between you?" came the question.

Dyer did not pause. "It was mutual part of the time and part of the time maybe mostly myself."

It was quite horrifying to see only the back of Billy's neck. What was his face doing? What was his heart doing as Dyer said this? Dyer was marking this boy. Dyer was not taking the entire blame. He was marking the boy with equal blame, with officially bestowed shame and guilt. A child. Dyer kept on looking at Billy with the tenderness of a father. He was pulling the proceedings into his own safe territory, pulling the courtroom off course with his tenderness. But what, indeed, had been the court's charted course before that moment? What was supposed to have happened? I was no longer sure.

Dyer finished, and the judge told him to take his seat.

Dyer's wife, a small, sweet, sad, blond woman, crossed the room and took the stand then. She said that Ed "feels really bad because of what he's done and how people feel toward him. He feels really bad. And he feels bad for the people he's hurt."

She seemed loyal, masked. Or was there something else going on? Something to do with witnessing, the way it's done in the Mormon Church? It was as if she were witnessing: "You don't always look at the thing that someone does wrong," Ed's wife told the courtroom in a steady voice. "You look at the other qualities a person has, too. And I think if you care about someone, you expect that these people are good and maybe they'll be able to crack this problem." Amen, I thought she said then. Do they say Amen as punctuation in the Mormon Church?

The judge nodded his head when Mrs. Dyer stopped. I began to understand, then, that the hearing wasn't really about a pedophile, about Billy, the victim, and about Faith, his powerless mother, or about what happened to the relationship between mother and son because of Ed Dyer. It wasn't about where the money might come from to pay for counseling for Billy if he wanted it. The hearing was about a decent, upstanding, remorseful human being, a man of strong passions who had faltered and was going to be forgiven. He was going to be forgiven by his clan.

People in his clan did get up and testify then about Ed's enormous contributions to the community through the Forest Service and Scouting, and about how much pain it had caused Ed to have to retire from the Forest Service because of "his problem."

No one spoke of Billy's pain, of Faith's pain.

The judge pronounced thus: "From what all the witnesses have testified to," he said directly to Dyer, who looked both harsh and regretful at once, "why you're a fine fellow, with a good work record, who's done a great deal for the community. If you feel positive about yourself, why these episodes aren't going to mar your life, and you can make the best of it." The judge smiled at Dyer then, and Dyer nodded his head in accordance.

"I sentence you to twenty days to be served at your own convenience," the judge said solemnly, and Dyer lowered his head and moved his lips as if in prayer.

The mood in the courtroom was muted, diffuse, confused, repressed.

Faith and Billy moved quickly outside, both of them still

looking blank. They got into Faith's truck, parked in front of the Justice Center. They drove away and left everyone standing there not knowing what to think.

Back home I wanted very much to tell Peter what had happened at court. I started in while we were eating lunch, even though I knew it was risky. Peter was agitated listening to me, and when I said that Ed got twenty days, to be served at his own convenience, Peter exploded angrily, his face twisted into disbelief. Then he got up and simply left, went outside.

I felt very alone and sat there at the kitchen table for a long time with my head propped in my hands, as if it were too heavy to hold itself up. After a few minutes, I heard a karate-chop shout outside — "ka-pow!" I think it was — and then the heavy thud of something very dense hitting the ground. I walked to the living room window, looked out, and saw Peter near the corral stalking a huge, black turkey vulture. Peter had the ax in his hand and swung it at the huge bird, which jumped back awkwardly, not taking its beady eyes off Peter. Peter moved slowly forward. The bird stumbled and flew up flapping, and in a single motion Peter swung the ax in an arc, severing the vulture's head from its body, and then the ax hit the ground with a dread thud. Peter went rigid. His hands clenched. He kicked his legs stiffly out in front of him, the way I'd seen him do once before. He went around in a circle that way for a few seconds, breathing heavily, and then he stopped. I stopped watching and went in the kitchen and cried.

I heard Peter get in the Scout and drive off. I was still sitting at the kitchen table, paralyzed, when he came back an hour or so later. He came into the kitchen, looked down at me. He was holding a huge bouquet of red roses.

"I'm sorry," he said, handing me the flowers with gentleness in his eyes. I was so touched and smiled up at him, but my smile froze when he said, "Buckner's dead. I heard in town they found his body alongside the creek, in his camp, just downstream from here. He probably drank himself to death, they think. The drink triggered some kind of epileptic fit. Whiskey. He had apparently drunk two bottles of it. Chin was sitting right there beside him."

I wailed finally, right from the gut.

THIRTEEN

F IRST THING I DID when Peter told me Buckner was dead was yowl and scream. Then, as I recall, I threw my arms around Peter and frantically rubbed my body against his, and during this, I clamped my jaw shut with a certain intensity, thereby cracking a back tooth in half.

A couple of hours later the Saints dentist looked in my mouth, poked around. He said I'd need a crown, and it would run me $450. The news played on my financial fragility, pushed me over the edge, made me hate Viorst. I hated him for exploiting us, hated him for not paying us, for not having put us on his corporate health insurance plan, something that would have cost him no effort whatsoever, but that he did not do, because he thought roughing it was good for us: toughened us up. I told the dentist I'd get back to him, drove home wildly, angrily, told Peter about the $450.

"A ranch is a fucking dangerous place to live with no money!" I raved. "What is Viorst fucking thinking about? We're constantly injuring ourselves. I'm destroying my back on his lousy gorgeous horses. We're just withering away here, and for what? For his pleasure?"

Peter encouraged me to play it out, took on my coloring. It felt obvious it was long overdue that I should get angry at

Viorst, and it was especially gratifying having Peter get angry with me.

Later, in the pause after our venting, Peter said, "I'll pay for the crown." He was terribly endearing the way he said it, with so much consideration, and after four more days of fretting, I had the new crown.

The next day I got a deadening headache and felt myself slipping into depression. I found it hard to hold up my head. I had to stay horizontal, in bed, in the fetal position. I had my jaw clamped and shoulders tensed, warding off danger, animal-like. I could have snarled in rage at this point, even at a friendly hand.

There are those who can look at a raging animal or person and see what's going on. There are those who can see what to do for the raging one, although such saints are not common. When we find one we cling to him. Most people react fearfully or hysterically to another person's wildness, aggravating the pain, compounding the problem, sometimes getting injured. Peter went on instinct and did beautifully.

"You need to be alone," he said to me intuitively a week after Buckner's death, and left. He filled up the fridge and told me carefully where he was going and for how long. He was brilliant. For him, the hardest part probably was being sure I'd really registered what he'd said, about where he was going, et cetera, because I mustered only a grunt. But I did hear him and registered especially how great it was to have someone speaking, almost unexpectedly, to my inner self. After that, I heard him drive away in the Scout and felt released from some kind of straitjacket, from the responsibility of . . . of what? Peter had freed me up, was what I felt. What a good man! Like a babe, I rolled over, lay spread-eagled on my back, and studied the ceiling.

After another day, I got up.

*

"You get dragged by a horse or something?" the Saints chiropractor asked me jovially when I drove myself in to see her. She performed her usual broncobusting chiropractic on me, and then I drove the five miles home slowly and carefully, not wanting to be jostled. There was no one anywhere around, not on the road, not alongside the road. Back on the ranch I was alone. I hollered for the horses, who came in perfectly like good children without me lifting a finger. I went back to bed and slept twelve hours.

The next day I was definitely on the mend. I spent the afternoon sitting in the sun in the front window, soaking up the heat of the late-season rays, back to the Spectacle. I listened to the wind blowing thousands of yellow and red leaves off the cottonwoods in an autumnal lament, fell asleep curled up on the rug in the fading sun.

When I woke up the third day Peter'd been gone, I was calmer. After a big breakfast of oatmeal and bacon, I took up my journal of Saints and began to write. I didn't write about Faith and Billy, whose experience left me deadened. I wrote about Buckner, who was dead.

Buckner is dead, I wrote. Buckner has died, and is not out there anymore. I do feel differently about this place with Buckner gone. It seems empty again, like when we first got here. But also he had made it safe, or at least I had imagined it thus and was released from unnecessary worry. For me, Buckner had invested the place with definitions that sprang from the idea of him being on patrol in our forest, still in Nam in his head but out there in our forest, having brought the war home, after all. I had wanted him to prevail.

There was much to be said about Buckner's presence on the ranch and about the fantasies he had aroused in me — about territory, about being in somebody else's territory; or fantasies of being watched and being made to accept certain behavior in exchange for protection; or sexual fantasies.

It was utterly depressing to imagine, as I was now allowing myself to do, that Buckner was dead because he'd traded meat from that buck the two of us had watched stumble, fatally injured in battle, for two bottles of whiskey that he'd drunk straightaway, thereby killing himself.

After crossing the meadow to the injured buck that afternoon, Buckner had apparently tossed a rope over a tree branch right near where the buck had collapsed, in the ponderosa stand half-way between our cabin and the Main House. Like any hunter, he had probably tied the rope around the animal's rear feet, hauled it up, and cut its throat. He'd gutted it as it hung, thrown the innards in a pile. The dark blood had spread and puddled on top of the pine-needle mat and then sunk, leaving a stain I actually saw, a stain that, along with the guts, would attract flies, bees, coyotes and a single vulture.

Leaving the hindquarters hanging, Buckner no doubt cut off the forequarters, then the head with its magnificent rack. Buckner would have shouldered the headless forequarters and carried them to his own encampment on the creek just downstream from the ranch, returning at least two more times, first for the head and then for the hindquarters.

At his camp, he would cut the forequarters in half, hang one half high in a tree along with the hindquarters. I imagine he pushed the head with its rack onto a tree prong at eye-level where it hung like a giant mask similar to one he'd probably made a long time ago, from the huge head of a water buffalo. After that he stirred his campfire into life with matches and dry twigs, cut some prime backstrap from the remaining half of the forequarters, and grilled himself pieces of the steak, tossing morsels plus a bone to Chin.

As he ate, maybe he wondered: Had I wanted some of the backstrap or hadn't I?

Next, I imagine Buckner doused his campfire with creek water, took up the deer quarter at his feet, and headed into town on foot with Chin trotting along beside him. In Saints the first person he asked, someone who knew him and occasionally let him sleep in his shed on cold nights, this person maybe gave Buckner twenty dollars or so for the deer quarter. Soon after that Buckner stepped into the darkened back room at the B-Bar-B, where he stood for a moment in the darkness, then ordered and drank a triple straight shot of bar-brand whiskey in the company of other solitary men. He would feel tense after a while, want to be outside, so he gave the bartender his twenty dollars in exchange for the rest of the bottle of whiskey plus an unopened one. He put the two bottles in his pack, went to the place under the bridge just south of town where he sometimes met up with his two friends. Maybe no one was there. Buckner lay down to wait, his thoughts like lasers in the jungle churning up some incredible untold memory.

Sometime after that, I guess he would have thought about giving me his Purple Heart. Why not? He was feeling the whiskey after such a long time without a drink. Maybe I would think he wanted to surrender? He would laugh out loud, and the laughter echoed against the concrete bridge pilings in the gathering dusk. After a while, maybe he'd fallen asleep. Later, he would get up, hike back up the creek in the dark to his camp, where he made sure the smell of fresh deer meat hadn't attracted anything rare, like a cougar. Then he dug up the Purple Heart from its hiding place. He dropped the medal into his vest pocket and hiked upstream to the edge of the forest next to the clearing where our cabin sat.

He would have stopped to reconnoiter. All of our vehicles were there at the hitching post — the Mustang, the Scout, the Toyota. There were no lights on inside the cabin, so he couldn't see inside the bedroom with no curtains. Buckner probably walked quietly across the yard to the house then and up onto the porch, where he hung the Purple Heart on the doorknob. Swiftly, he turned and went back down the creek to his camp. Once there, he built a little fire in his fire ring, sat down next to it, and drank himself to death, having survived, up until then, on wits and heart and a slow-draining reservoir of luck.

Buckner was a rogue male, I wrote in my journal. He'd been living his life here in our forest as an expression of extreme anguish. I set aside my journal, put on my parka, a big muffler, and a hat, took Buckner's Purple Heart out of my jewelry box, and hiked downstream until I came upon what looked like it had been a campsite. I wasn't surprised to discover it was not far from our house, not close, like a city next-door neighbor is close, but only about a quarter of a mile away. The forest seemed desolate there, silent, empty, cold, the sky overcast. The air streaming north off the mountains was full of ice. At the camp I saw that the only thing left of Buckner's very own place on earth was the fire circle made of blackened rocks arranged on the sand next to the creek. And maybe that green stick lying there was the one he'd sharpened to skewer and grill the backstrap for his fine last meal. Aside from that the camp was utterly empty, no longer a camp. I looked up in the trees and saw that the impressive deer-head mask with its magnificent antlers was not there, if it had ever been there in reality. But Buckner would have kept such an outstanding animal's head. Perhaps the people who found him had taken it.

There was nothing anywhere, nothing to find, no message from the beyond, no feeling, no trace of suffering, nothing. I turned and left, taking the Purple Heart back home to keep as a talisman.

When Peter came back the next day, I was happy to see him. He took me in his arms and held me. He held me and held me. He held me for as long as it took.

Many days later when Peter and I were curled up like spoons on the couch, there was the sound of a gunshot not far from the cabin, closer than it ought to have been. Peter sighed, looked at the date on his watch, and said, "Deer season starts tomorrow. It's time to go outside, mark our territory." By then it seemed possible to me, this going outside business, this return to perambulation. The pacing was good.

Outside, Peter got a stack of No Hunting signs from the Scout. I don't know how long they'd been there — whether, for instance, they'd been purchased before or after Peter had learned about Buckner's death more than two weeks earlier. In my mind the events were connected, as if our flanks were now exposed to danger — in this case danger from hunters — without our man Buckner on patrol.

Hunting season was indeed upon us. It would last for two weeks, marking the end of summer, a timing selected by the Fish and Wildlife people to cull the herds for the harsh winter ahead, when forage would become slight. The thing was, sensible or not, Peter didn't want anyone hunting on our territory, and neither did I. There was no reason to risk our getting shot or a horse getting shot, as had apparently happened one year. Coco dead like that? Huh-uh. Peter and I took the No Hunting signs and hiked the boundaries of the ranch, attaching signs to trees along the perimeter, especially where hundreds of small, sharp hoofprints revealed obvious deer trails passing onto the property from the surrounding national forest.

Energized by our land, we walked the full length of our irrigation network to assess the damage wrought by a season without water. Larry Lazio had opened our water gate just below the irrigation dam when Peter had finished clearing the pipe, but the water was so low in the creek by then it scarcely flowed. What water there was petered out in the upper ditch system before it got to the first gate.

All along the dried out network, the wildflowers were dead, as were all the alder, the willows, all the grasses except cheatgrass, bunchgrass, and crested wheatgrass. All this death gave the sensation that life, not to be found here, must therefore be happening elsewhere — in some other country perhaps. It was the first time I'd had that feeling for some time, the feeling of having made a grave mistake. Peter and I were very careful with each other, very solicitous, very close, as if each recognizing fully the life that lay within the other.

It was into this new mood that Isabel phoned one day from Rancho Rajneesh. I hadn't been up to Rajneeshpuram or elsewhere in Wasco County for a month.

"Listen, I have something to tell you," she said with a controlled urgency in her lovely accent. "You have been gone for a while. Things have happened. I remember the first time we spoke you said you would like to talk with Bhagwan. Well, you can, but it must be now," she said compellingly. "It must be tomorrow."

How strange! My first reaction was that I didn't want to do it anymore, and now Isabel was offering it to me on a silver platter.

"And you must come see Siddha," she added, sensing my hesitation. "I think he might be leaving."

"What?" That got my complete attention. Isabel was so smart. Or was she cunning? She knew I really did care. She paused for a beat to let it all sink in.

"You will have to ask Siddha about it. I'm not sure of the details. He'll be here tomorrow for your séance with Bhagwan if you come." She was using the word *séance* in the French sense, as in *session,* not in the Webster's sense of a meeting where you try through a medium to communicate with the dead.

I went, of course. I was ambivalent about talking with the guru but nevertheless eager for some kind of closure. I was not ambivalent about seeing Siddha. I had been wanting to talk to my shrink, but I was surprised to learn that it might be for the last time.

FOURTEEN

THE DRIVE UP NORTH to Rancho Rajneesh seemed longer than ever before, the landscape not unique, not even interesting. The security at the Rajneeshpuram checkpoints was tighter than usual, due, I imagined, to the increasing telephoned death threats. I was stopped, and a guard looked into the Mustang several times. At Rajneesh Reception, I expected to be taken to shower down as before, maybe even body-searched, but Isabel came out to greet me and said, "No, it's not necessary." She looked me over in my layers of clothing and said, "Good. That's the way to do it. You won't get cold." She was lovely. There was no one like Isabel. That day, in spite of tensions around her, she was a generous seductress in her Italian knit dress and red silk parka, her smile flashing, her South American derriere undulating as she led me out the door of Rajneesh Reception to a waiting car. She smiled at me radiantly over her shoulder several times as I was noticing her behind, and I realized that the smile was the same one I'd found in a photo of Isabel published five years before in *The Dalles Weekly Reminder*, a tiny Wasco County newspaper.

The photo was from the earliest moments of Rajneeshpuram, from just after the Rajneeshees came to the high desert, long before things had gone bad between the cult and the clan. In it, Isabel was standing with the Wasco County judge, the two of them smiling hugely, enormously, at each other. I'd hung a copy of the photo on my photograph wall. The Wasco County judge looked like he was in love. It was one of those stolen moments photographers sometimes capture. And there it had been in that little weekly rag. What had people thought of that photo back then? I'd wondered.

I'd asked dozens of people around Wasco County what it had been like then with the Rajneeshees, hoping people could remember before they got mad. I'd been told a number of times that, from the first, all kinds of people had been in love with Isabel. She'd created a local sensation, become the object of countless sexual fantasies, a few of which I'd even heard recounted by the men who had had them. My sources told me that two Wasco County men had gone so far as to propose marriage to the femme fatale, they'd wanted her so much. She'd had the finesse never to humiliate anyone, even as she was rejecting the advances. Eventually, Isabel had married a Rajneeshee, an American, a former corporate lawyer from San Francisco who now lawyered for Rajneeshpuram. Everyone in the county believed she'd married only for her green card and not for love, so Isabel's extraordinary appeal remained undiminished. Her heart, they fantasized, was still to be won, her body still to be possessed.

Watching Isabel move so beautifully that day on our way to the car, imagining her out and about in Wasco County moving that way, especially in the early days, I marveled that I might be looking at the real reason Rajneeshpuram could never have lasted long on the high desert.

On the way to the meeting with Bhagwan, Isabel turned and smiled at me again, breaking into my thoughts. "How is Peter?" she asked as we rode the short distance to the modular building housing the guru. "He is a good man, isn't he?"

"Yes," I told her, puzzling to myself about her line of thinking. "Peter is a very good man," I said.

"And you worry about him because he is such a good man?"

"I worry about offending the good part."

"I am married to a good man as well," she said. "I worry about him, because Sheela keeps asking him to do lawyer things he doesn't want to do."

"Ha. Ha. Like file suits against everyone?" I asked.

"*Oui*, the lawsuits are unpleasant for him."

"Is your husband morally offended by Sheela's requests?" I asked.

She paused reflectively. "It is interesting being married to a lawyer, isn't it?" she said finally. "There is so much compromise."

We had arrived at our destination. The Rajneeshee musicians stood outside Bhagwan's quarters, dancing in place rhythmically in a semicircle, sort of Hare Krishna style. They were playing a folkloric Rajneeshee new-age–raga hybrid composed on a pentatonic scale, with no chord changes, no tension, no disharmony. The sound was a friendly, brilliant D chord forever. The floor was scattered with rose petals. The guru's peacocks were strutting around exotically in the courtyard, stimulated into a strange dance of their own by the music and the bobbing Rajneeshees. Suddenly, out of nowhere, there was Siddha, looking at me with weeping eyes, totally incongruous midst the ecstatic scene. He took me by the hand, and we went into an anteroom, sat down.

"What is it?" I asked and squeezed his hand. He was slipping away. He had already slipped away, in fact, and it was clear he wasn't going to tell me what was happening. I had a violent sense of being rejected, cut off, abandoned. So this is it? I thought. This is how it goes? He owes me nothing, is that it? He has no responsibility, no answers? I get no closure, no epiphany? No lingering friendship?

Siddha read my thoughts, shook his head slightly, snorted endearingly, almost ironically, smiled, soured, turned and was gone. Isabel was beside me then, smiling, pulling me by the hand into Bhagwan's chambers, where she directed me to stand and wait. She let go of my hand, turned, and took her place with the other Rajneeshees standing off to the side of the room. I sat down in my chair opposite Bhagwan. I saw that next to my chair there was a table on which were arranged a silver pitcher of ice water, a bowl of fruit, and a tray of chocolates. I thought about eating a chocolate, but I wasn't hungry.

The guru studied me and waited for my questions. I couldn't think of a single thing to say. This was blankness with a certain calm. My eyes were locked onto Bhagwan's, and time passed that way.

"What is your question?" he said finally, and all the Rajneeshees sitting off to the side of the room laughed. I liked that they laughed. It felt good. I thought about how it was my line now, as if there were a dialogue to be had, a particular dialogue. My eyes were still fixed on the guru's infamous hypnotic gaze. I let the time pass comfortably.

He didn't wait. "The Oregon idiot is a special idiot," he began, starting in on a tirade. I was terribly disappointed. He went on in that vein. I felt my face fall. I felt disapproval and distance, and my gaze on his was judgmental. I looked down at my prepared questions:

1. Aren't you getting tired of all this?
2. When are you going to fall silent again?
3. Isn't this Rajneeshpuram thing about over? Or (to put it in his language): Is the ripened fruit ready to drop from the tree?

I decided to begin with the first question. I looked back up at Rajneesh, who was still talking in a way that did not seize my attention. I sat, impatiently poised, ready to ask my question the instant he stopped, perhaps the instant *before* he stopped, if I could sense when that might be. I was by then familiar with his style of circling around and around a subject, sometimes repeating himself, so I knew I was in for a spell. As he droned on, I wondered if he ever stopped and changed to another course before finishing the first one. It occurred to me then that he was doing this to goad me in some way.

I smiled at the guru then, and he smiled back and stopped.

"Is the ripened fruit ready to drop from the tree?" I asked him quickly.

"Yes," he said, paused, then asked, "You know I have been dancing again lately?"

"Dancing?"

"Yes," he answered and succeeded in locking my gaze on his again. "Moving toward happiness is such a difficult thing to do," he said.

There was a pause full of anticipation when I, at least, didn't know what was going to happen next, then Bhagwan clapped his hands and stood up, moving his feet to the music, which had started up on cue. He reached toward me, gestured for me to lift my hands. Our palms met, and we danced slowly, palms together, turning in a circle a few times, gaze still locked. I felt the Rajneeshees off to the side rise and dance in place. Suddenly, Bhagwan dropped his hands, turned his gaze away from mine, moved for the door, still dancing, and was gone. Then Siddha and Isabel were there next to me, telling me how good it had been for them. Everyone rushed off. It was over, and I found myself back in the Mustang before I knew what was happening.

*

The night was icy, frigid. It had rained that day, and now the steep gravel road was covered in black ice. Peter had planned for this eventuality and weighted down the rear of the car with logs in the trunk, but I was still nervous about driving on the ice. I cautiously inched along the road climbing the side of the canyon. On the steepest rise I suddenly got no traction, slid sideways, stopped. I was terrified. I put on the emergency brake and got out fast. I didn't even slam the door for fear doing so would push the car into a slide.

I walked slowly up the slippery road to a security checkpoint, where I told the Rajneeshee inside I needed to be towed up. The guy asked my name, checked me out on his walkie-talkie, then asked for the garage. Somebody answered, even in the late evening. He explained the situation, listened a minute, then told me someone would be up to help.

It was a bloody cold wait. The tiny checkpoint building wasn't big enough for two people, so I waited on the road. When the tow truck came, it squeezed uphill past the Mustang, stopped, and two Rajneeshees got out. One of them half-walked, half-slid down to Stang, dropped to his knees to check out what he could hook his tow chain to. When he touched the car, the weighted rear end swung around, pointed itself downhill, and Stang began a slow, sickening descent, alone, down the narrow, steep road. We all watched silently, breathing hot plumes of breath, or not breathing at all, as the car slid, veering toward the drop-off along the outer edge of the road for a good ten seconds, before it gradually, miraculously, hove to the inside, where it ground up against the canyon wall and stopped.

Silence, then one of the Rajneeshees farted long and low.

Later, after they had towed the Mustang up to the top of the canyon, I drove away tortoiselike, only as far as the town of Antelope, or Rajneesh, or whatever it was. When I saw

Margaret Hill's yellow ranch house all lit up against the night, I steered toward it and parked.

Margaret opened the door and smiled, startled perhaps at seeing me unannounced late at night, but her smile turned to concern when I told her something had happened and asked if I could use her telephone to call Peter. I talked to him in front of her, didn't seek privacy, and when Margaret heard everything, she offered to let me spend the night there rather than drive home in such an agitated and chilled state.

After breakfast early the next morning, when I left Margaret's to drive home, a silver thaw covered the rocks and fields on both sides of the road, and all the hoarfrosted cattle standing in the fields were immobile, their faces turned like mine toward the rising sun.

The next day Isabel phoned me at home to say that Siddha had disappeared from Rajneeshpuram. She and I did not even mention the preceding evening's events. "A car is missing," she said urgently. "I think Siddha discovered that Sheela had been planning some kind of murder plot to get rid of all her imagined competition, and so I think her people had the idea to kill him. I think Siddha took a car and drove off."

Later that day Isabel called back to say Siddha had just phoned her from Seattle to tell her he was leaving the purloined car at the airport parking lot and mailing the keys to her. She added, with what sounded like relief, "He told me no one at Rajneeshpuram would be hearing from him again."

"But I didn't even get to say good-bye to him," I said from my kitchen.

"You didn't say good-bye, so that means you will probably see him again," she answered, sounding almost comforting, a trait I'd never detected in her before.

"I doubt I will ever see Siddha again," I said. Then: "Are you leaving too?" I surprised myself, it was such a whine.

Isabel answered me: "For now, no, I'm not leaving, I'll stay here and do my job . . . the phone is ringing day and night. You know, it's crazy," she said calmly, as if it weren't crazy at all, as if she thrived on craziness. "As long as Bhagwan is here, my life is still here, because this is the path I have chosen."

Could I say the same thing about my own life? I wrote in my journal after I hung up. I admired Isabel for sticking it out. I was already wondering what life would be like without her, without Siddha, without an Indian guru looming large up north.

Sure enough, soon after that Bhagwan wasn't there anymore. In a kind of truth-is-stranger-than-fiction episode, Bhagwan fled the high desert in the middle of the night in a small plane with his physician and a few other Rajneeshees when they were tipped off that U.S. marshals planned to arrest the guru the next day for, of all things, immigration fraud — all those green-card marriages. Federal marshals did indeed arrest him the next day, but on a distant Caribbean island, where the plane stopped for refueling. Then, for more than a week the marshals and their prisoner hopscotched west across the United States on a media tear from one federal prison to another. Bhagwan was finally brought back in chains to Oregon for a short stay in prison and official deportation.

"Why'd they bring him back?" the current Wasco County judge asked plainly from the headlines of *The Bulletin* and *The Oregonian*. "Why didn't they just let him leave?"

Isabel cried tears of disappointment in front of the media. On the phone to me in my dark kitchen, where I paced around, she said, "I have lost all interest to do this job with Bhagwan no longer here. I have no reason. I can't do it now. I want to move on."

"So are you leaving now?"

"I would go now, yes, I am through. But my husband now has all the legal questions to handle, everything unraveling and all. He doesn't feel done with the whole thing yet. So I will stay with him for as long as I can, but I can't push it. You can't push it," she said. "When you have to leave, you have to leave."

"You have fallen in love with your husband, I think," I told her, but she didn't answer. It was the last time I would talk with her.

"Go ahead and write about it," Peter said when I tried to explain it all to him. "Even if you end up throwing it away."

"I thought you were going to say even if I end up throwing up," I said.

We were standing on the edge of the cliff upstream, looking down into the gorge of the creek where the big Doug fir and all the other trees were now dusted with snow, still there, reprieved from logging at least for then. The faithful Scout had managed to plow to the site in four-wheel drive through ice, mud, and a foot of snow. The high elevation meant it would soon be deeper in snow and inaccessible for the rest of the season. The Three Saints loomed hugely, just out of reach, already modeling good snowpacks. They were virginally garbed against the azure sky.

"I can't write about it yet, not for a while anyway," I said. "It doesn't feel like it's over yet."

Out of the blue a few days later, a forgotten coal burst into flame, following its own high-desert logic. This was in *The Bulletin*:

Saints Teen Held in Death of Redmond Man

A seventeen-year-old Saints youth was arrested Wednesday afternoon in connection with the fatal shooting of a fifty-year-old Redmond man.

Billy Gaines, who lives in the Tollgate subdivision west of Saints was being held in a juvenile detention facility in Klamath Falls this morning.

He is accused of shooting Edwin Ellis Dyer, fifty, at Dyer's home at 5508 West Highway 126 at about 12:30 P.M.

Gaines was arrested at 1:40 P.M. by Oregon State Police detectives in a field along State Highway 126 about three-quarters of a mile west of Dyer's residence. . . .

Deschutes County Undersheriff Darrel Davidson said Gaines apparently walked to Dyer's house after attending classes at Redmond High School, where he is a sophomore. Dyer's house is about 2½ miles west of the school.

Davidson said Gaines was admitted into the house by Dyer's wife, Tona, and asked to talk to Dyer. Dyer, who was in another room, refused to talk to the boy, he said.

Tona Dyer then offered to drive Gaines back to the high school and Gaines went outside, Davidson said.

He said Gaines was standing by a pickup truck in Dyer's driveway and Tona Dyer still was inside when Edwin Dyer came out. Davidson said Dyer and Gaines exchanged words before Dyer was shot.

He died at the scene from a shotgun blast to the chest.

Oh, my. Oh, Billy. Oh, Faith. I had looked away from Billy and Faith after Dyer's court hearing and lost track. Dazed by the news and by miserable feelings of having let Faith down, and maybe therefore Billy, I went outside looking for Peter in the cold, dry air and saw that his Mustang was gone. I had vaguely seen him come in the house, go in the kitchen briefly, then go outside again. This must have been when he left *The Bulletin* for me on the kitchen table, so he obviously already knew. I'd even heard Peter drive away after that, now that I thought about it. I felt panicky, with a free-floating anxiety, not really sure this horrible thing had happened unless I could verify with somebody else who had read it, too. I picked up *The Bulletin* again and saw something I hadn't seen earlier: Next to the article, Peter had written "YO, BILLY!!!"

So Peter had felt jubilant for Billy. At least momentarily, in any case. Then he'd felt the need to take off. Why? Where? On what mission? He didn't want to talk to me about it? Why not, goddamnit? I was jumpy, wanted to be up and running, too.

The Scout started right up even though it was already very cold and dark in the middle of the afternoon. I hurtled into town, angle-parked in front of the E-Z Mart, and went in. Inside, two middle-aged local men were talking quietly. They were drinking coffee out of styrofoam cups. I passed close to them, close enough to eavesdrop on my way to the magazine rack, as good a destination as any.

"It's clear the kid set him up," one man said out of the side of his mouth to the other man.

"You have to watch out," the second man said, shaking his head woefully.

I turned and stared openly at them as they continued saying the same things again and again, sounding otherworldly, alien, to my present state of mind. Just then a teenager with green hair came in and walked over to where his friend was playing the video machines along the wall near the cashier. I turned away from the two men, picked out some cat food from the shelf, and went to the counter to pay. The kids were making sounds of stunned disbelief.

"You saw it, man?" one kid said, dancing his weight from one foot to the other.

"Blew his fucking head off!" said the green-haired kid in a loud whisper, lopping off Dyer's head as surely as Dorrance's had ever been lopped.

I went outside and stood in the crisp air by the Scout. A triple-trailer truck thundered down the main street of Saints, scarcely slowing down. It roared past the five blocks of candy-colored, illuminated western storefronts lining both sides of the street. The driver inside his high, enclosed cab must have been seeing just a flash of color and then darkness, like a synapse. Sometimes a synapse is all we get, and we must deduce the rest.

I wanted to be back in the safety of my kitchen, with Peter, and I drove home fast. Back home I found Peter in our cold bedroom packing a bag. He was leaning over his task at a strange angle, listing, as if he might capsize.

"Where are you going?" I asked him angrily, then repeated it warily, aware for the first time of just how far the bedroom was from the woodstove, how cold it really was now that winter had apparently arrived.

"I'm going up to Rajneeshpuram to a meditation workshop. You asked me to, remember? They're having their last one, now that the place is falling apart, seems kind of appropriate, don't you think?"

Now? was all I could think. I sat down on the bed and watched him. "It started today," he said, pressing his hands against his lower back where it must have been aching. "So I've missed a day, but I'm going anyway."

"How long's it last?" I felt detached. What he was doing felt foreign to me, as if some kind of transfer had actually occurred.

"Six more days."

I nodded my head, and we looked at each other.

"You're driving up there tonight?"

"No." He shook his head for longer than necessary then resumed: "Tomorrow morning at four-thirty." He was breathing shallowly. I moved toward him and our foreheads bumped. We moved apart.

Later, lying awake in bed, I reached my hand out for his warmth and asked him why he had decided to go up to Rajneeshpuram. His leg jerked as if he were falling asleep, but I was sure he really wasn't. He was coding his withdrawal in a body language I was sure to understand. It made me think about Billy trying to communicate with Faith but not able to do so, because he didn't know her secret code.

The next morning when I awoke, Peter was gone. It was overcast and gloomy, and when I went outside, the stray peacock who'd turned up when nighttime temperatures had started to plunge ran at me shrieking. The horses were nervously braying, hungry for good hay and high-calorie oats now that it was zero degrees Fahrenheit. The geldings butted ferociously up against one another, kicking and whinnying. Coco lunged to push them back into the corner of the corral so she would be first served. I saw that I'd forgot to plug in the water-trough heater the night before, and the ice was two inches thick in the trough, so the horses were thirsty. I threw a flake of hay for each horse far apart from the others to get rid of the herding action, to calm them. Then I chipped away the ice on the trough. After that I began untangling dreadlocks from tails and manes.

After he finished his hay, the big white Arab Granite came over to where I was struggling with Coco's matted tail. He began fooling around seductively with me, nibbling on my hair. He was obviously trying to get Coco's attention, to arouse her jealousy by fooling with me behind her. It was extraordinary behavior, new to me. I went in the house and got my camera and three rolls of black-and-white film and passed at least an hour photographing Granite positively showing off, an exhibitionist of a horse. Was it the proud cut in him? I don't know, but after a morning of so much attention, Granite suddenly bolted out of the corral away from me, then stopped again for more fooling around with Coco, without me in the way. The prancing white Arab sidled after Coco while she trotted desultorily away, not yet taking the big male seriously. As I watched, Granite stretched out his long arched neck and bit Coco on the ass. She looked round over her shoulder, startled, it appeared, ears back. She kicked her legs behind her into the air, came down running. With great aplomb Granite avoided her kicks and pulled up running beside her, stretched out his neck again, and, in a gesture of dominance, bit her smoothly on the neck.

It all happened so naturally, this change in the pecking order, this transfer of equine power, and the two horses went on celebrating it for the rest of the day, bucking and starting, chasing and getting caught, rubbing their necks together almost violently. Coco was more exhilarated than I'd ever seen her, and Granite was a superb cock of the walk, mounting Coco repeatedly, hard, again and again.

The change, it would turn out, was permanent. I told Peter about it on the phone that night when he called from Rajneeshpuram. He seemed charmed to hear me so excited.

"Hey, listen," he said. "There's two old rednecks here from Madras, dancing in the disco, with Rajneeshees!"

"Noooooo," I said.

"Yeah, I swear. And I did see your friend Isabel, and I said hello from you. Listen, I'm rooming with two Germans who just got here, they have no idea what is happening, they just arrived from Germany, they didn't even know that Bhagwan wasn't here anymore. All they want to do is fuck."

"Well, you can hardly blame them," I said lamely.

"Well, no, I didn't mean me . . ."

"It's okay, don't tell me anything. Wait till you get back."

For a number of reasons I didn't want to think about whatever was going to happen to Peter up there. And I didn't even mention to him I'd decided out of morbid curiosity to go to Ed Dyer's funeral the next day.

The following morning driving through Saints to the funeral service, I saw that the sign in front of the Church of the Second Coming had been changed to read THOU SHALT NOT KILL. The civilizing factor was already at work.

At the Mormon church in Redmond, Ed Dyer's funeral was stiff and impersonal. I heard a prayer or two and some nonspecific testimonials that made no reference to the man, to his life, to his abuse of Billy, or to his actual death. The service could have been for anyone, for anyone who'd died any kind of death. After the ceremony everyone filed past Dyer's open casket. I looked, and he didn't appear anywhere near as big as he'd been when he was alive. He scarcely looked like the same man. Neither Faith nor Billy was there to see that Ed Dyer was now utterly diminished, utterly puny. Neither one would have been able to take this in anyway, probably not then, not ever. Instead, Faith was occupied getting a criminal lawyer to defend Billy. As for Billy, he would eventually serve a short sentence in a juvenile facility and then take up body-building and become powerful and thick-chested himself. Never again, he would be saying, never again would he find himself vulnerable to aggression from someone stronger than himself.

On my drive back home after the funeral that cold, wintry day, I was almost to the ranch when I passed Hamilton Jones in his pickup going the opposite direction. In my rearview mirror, I saw Ham stop and back up toward me. I stopped my car and waited till we were face to face, our vehicles blocking the road. Ham regarded me for a moment before speaking.

"What've you guys been up to?" he said finally, checking me out very flirtatiously in a way he never did when Peter was with me. I wasn't really surprised. When I told Ham I'd been to Ed Dyer's funeral, he acted appreciatively shocked. "You are really weird, girl," he said.

"You can get weird when you have a whole ranch to yourself, Ham, know what I mean?" I was ready to talk his talk.

"You have the ranch to yourself? Where's Peter?" he asked, winking at me.

"He's gone up to Rajneeshpuram for a meditation workshop."

"He has not," Ham said, looking hard at me. Then: "He has?" He was startled for real this time.

"Yeah."

"How long's he been gone?" he went on, the honey-cured Ham.

"Three days."

"Three days?" Ham was now smiling hugely, tauntingly at me. He pointedly reached and switched off his engine. "Three days," he repeated, leaning his head back against his headrest.

"Uh huh," I said.

"You let him go up there and leave you all by yourself?"

What was he getting at? "Why not?" I asked, revving the Toyota's engine for emphasis.

"Hah," he said. "You're not afraid?"

"Well, not so far, thank you very much." He was starting to irritate me.

"You're not afraid of what or perhaps I should say who might happen to Peter, up there?"

Fuck! It was that Ham. "Ham, you pig," I said to him, shaking my head, "you bring out something awful in me . . ."

"You want to kiss my ass, don't you?" he said.

I took off in second gear, not a very wow exit, but still satisfying. At home I got in the shower, trying to wash off Ham before I got contaminated, but it was too late. He'd already planted a little seed of fear in my heart, which sprouted and grew as my imagination fertilized it. Soon, unable to stop myself, I was fantasizing how perfect Isabel and Peter would look naked, making love, each of them such a fine specimen.

It made me miserable, this excruciating fantasy, and I saw myself hoist belatedly on my own petard. For I was now stricken with the feverish blow that had struck the women of Antelope and Wasco County that fateful night long before, outside the Antelope City Council meeting, when an angry Sheela had told them they were all just waiting to die. Because after telling them that, she'd said something else, something far more cunning, something the delicate Darlene Osborn had not been able to bring herself to repeat to me. I had eventually heard from others what Sheela had said that night, heard the story several times even, in widely differing versions, but the gist was always the same. Sheela had told the women of Wasco County to watch out or the Rajneeshee women were going to fuck their husbands.

FIFTEEN

I WAS DOZING, escaping, in the middle of the day on the couch next to the woodstove when Larry Lazio's daughter Lisa came by wanting to talk. Lisa, guileless and lively, a young woman no bigger than your thumb, had a short stack of red-gold hair and skimpy running clothes. Lisa was earnestly preoccupied with the morality of Billy Gaines having killed Ed Dyer, or so she began the conversation. This was not the first time Lisa had stopped by to talk to me about something troubling her notions of morality. She had previously asked me what she clearly thought were outrageous personal questions, about Peter and me cohabiting while unmarried, about true love: Did I believe there was a one-and-only mate for everyone, or do we just love the one we're with? Once she had asked me about who — the man or the woman — sleeps on the wet spot in bed after sex. Lisa's visits had frequently ended abruptly, as she in red-faced embarrassment bolted out the door with my answers to her questions. Lisa had an active imagination and, I gathered, no one but me to share it with.

On this occasion Lisa came in out of the chill and planted herself next to the intense heat of the woodstove. After several false starts she opened by saying she was sympathetic to Billy Gaines but balked at the idea of murder and thought he had

committed a sin. She was consequently troubled by her resur-
gent waves of empathy for Billy. The dilemma was indi-
gestibly stuck crosswise in her gullet like a huge pill.

"The thing is," she said, her tiny frame shaking in spite of
the stove's outstanding performance, "the thing is, I think, I
know, I do know, I feel . . . that I'd feel like . . . killing somebody, a guy I mean, somebody who, you know, somebody who
forced . . . me to . . . I mean . . ."

I waited, but like a true high-desert girl, Lisa repressed her
obsession and fell silent. The kettle on the stove hissed steam
into the dry air. Lisa failed to reignite her courage. I struggled
to find the energy to respond to her aborted effort and failed.

Rolling her eyes heavenward, Lisa jerked herself toward the
door. "You're . . . ," she muttered, seeming to notice for the
first time that I might not be my usual self. "I'm outta here,"
she blurted and then was. Disappointed in my new helplessness, I roused myself and made coffee and thought about my
one-and-only mate up there at Rancho Rajneesh loving the
one he was with.

Ten minutes later there was Lisa again, thrusting into my
hand as I opened the door a poem she'd written earlier for Peter and me, then leaving again. This was the poem:

> This country is yours
> the hills will forever keep your footprints
> intact in soft earth
> Remember:
> Keep this place
> if not in truth
> keep this place in your heart.

I wasn't surprised to see Larry Lazio pull in later in his
pickup. He caught me just as I stepped outside hauling a big
bucket of hot water to the horse trough to keep it from freez-

ing up so fast. When I saw him coming I dropped the bucket on purpose and settled to the earth in a pile. Alarmed, he parked his rig and came over to see if I was all right.

"Made you look," I said, jumping up, and Larry laughed.

"You are a funny one," he said. "Well, I guess you're all right. Lisa said she wasn't sure." He walked back to his truck, got in, rolled down the window, and stuck out his head. "Watch out you don't slip on that puddle when it turns to ice," he said, pointing at where I'd dropped the bucket of water. He was sweet. I waved, said, "Daddy," and wept bitter tears as Larry drove out the drive. Just then Boyd the peacock came noisily around the side of the house looking disheveled. He had scarcely any feathers left at all and was clearly having a rough time of it. I gave naked Boyd a pan of grain and went inside for a fresh bucket of hot water for the horse trough.

His fifth night at Rajneeshpuram, Peter phoned again.

"I saw Boyd," I told him.

"Boyd?"

"The peacock. He's totally bald."

"Oh, really?"

"I thought you would have run off with somebody by now." I gasped.

"What?" He sounded shocked.

"You haven't?"

"What are you talking about?" He sounded really concerned.

"Oh, God . . ." I was humiliated.

"Are you all right?" he asked me solicitously.

"Do you want to come home?"

"Now?"

"Ever?"

There was a long silence over the wires.

"What's wrong?" Peter said finally.

"I don't know, I'm crazed."

"Do you need me to come . . . ?"

I felt like a complete fool. "To be my caretaker?" I asked in a small voice.

"I'm not your caretaker," he answered steadily. "But I do care about you."

"But what about your caretaking?" I said, shifting the tone of the conversation.

"Actually, I've been thinking about my caretaking."

"You have?"

"About the actual caretaking. I've been thinking about the blocked pipe. What was that all about?"

"Hah! I don't know. The earth calling for her man!"

Peter chuckled easily. I was starting to relax.

"You know," he said, "I like the commune here. I like that part a lot. Things would be more diffuse if you lived in a commune. You wouldn't narrow down and obsess so much."

"The commune has seduced you," I said, tightening up again.

"Well," he said, "there is a lot of seduction going on here. I've been asked. I'm not here for that. It just doesn't . . . It's easy for them to ask, you know how direct everyone is here. They say what they want. And it's easy to say no. That's the good thing about the place, remember? You already knew all this. Now I know it too."

"Oh."

"I love you," he said then, "but I'm not you."

"What's that supposed to mean?" I was aware of feeling terribly at risk.

"I want to give away the rest of my money," he said.

"To people you've met?"

"They're leaving and don't have any money of their own."

"They spent everything they had to get there?" I suggested,

knowing what was going on up there. "And you want to have no money left as well?"

"That's enough thinking for now," he said, and we hung up.

When Peter came back I could scarcely look at him. I'd been breathing shallowly, waiting for the sound of the Mustang on the drive, and now, as I ran to him at the door, my midsection caved in, and I could not look at his face for fear of what I might see in his eyes. I saw instead that in his hand he was holding a shock of luminous green-and-blue peacock feathers — there must have been twenty of them — gathered, I knew, from those dropped by Bhagwan's peacocks. Peter held them out to me.

"Maybe we can glue them onto Boyd?" he said, smiling hugely at me.

I reached to hug him, my heart pounding, and he stood hugging me warmly, but it was almost an institutional warmth, nonspecific. I stepped back and looked at him and felt that he looked different somehow as well as purposeful, as if there were something that was supposed to happen now. What was it? Did he want to talk?

"Maybe I should tell you about it," he said. He was still standing at the door in his coat, hadn't even really come in yet.

"You don't have to," I said quickly, stepping back farther.

"But we should do an interview, or something," he said, quietly insistent. "A debriefing."

"Well, all right." I felt his coldness, his need to set things straight, or was he just being methodical?

It was only then he took off his parka, hung it up in the long, dark hall of our beloved cabin, and led me to the couch.

"Aren't you going to write anything down?" he asked, looking at my empty hands.

"Of course," I said and ran for paper and pen. I came back and fell clumsily onto the couch, totally adolescent.

"Okay," I said, but then I asked nothing, because I didn't have any questions. I did not want to know anything.

"Aren't you going to ask me anything?" he nudged gently.

"No, yes . . . are you glad to be home?"

He stared at his hands a long time, and one of them floated up almost absently to stroke his upper lip. I realized I hadn't seen him float like that for some time. He gazed at me while he worked something through.

"Okay," he said finally and, after a pause, repeated his statement from our earlier phone conversation: "I love you, but I am not you."

I sensed he would have said this no matter what I'd asked. "Yes, I know, you said that. Of course you're not," I rushed to say, but he held up his hand to stop me.

"But I don't think you were really listening to me." Peter said this with all his first-degreeness, which, as always, was impossible to deny.

Eventually, after what was probably an eternity, I nodded my head. "Yes?"

Nodding with me, Peter said, "Now, I'm going to drive two Germans I met up at Rajneeshpuram down to Arizona where some people are starting a commune."

"You are?"

"I am. I'm leaving in a few minutes. They're waiting for me in town, in the café."

I was poleaxed. I mustn't say a thing, I mustn't interfere, I mustn't interfere, I repeated to myself like a litany, followed closely by Why the hell not? and, Can I live like this? Peter disappeared with his bag down the hall to the bedroom, where, I suppose, he exchanged worn underwear and socks for fresh ones. And then, with a smile to melt my heart but without the longed-for reassurance of his body in mine, he was gone.

Right away after Peter was gone, I had a revelation: I had formed one of those dread expectations. I expected him not to abandon me. I had promised as part of our deal with each other to keep Peter informed if I developed any expectations, but I hadn't done so.

Then, I found Peter's journal. I hadn't been looking for it. It was there, in plain sight, on the mantel. I had never hidden my own journal from Peter, had left it around in plain sight, trusting that he probably wouldn't read it. I was actually quite certain Peter wouldn't ever read my journal to see what I wrote about him, about us. Nevertheless, I imagined that if he did read it, the kinds of underpinnings he might find there would only reinforce our relations with each other. I wasn't worried. If there was one thing my friend Peter could do, it was process stuff.

I opened Peter's journal to the first page, which, I soon realized, had been written during that period when we'd had our differences about drifting, about him thinking he was circumscribing his behavior to please me. That whole time had been a nervous dance, I recalled. Peter's touchiness about why he was madly clearing out the irrigation pipe had coupled dangerously with my inability not to find humor in it. And then there was Viorst's wish to get Buckner off the property. I had rejected this explosively, and Peter had withdrawn to his bath. The next day I'd done a kitchen-table tirade, loved Peter for not retreating from my outburst, felt things were all right between us. Then, later, I'd seen Peter go off into the forest carrying this little notebook, this journal I was now holding. This is what Peter had written that day: I cannot bear her anger. She makes me feel very bad. I have thoughts of violence. It takes me days to realize it is all a projection on my part. It takes her no time at all.

Perhaps things had not been all right between us, I realized. Sitting down hard at the yellow table, I ran through in my mind the events surrounding the blocked pipe. I went back in my journal to all the entries about Faith and Billy and Ed Dyer, remembering how painful that had been for Peter and me. The thing was, though, we had gone on past the nervous dance, the two of us. We had gone on into a partnership phase. We had become comrades out in the gorges and ravines of the forest, out in the arroyos of the high desert. As a result, I wasn't too troubled by what Peter had written in his journal at that earlier time; I was even glad. He might take days to sort through his thoughts, but I was leaping ahead, getting excited now, jumping up from the table, bounding around with energy at these insights. I was self-curing.

My frustration, slower to come, took over a bit later, when I realized this wasn't a conversation I was having with Peter. I saw our situation so clearly in the wake of numerous startling events. Wouldn't he? I was fairly certain, yes I was, that Peter would move through his own complex thoughts, through the wonderful tragedy of his own person, and that he, clear once again, would come back to me.

While waiting, I sat in the evenings at the yellow table and wrote within a circle of light thrown by a lamp hanging low from the ceiling. The rest of the house was dark, and on the woodstove the teakettle steadily pumped steam into the dry air.

I started writing about the immense heap of horseshit piling up along the fence right outside our big southern window. The point was that the horses had never shit there before our arrival, but that Peter and I had drawn them there simply by opening up the blinds to reveal to anyone out there our own well-lighted spectacle inside the cabin. Out of curiosity the horses now stood there all the time, watching us or dozing off or shitting atop the ever-growing mass along the fence. Every day the pile grew taller, the fence seemingly lower. Clearly, I wrote, if we didn't do something about it, one of the horses was soon going to step right over the fence and walk away. The point was that Peter and I had inadvertently written this shit-pile scenario.

While waiting for Peter to come back to me, I also decided not to spend my scarce money on health insurance and to spend it instead on film. I bought fast black-and-white for the oblique shafts of cold winter sun stabbing weakly out of the horizon. The high desert was extraordinarily subtle in the dead slant of winter. Each spiky blade of grass, each sprawling, naked cottonwood, each warmth-starved, slow-moving animal cast its double in long, spooky shadow.

Dressed in a khaki, knee-length, arctic-weight parka, I shot ten rolls of close-ups of the horses sprawled on their sides in a circle on a high spot in the pasture. They were so profoundly asleep in the winter sun you'd have thought they'd had no sleep at all recently, the nights had been so cold. All that muscled horseflesh looked like so much meat, spreading, loose, barely contained by skin stretched taut under thick winter coats. I took pictures of Coco and Granite dreaming, maybe about each other, their drooling lips and exposed teeth twitching to follow some unimaginable stimulus. They opened their moist eyes momentarily and grunted as I moved in and around them, clicking away. And then they let me lay there comfortably amongst them on the hard, frozen earth until I got cold. I reluctantly went inside, but not before I took one last picture of a frozen, pear-shaped tear dangling like an ornament from the edge of one of Coco's beautiful, long-lashed eyes.

That clear, cloudless night, the temperature dropped to

eighteen below zero. I set the alarm and went outside twice with hot water for the horse trough and treats all around.

Peter came back a week later. It seemed like years. I was nervous when he actually walked in the door. He'd called the night before to say he was coming, and I'd made boeuf bourguignon. "This is where I want to be," he told me as we ate the rich stew. "I want to be here with you, with you, here, with you," he said, his hand rising slowly in the air till it was level with his face. I noticed the tiny indentation in the end of his nose. I hadn't touched it for weeks. He tilted his head slightly, went on: "We've got things we want to do, right?" He snorted then, clowning around, chortling at some inner thought. "Right?" he repeated. He was very funny. "Right? Right? Right."

AFTERWORD

THE FIRST TIME PETER and I attended Ham Jones's annual summer garden party, the normalizing of our lives on the high desert commenced. For his big do, Ham served a midday dinner under striped awnings to guests imported from Florida, Paris, London, Portland, et cetera. The blond earthwoman Sally was gone, replaced by a flashy, brainy brunette.

"A new era," Peter said to me, taking it all in as we arrived, and headed for the pool. The afternoon was nonpareil. I stood in the shade of an umbrella and drank a bottle of champagne with a stranger. We spoke of France and Italy, eating tartine after tartine spread with *crème fraîche aux fines herbes* the man had made himself. A delicate breeze wafted off the Three Saints, moving strands of loose hair off hot faces. The dry red dust that might usually have been swirling around Ham's ranch was buried under hundreds of square yards of newly in-stalled, springy green turf. His black Lab, Jake, bounded across the strange grass with a coyote skull in his mouth. One group of five white-clad guests moved slowly across the lawn, entirely absorbed in their game of *boules*. A woman, whose husband would turn out to be a psychiatrist, talked to me of a story she'd read in *The New Yorker*. Later we all played a genteel round of volleyball in the shade of a cottonwood, and the woman threw herself happily to the plush turf like a child. Inspired and in a kind of ecstasy, Peter did the same. The psychiatrist and I laughed together. The woman would follow up on this with an invitation to dinner, and we would all become friends.

When we left Ham's that evening, hugging and kissing people we had never seen before that day, we saw things differently, as if we'd been traveling. The drama of our lives would soon thereafter turn into a story about us and the four or five people who became our friends. And I always saw Peter's and my paths joined, like the arc of a single meteorite.

For Peter and me, work became the drama. I was forced to abandon the idea of financial independence, but I did make money doing Viorst's tree plantation, for which I earned about $1,500 a year at $10 an hour, primarily for irrigating. With some bitterness, as well as a certain contentment, I came to think of myself as a serf. A peasant. I chased water for long hours wearing gum boots and a coolie hat bought from a Vietnamese war bride who lived, briefly, in Saints. The work tamed me, made me willing but also more apt to hide my light under a basket, as the saying goes. Sometimes, when I focused on it, I felt underutilized and underemployed, isolated and untapped. I had fantasies of becoming a highly paid executive. But for the most part I found pleasure in the physical life for years. I remember standing in the fresh mud with satisfaction as water oozed down a waterway I'd just built toward newly planted seedlings. And I remember Peter coming out to find me, following the water, moving toward me across the land like a desert mirage.

I always told Peter not to come back unless he wanted to, to always consider this, this possibility of not coming back. It made it all the better when he did come back. I remember the way he would look at me, moving across the land toward me.

I remember how, when he got there, he would lay down with me.

While I learned to stay put, Peter now was often off the ranch doing paid legal work, as I believe he had indeed given away most of his money to lost souls up at Rajneeshpuram. As for the Forest Service, the district ranger's earlier promise to pull the infamous timber sale away from the creek had been only a beginning. Peter had painstakingly negotiated the timber sale down to a thinning operation, an intensity of logging that even Forest Service biologists recommended as a way to retain the old-growth characteristics of the national forest, including the old-growth-dependent wildlife. Then, after it was all settled, to Peter's horror the logging company hired by the Forest Service clear-cut the whole area anyway. They took everything, every last tree, even the famous landmark tree.

"Oh, they borrowed the big one, too?" said the forester when Peter phoned to report what he'd found. The forester claimed to be unaware of what had happened, although there is normally an official postsale visit by a Forest Service official. They played very dumb. Too dumb.

After Peter made his discovery known to the newspapers, we got obscene and threatening phone calls ("How'd you like to eat my onions, little bitch?" or "Just step outside, little lady, and see who's waitin' for you right now.").

One night someone in a big, noisy pickup drove right up on the grass next to our cabin at 3:00 A.M. and shone a spotlight directly into our faces as we looked out our bedroom window. They fired shots. They didn't hit anything, so they weren't trying to. We were a little slow on the uptake, and the dark-colored rig escaped before we could give chase. I target-practiced the next day with the rifle and made some progress in my skill level.

The investigation of the timber theft went on for some

time. When it eventually reached the courts, *The Bulletin* reported:

> When the long-awaited timber theft trial of Bend's Layton & Bartlett logging company gets under way . . . in Eugene, the U.S. Forest Service is likely to come under nearly as much scrutiny as the loggers who are charged with stealing millions of dollars worth of public timber. . . .
>
> "This is, if not the most significant, then one of the most significant timber theft prosecutions ever by virtue of the value of the timber alleged and the duration of the alleged theft," [Assistant U.S. Attorney Jeffrey] Kent said this week.

For Peter, it was his war come up out of the basement. He was ready with all his sound effects. As the picture came into focus over the years, the great federal forests of the Far West were found everywhere to be unraveling ecosystems stressed by government policies of overproduction and overharvesting. Peter was an authentic caretaker of the forest, accusing the impostors. He pursued them appeal after appeal, survey after survey, negotiation after negotiation. He wouldn't give up, held on like a crab, financed his efforts by writing law briefs for firms with offices in the county seat.

Eventually, everyone would know about Peter. Everyone in the territory would phone Peter the caretaker when they found bizarre logging activity in some remote corner of the national forest. Peter and I became a local institution, a condition that eventually leads, as everyone knows, to a diminished quality of experience. I often replaced him when he had no more energy, when he couldn't be everywhere at once. We were partners after all, collaborators. I became a forest spokesperson in my own right, then an occasional lobbyist in Washington, D.C. We were in this fight to the finish.

One day in a meeting the national forest supervisor aggressively thrust the back of his hand in my face to prevent me from contradicting him even though he was lying through his teeth about some logging practice or other. I could feel my anger accumulating. Some days I felt angry alone on the ranch and thought I would surely die there angry and alone and no one would know. Feeling this one day after seven years there, I became aware of my ambivalence about the place. I wanted to leave.

Unexpectedly, Viorst gave us a little shove. "Bob wants to pull the cabin down, rebuild on the same spot," Peter told me one day as he flipped grilled cheese sandwiches in our kitchen haven. "You know . . . decent kitchen, bathroom, laundry room, insulation, the basics."

"A suburban fucking tract home?" I looked hard at the ancient pine-board flooring, the rough yellow cupboards darkened with smoke.

"He thinks the place is falling down," Peter explained, fully aware of the effect his words were having on me. "The county's changing to no more building on woodlots, and we're officially a woodlot now, so it's rebuild now or never."

My commitment to the place ended irrationally then. I cut a picture of the Eiffel Tower out of a magazine and set it on Peter's plate for dinner. It became a goal.

A year later in the fall, after a winter spent fixing up my Victorian house to rent out, we left the ranch for good. In Paris we found a tiny apartment with water flowing underground. In the courtyard of the building, you could hear the water gurgling at the bottom of an old well. I got myself a typewriter and settled in. Peter was anxious and out of sorts. He worked on his lawsuits in cafés, sent and received faxes at the *papeterie*, explored Paris on foot, but his mind was back in Saints. I imagined it was just a question of me making a rapid adjustment while his would be slow to develop. Through an old friend, I got work looking at the international trade/environment link from the perspective of greening the GATT. Peter looked desultorily for law work, which turned out to be impossible to find in the French recession, and this lack of professional status, for all that he had maligned it at the beginning of our stay in Saints, now mattered considerably. He got word that his Mustang, left in Oregon, had been stolen, then found, but in damaged condition. "You should never have left," Stang whinnied from a distant police garage. Goddamn car.

Our Paris place was so small — 350 square feet — and there were no wide, open spaces outside for Peter to recuperate in. There was something about the coldness of the French that deeply offended him. He couldn't get their rudeness to not matter. He was done in time after time by cultural interference, like a bird dive-bombing into invisible windows. We began to have suspicious, doubtful, even painful exchanges the likes of which we hadn't had since our first year at Saints, only where the balance had lain one way before, now it went the other. After a year and a half, we stopped having sex.

At about the same time, Peter ran absolutely out of money and went back to the high desert to earn some and to tend to legal details. When he left he thought he would return in six months. I didn't want to leave with him. I was earning money in Paris now and had no prospects on the high desert. He wrote me from there: "I can't live your life. I want to be who I am, not who I think you want me to be. Like when I went to Rajneeshpuram that time. I went there because you wanted me to go, and I came back afterwards because you wanted me to. I never figured out what I wanted."

It was the sudden violence of a twister tearing into my heart. "My life is here on the high desert," Peter wrote me later, and I saw how much of what we had been together was because we'd been there, together. "It's like you went out for a pack of cigarettes," I lamented. "You don't mean it. I will wait for you." I said this for over a year, until one day, as if carefully considering the effect, he wrote he'd dreamed of killing me, the kind of cruel, definitive thing lovers say to each other when they want to make a complete break.